D1327398

International Financial History in the Twentieth Century

SYSTEM AND ANARCHY

The essays in this book, written by some of the leading experts in the field, examine the long-run history of the international financial system in terms of the current debate about globalization and its limits. In the nineteenth century, international markets existed without international institutions. A response to the problems of capital flows came in the form of attempts to regulate national capital markets (for example, through the establishment of central banks). In the interwar years, there were (largely unsuccessful) attempts at designing a genuine international trade and monetary system; and at the same time (coincidentally) the system collapsed. In the post-1945 era, the intended design effort was infinitely more successful. The development of large international capital markets since the 1960s, however, increasingly frustrated attempts at international control. The emphasis has shifted in consequence to debates about increasing the transparency and effectiveness of markets, but these are exactly the issues that already dominated the nineteenth-century discussions.

Marc Flandreau is Professor of International Economic Relations at the Institut d'Etudes Politiques de Paris.

Carl-Ludwig Holtfrerich is Professor of Economics at the John F. Kennedy Institut für Nordamerika Studien at the Freie Universität Berlin.

Harold James is Professor of History at Princeton University.

PUBLICATIONS OF THE GERMAN HISTORICAL INSTITUTE,
WASHINGTON, D.C.

Edited by Christof Mauch
with the assistance of David Lazar

The German Historical Institute is a center for advanced study and research whose purpose is to provide a permanent basis for scholarly cooperation among historians from the Federal Republic of Germany and the United States. The Institute conducts, promotes, and supports research into both American and German political, social, economic, and cultural history; into transatlantic migration, especially in the nineteenth and twentieth centuries; and into the history of international relations, with special emphasis on the roles played by the United States and Germany.

Recent books in the series

Norbert Finzsch and Dietmar Schirmer, editors, *Identity and Intolerance: Nationalism, Racism, and Xenophobia in Germany and the United States*

Susan Strasser, Charles McGovern, and Matthias Judt, editors, *Getting and Spending: European and American Consumer Societies in the Twentieth Century*

Carole Fink, Philipp Gassert, and Detlef Junker, editors, *1968: The World Transformed*

Roger Chickering and Stig Förster, editors, *Great War, Total War: Combat and Mobilization on the Western Front*

Manfred F. Boemeke, Gerald D. Feldman, and Elisabeth Glaser, eds., *The Treaty of Versailles: A Reassessment After 75 Years*

Manfred Berg and Martin H. Geyer, eds., *Two Cultures of Rights: The Quest for Inclusion and Participation in Modern America and Germany*

Manfred F. Boemeke, Roger Chickering, and Stig Förster, eds., *Anticipating Total War: The German and American Experiences, 1871–1914*

Roger Chickering and Stig Förster, eds., *The Shadows of Total War: Europe, East Asia, and the United States, 1919–1939*

Elisabeth Glaser and Hermann Wellenreuther, eds., *Bridging the Atlantic: The Question of American Exceptionalism in Perspective*

International Financial History
in the Twentieth Century

SYSTEM AND ANARCHY

Edited by

MARC FLANDREAU
Institut d'Etudes Politiques de Paris

CARL-LUDWIG HOLTFRERICH
Freie Universität Berlin

HAROLD JAMES
Princeton University

GERMAN HISTORICAL INSTITUTE
Washington, D.C.
and

 CAMBRIDGE
UNIVERSITY PRESS

PUBLISHED BY THE PRESS SYNDICATE OF THE UNIVERSITY OF CAMBRIDGE
The Pitt Building, Trumpington Street, Cambridge, United Kingdom

CAMBRIDGE UNIVERSITY PRESS
The Edinburgh Building, Cambridge CB2 2RU, UK
40 West 20th Street, New York, NY 10011-4211, USA
477 Williamstown Road, Port Melbourne, VIC 3207, Australia
Ruiz de Alarcón 13, 28014 Madrid, Spain
Dock House, The Waterfront, Cape Town 8001, South Africa

http://www.cambridge.org

© German Historical Institute 2003

This book is in copyright. Subject to statutory exception
and to the provisions of relevant collective licensing agreements,
no reproduction of any part may take place without
the written permission of Cambridge University Press.

First published 2003

Printed in the United States of America

Typeface Bembo 11/13 pt.   *System* LaTeX 2_ε [TB]

A catalog record for this book is available from the British Library.

Library of Congress Cataloging in Publication Data

International financial history in the twentieth century : system and anarchy / edited by
Marc Flandreau, Carl-Ludwig Holtfrerich, Harold James.
    p.   cm. – (Publications of the German Historical Institute)
       Includes bibliographical references and index.
          ISBN 0-521-81995-4
  1. International finance.   2. Monetary policy.   3. International economic integration.
 I. Flandreau, Marc.   II. Holtfrerich, Carl-Ludwig.   III. James, Harold, 1956–   IV. Series.
             HG3881 .I607283   2003
          332′.042′0904–dc21   2002073594

ISBN 0 521 81995 4 hardback

Contents

Contents

Contributors

Werner Abelshauser is professor of economic history at the University of Bielefeld.

Marc Flandreau is at the Ecole des Hautes Etudes en Sciences Sociales, Paris.

Eric Helleiner is professor of political studies at Trent University, Ontario, Canada.

Harold James is professor of history at Princeton University.

Charles P. Kindleberger is professor emeritus of economics at MIT.

Kenneth Mouré is professor of history at the University of California at Santa Barbara.

F. Taylor Ostrander lives in Williamstown, Massachusetts.

Louis W. Pauly is professor of political science at the University of Toronto.

Stephen A. Schuker is professor of history at the University of Virginia at Charlottesville.

Robert Skidelsky is professor of history at Warwick University.

Jakob Tanner is professor of history at the University of Zurich.

Mira Wilkins is professor of economics at Florida International University.

Preface

This book originated in the papers and the discussion at a conference organized by the German Historical Institute and Princeton University's History
Department and Woodrow Wilson School in April 1998. The conference
had initially been planned by Diane Kunz of Yale University and Carl-
Ludwig Holtfrerich of the Freie Universität Berlin. At a later stage, Marc
Flandreau and Harold James were involved in the planning. The aim of the
conference and the volume was and is to examine major episodes in the
history of the international financial system: the gold standard, the Great
Depression, the creation of a new international and European order after
the Second World War.

We are grateful to the German Historical Institute and its Director,
Professor Detlef Junker, who enthusiastically supported the project from the
beginning, and to the staff of the German Historical Institute, in particular
its editorial director, Dr. Daniel Mattern. Princeton University provided an
agreeable setting for the discussions.

Marc Flandreau
Carl-Ludwig Holtfrerich
Harold James

Introduction

MARC FLANDREAU AND HAROLD JAMES

The long-run history of the international financial system in the course of the twentieth century can be described in terms of the current debate about globalization and its limits. At the beginning of the new century, there existed a substantially integrated world economy, tied together through more or less unconstrained flows of capital, goods, and labor. During the next decades that "one world" economy disintegrated, in part as a response to World War I, in part as a result of growing political expectations about how the state might limit the shocks emanating from the global economy. The years after 1945 saw the creation of an institutional infrastructure – in particular the Bretton Woods institutions – that altered the calculations about appropriate state policy and permitted the recreation of a world in which trade expanded more quickly than production, capital flows increased (especially after the 1970s), and labor also began to move.

The course of the twentieth century can be described from this perspective as a U-shape. First integration collapsed, and then the pendulum swung back. Can there be another dip in the U? If so, what does history tell us about "backlashes" against globalization (to use the expression of Kevin O'Rourke and Jeffrey Williamson)?[1] What exactly is a "backlash" – an attempt to reverse the previous course of globalization, or an attempt to secure that course by directing it along more stable tracks?

In the nineteenth century, international markets existed without international institutions. A response to the problems of capital flows came in the form of attempts to regulate national capital markets (for instance through the establishment of central banks). In the interwar years, there were (largely unsuccessful) attempts at designing a genuine international

---

1 Kevin H. O'Rourke and Jeffrey G. Williamson, *Globalization and History: The Evolution of a Nineteenth Century Atlantic Economy* (Cambridge, Mass., 1999).

1

trade and monetary system; and at the same time (coincidentally) the system collapsed. In the post-1945 era, the intended design effort was infinitely more successful. At first, it was designed to regulate and indeed control financial markets. The development of large international capital markets since the 1960s, however, increasingly frustrated attempts at international control. The emphasis has shifted in consequence to debates about increasing the transparency and effectiveness of markets.

Much of the tragedy of the interwar period, when globalization went into reverse, can be attributed to the collapse of world trade and, in policy terms, to the position of the United States. Whereas in the globalized nineteenth century, Britain as a hegemonic power had followed a liberal trade policy, in and after the First World War and above all after 1932 Britain moved decisively to trade protection. U.S. commercial policy, in particular the Hawley-Smoot tariff of 1930, had even wider repercussions and was a decisive element in the upward ratcheting of protective tariffs, quotas, and other types of trade discrimination. After the Second World War, by contrast, the United States was in a position of unchallenged hegemony and was able to set a worldwide liberal trade agenda, which reached an initial peak of success with the Kennedy round of GATT negotiations in the 1960s. Liberalized trade markets came out of the bottom part of the U-curve more quickly than did capital markets. But financial flows may be needed to help in cases in which trade adjustment is sticky, in other words to finance current account imbalances. In the 1960s, as global commerce expanded, countries began to worry about balance of payments adjustment and about the relative role of markets and international institutions in making this adjustment.

There has thus been a long-running debate that from the beginning accompanied the evolution of the global economy – a debate about the appropriate institutional design of the international financial system. "Peel's wisdom, Bismarck's precision, Descartes' logic, and Franklin's common sense, should meet to draft a new monetary order: then the world monetary peace would be signed." These words were not the product of a speechwriter in the U.S. Treasury. The reference to a new "monetary order" – a nineteenth-century equivalent to the recent concept of a "new architecture" – was really made more than a century ago by the political economist, philanthropist, and leading bimetallist Henri Cernuschi in his *Diplomatie Monétaire*, published in 1878.[2] This parallel should remind us that the quest for an appropriate – if not ideal – monetary and financial architecture did not begin in the midst of the recent East Asian crisis. Rather, modern advocates of monetary reform

---

2 *La Diplomatie Monétaire en 1878* (Paris, 1878).

are just the latest offspring of a long and venerable tradition dating back to the nineteenth century. We may find it wholly discouraging and suggest, with Paul Krugman, that calls for comprehensive monetary reform are a bit like calls for global brotherhood: good for your self-esteem, but not quite practical. Yet even pessimists may find a short detour through history useful. The past has lessons that are relatively cheap to learn, and, as we shall see, they are telling and compelling.

Put simply, these lessons are: (1) attempts at international coordination or control rarely work; (2) such attempts are most unstable when they are politicized as a result of unstable international politics; (3) the markets are themselves possible only on the basis of powerful institutional, political, and social forces.

These issues provided the major themes of a conference that was organized by the German Historical Institute and held in Princeton, New Jersey, in April 1998. The participants were mostly economic historians, but the discussions were attended by the two retired heads of the world's most powerful and respected central banks, the Deutsche Bundesbank and the U.S. Federal Reserve System. There was something of an atmosphere of latent crisis, with fears that the Asian financial crisis, which had emerged originally in Thailand in the summer of 1997, might present a global contagion. In the middle of the conference, one of the central bankers, Helmut Schlesinger, was called away to Indonesia to advise on the reform of its central bank. Meanwhile, Paul Volcker delivered an insightful but gloomy address on the likelihood of a mass popular rejection of globalization and financial and trade liberalism (the so-called Washington consensus).

Like the conference, this book examines the three phases of the modern globalized economy – the creation of the global world in the nineteenth century, interwar disintegration, and postwar restoration – in a very broad context, looking at the economic history but also at the institutional and political and security debates that provided a context for the financial developments.

THE CLASSICAL GOLD STANDARD

In regard to the first era – the gold standard years of an integrated global economy – three questions arise. The first is the question of how the financial markets processed and evaluated information. Particularly, what institutions handled flows of information in that era? How did global capital movements respond to opportunities? Was there any or much political intervention – as has often been claimed in the case of British, French, and German lending in the era of imperialism? How did the private sector manage uncertainty and crises in a world without international institutions?

Marc Flandreau's essay (Chapter 1) examines the Credit Lyonnais's economic intelligence department, and he establishes that a quite sophisticated (and remarkably de-politicized) credit rating system was already in operation before World War I. Its existence gave the bank a competitive advantage through superior access to information.

A second question relates to the nature of the capital movements that occurred during this period. Capital flows not only in the form of short-term credits, bond issues, and the issue of securities. The existence of a substantial amount of industrial investment, in which transnational corporations sought foreign activities and investment, is part of the remarkable story told by Mira Wilkins (Chapter 2). Her essay raises the question of the linkage of such very stable and long-term flows to the more volatile securities markets. The investments of companies depended on a great deal of knowledge about local markets. Here was another channel through which information was disseminated. Did such information spill over into other markets and affect the securities and credit markets?

Third, what sort of institutional setting was required? How far was the gold standard managed? There are some paradoxes, as Eric Helleiner demonstrates (Chapter 9). The gold standard of the last quarter of the nineteenth century was perhaps the first truly global system; but at the same time it might be said that the gold standard was a profoundly nationalistic construct. In the previous period, there had long been a plurality of international currencies, with gold and silver coins circulating widely across national frontiers. The second half of the nineteenth century was an age of nationalization, in which powerful nation-states emerged (in part at least, it might be argued, as a defensive response in the face of globalization). They imposed national moneys. Yet at the same time, this is the age that we think of in retrospect as the era of a truly golden internationalism.

The origins of the gold standard are indeed deeply interwoven with the acceleration of international exchanges that took place after 1850. This era was accompanied by an expansion of free trade, at least in Europe. Globalization in commerce seemed to call for a corresponding globalization in money, and the supporters of lower tariffs were often as well the advocates of a "universal" currency system. Each period has challenges of its own: At that time, reforming the world monetary architecture involved replacing heterogeneous national standards (gold, silver, and bimetallism) by a uniform one. There was widespread agreement, notably among European elites, that such a reform was needed. But when it came to deciding what the basis of a universal currency should be, policymakers disagreed. The costs of monetary reforms would be unevenly spread between countries, depending on the mismatch between their current regime and the one that would be eventually selected – and this created considerable tensions. From a purely logical point of view, the standard that should be adopted eventually appeared straightforward. Gold was a natural choice in the 1860s because of the network externalities generated by England's leading position in international trade and finance, and by its early choice of that standard. In addition, the gold discoveries of the 1840s and 1850s had created a situation of flux that reinforced this rationale: The proportion of gold in bimetallic countries had dramatically increased, and a few former silver countries had taken advantage of the gold glut to switch to what appeared then as a soft money standard.

Yet putting this economic logic into action required political actions: Such was the origin of the making of monetary diplomacy in the second half of the 1860s. The concerted move of bimetallic countries on the Continent that resulted in the drafting of the Latin Monetary Union in 1865 and its ratification in 1866 was a first step toward the recognition of the need for coordination. A new architecture required a new consensus. An international conference was gathered in Paris during the International Exhibition of 1867 to discuss the practical transition to gold. The exhibition's motto was: "L'Empire c'est la Paix," by which it was meant that civilized nations would no longer fight on battlefields but only through industry and trade. This was, if one excuses the comparison, the nineteenth-century version of Francis Fukuyama's "End of History" thesis. The agenda of liberalism was, as it is, comprehensive, and it thought it had in monetary reform – in a new monetary architecture – the ultimate step of economic globalization. Nonetheless, in the absence of any compensation scheme to buy silver countries into gold, the 1867 conference parted under a somewhat vague agreement to organize the international monetary system around a 25 French franc gold coin, but to leave each country time to adjust to the new regime. Each nation would have to find its own way to switch to gold, adjusting to the global standard in a fashion that would suit it best. French diplomacy kept preparing the ground, lobbying foreign governments in Europe and elsewhere. The whole scheme came close to succeeding. Recent research by Luca Einaudi has shown that in early 1870 even England came to recognize that it could be useful to debase its sovereign (worth 25.22 francs) to bring it in line with the new global currency.

But the one considerable obstacle in this projected transition to gold, some policymakers realized, was that one would have to dispose of the by then useless silver monies. This problem was nowhere bigger than in silver standard Germany, which would have to implement its monetary reform from scratch and convert huge amounts of silver into gold. A number of economists, on the other hand, warned that the resulting shrinkage in the supply of high-powered money would cause worldwide deflation. Thus, the "rational" system of the gold standard stumbled on considerable "irrationalities" with political implications: The heavy difficulties in moving to gold in turn acted as a powerful stabilizer of monetary architecture. The laissez-faire approach to gold globalization that had been adopted during the 1867 conference was really recognition of the incapacity of policymakers to actually agree on a global stance. Nation-states remained sovereign, and the question of architecture would have to be solved on-site through the actual strategies of the various countries involved. A new architecture, if it was to emerge, would be obtained "ex post" as the product of individual strategies, not "ex ante" from a grand design.

This became obvious in 1873, which marked the beginning of the decline in the role of silver. This date, perhaps not accidentally, does coincide with Karl Polanyi's chosen turning point when nineteenth-century liberalism took on a more nationalistic tone. At that date, Germany decided to switch to gold using the proceeds of the indemnity it had collected from France after the war of 1870–1. France had technically the capacity to exchange Germany's silver against gold. But it nonetheless decided not to facilitate Germany's reform. It took retaliatory action and first limited, then suspended silver coinage to block Germany's attempt to use French mints to dispose of its silver surplus. The collapse in the price of silver that ensued led to a worldwide flight away from silver. Such was the trigger that caused the emergence of the international gold standard.[3] Thus, the making of the gold standard was more an exercise in collapse than one in construction: The spread of the gold standard, as an international monetary regime, really reflected its nationalistic dimension. In the language of game theory, it resulted from a coordination failure between France and Germany. Problems of coordination were again evident when the bimetallic crusade developed after 1873. As silver depreciated, and as it became clear that those who had forecast a decline in price levels were correct, policymakers sought to rebuild a monetary architecture that, ironically, implied a partial reversal to a measure of bimetallism. This is where Cernuschi and the supporters of "international bimetallism" entered into the picture with a new agenda toward silver: The

3 On the transition from bimetallism to the gold standard, see Marc Flandreau, "The French Crime of 1873? An Essay on the Emergence of the International Gold Standard, 1870–1880," *Journal of Economic History* (1996): 862–97.

pendulum had swung again. In the views of bimetallists, a new monetary architecture was needed to avert deflation. The cooperation of at least four powers (Britain, Germany, the United States, and France) was needed to implement a concerted resumption of silver coinage. A better architecture, they claimed, required a larger role for silver, for this was the only way to escape the deflationary implications that the spread of the gold standard was bringing about. Conferences were held in 1878, 1881, and 1892 without achieving much. Each time it seemed that the critical mass required to reach an agreement was lacking. Moreover, here again, the gains and losses from such an action were unevenly spread. Europeans looked suspiciously at the Americans, for they – on top of monetary stability – would get a better price for their silver output. Domestic politics in Germany seemed to preclude any return to silver, and France would not move if Germany did not. Yet, again, as deflation developed, it appeared that bimetallists would finally have their way. This was in the 1890s, when in the United States the presidential campaign of 1896 focused precisely on the issue of bimetallism, and when in Britain, confronted with exchange instability within the Empire (India had remained on silver), even the Old Lady of Threadneedle Street appeared for a while to hesitate.

But with the gold discoveries of the late 1890s and the return to inflation, the silver question lost momentum, paving the way for the golden years of the gold standard. Some saw in the resulting system, by then no longer a subject for criticism, a kind of ideal of universalism. This illusion still affects many contemporary writers and policymakers. Yet the fundamentally national nature of the international gold standard after 1896 is not only evident from the point of view of its genesis, but also from its actual record. It is revealing, for instance, that after 1900 adopting the gold standard became a nationalistic slogan in semi-sovereign nations as different as India and Hungary. This was because the gold standard – as opposed to a London-operated gold-exchange standard for India or mandatory participation to a Habsburg-dominated currency zone in Hungary – required the establishment of a domestic central bank. And the corollary of having a national central bank was a measure of control in the shape and direction of domestic credit.

The gold standard required an institutional framework, though no international institutions. In a pure gold standard, no central banks are needed. The classic mechanism through which specie flow responded to price differentials and price changes, and produced a self-balancing order, as described by David Hume in the eighteenth century, needed no mechanism whereby a central bank influenced or controlled interest rates. It might be possible to interpret the introduction of central banks, late in the day in some countries, as a response to crises in which the international economy had an undesirable impact. Thus, the German Reichsbank of 1875 was in part a response to the dramatic stock market crash (the *Gründerkrise*) of 1873, whereas the debates that led to the creation of the U.S. Federal Reserve System were reactions to the abrupt crisis of 1907.

The way each nation adhered to the gold standard reflected a menu of choices (within political possibilities) that suited national preferences. For decades, scholars have puzzled over the question of the "rules of the game" that either explained or failed to explain the success of the gold standard but which in the end never existed. These somewhat irrelevant discussions (very much a product of the interwar years) are swept away if one recognizes that each country's record as a member of the gold club must be assessed not from the point of view of alleged rules that never existed but from the point of view of each country's needs, constraints, and potentials: England, with its global banking system, did stick to a rigid gold convertibility; Italy, a debtor country with a large public debt, gave itself much more flexibility; France, with a somewhat inflexible money market, stood in between. The greater homogeneity that characterized the years between 1900 and 1913, when more countries than ever before were found on gold or "close to gold," really reflected the positive effects that gold inflation had on national indebtedness: By inflating away public debt burdens, the South African developments and Klondike discoveries of the 1890s gave national governments enhanced maneuvering space, thus limiting the conflict between domestic objectives and exchange stability. This in turn permitted a steadier maintenance of gold standards on a national basis. Inasmuch as the gold standard had an architecture of its own, it was the product of history.[4]

THE INTERWAR CATASTROPHE

It is striking how much greater the state's role in domestic and international economic affairs became during the interwar years as globalization collapsed. That was in large part a result of popular political pressures and expectations. Again, national preferences and priorities played a decisive role, but this time the effect was highly destructive.

There was now a greater consensus about the undesirable political and social costs of unemployment that limited central bank actions and weakened

---

4 On this view, see Marc Flandreau, Jacques Le Cacheux, and Frederic Zumer, "Stability without a Pact? Lessons from the European Gold Standard," *Economic Policy* 26 (1998): 117–62.

credibility (the markets might believe that some policies were unsustainable and might thus launch speculative attacks). There was a greater mobilization of political forces demanding tariff and quota protection (while business interests in favor of trade protection were largely unaware of the bad consequences of such action for the functioning of capital markets). There were demands on the public sector for public spending in response to the consequences of the war that were fundamentally at odds with the equally powerful expectations of taxpayers and voters about the need for a quick return to fiscal stability and orthodoxy. These tensions generated inconsistent policy and further undermined credibility. The result was a vulnerability to crisis, not simply on the periphery (as had been the case in the pre-1914 system), but in the financial and economic centers.

What seems unique about the interwar situation is how completely and devastatingly the political process failed. It may be, as one of the editors of this book has argued in relation to the intense debate about whether there was political room for maneuver in Germany in the Depression era, that there was a willful failure of the political imagination.[5] It may be that policymakers were already subject to impossible constraints at this time.[6] But no one will doubt that one of the blights of the age was the politicization of the process – a politicization very eloquently described in Steven Schuker's essay (Chapter 3). In this account, everything was paralyzed by the sheer volume of political ill-will generated by the war debts and reparations issue. Even the most apparently idealistic institutions were affected by this blight of politics. The League of Nations, which at times offered what appeared to be apolitical, technocratic, and expert advice on stabilization politics, was in fact nothing more than an attempt by Britain to maintain its severely weakened international power.

The protective mechanisms that had already been established in the framework of the nation-state in the prewar era clearly failed. Trade policy became explicitly protectionist in every major country and helped to cause a dramatic and unprecedented contraction on world trade. Migration policy, too, became progressively more restrictive. In the international financial system, there was at first, in the 1920s, an uneasy tension between, on the one hand, attempts to restore a global system and to get back to the gold standard (the aim of the experts assembled in 1922 at an international monetary

5 Carl-Ludwig Holtfrerich, "Alternativen zu Brünings Wirtschaftspolitik in der Weltwirtschaftskrise," *Historische Zeitschrift* 235 (1982): 605–31.
6 See Knut Borchardt, "Constraints and Room for Manoeuvre in the Great Depression of the Early Thirties: Towards a Revision of the Received Historical Picture," in Knut Borchardt, *Perspectives on Modern German Economic History an Policy* (Cambridge, 1991), 143–60.

conference in Genoa) and, on the other, demands for monetary nationalism. Internationalism expanded on the basis of a fragile sense of international
central bank cooperation, but this prompted controversy about the role of
the central banks in domestic economic management. It produced legends
and myths about the baleful influence of the "bankers' ramp" (in the United
Kingdom) or the "*deux cent familles*" (in France). Then came the financial
panics and crises of the early 1930s.

Central banks and international central bank cooperation, which had for
a time been seen as the solution to problems of the international monetary
system, were both terribly discredited by the Great Depression. The Federal
Reserve System, torn between different regional interests, allowed the U.S.
money supply to collapse. The German Reichsbank, which had previously
exhibited a quite generous (maybe even overgenerous) commitment to
lender of last resort operations, was obliged to stand by in 1931 while the
German banking system failed. Perhaps the Bank of England was more
flexible (indeed, it is easier for central banks of creditor countries to be
flexible than it is for those of debtor states), and the end of the British gold
standard in September 1931 was a policy triumph. The critical issue, however, was the adjustment process in the surplus countries of the later 1920s,
the United States and France. The Banque de France, examined here in
Kenneth Mouré's essay (Chapter 4), maintained orthodoxy long after the
crisis of the early 1930s and helped to make the French depression longer
than it would otherwise have been.

THE POSTWAR BOOM

What accounts for the upward arm of the U after 1945? The traditional
story, most fully set out in the work of Charles Kindleberger, is that it was
the enthusiastic and generous U.S. embrace of internationalism that put the
world back to rights.[7] The most well-known embodiment of that benign
internationalism was the Marshall Plan (European Recovery Program), first
adumbrated by the new Secretary of State George Marshall in a speech
in February 1947 to Princeton University alumni (the speech formed the
basis of a later, and better-known, speech at the Harvard commencement
in June). Marshall explained:

We have had a cessation of hostilities, but we have no genuine peace. Here at home
we are in a state of transition between a war and peace economy. In Europe and
Asia fear and famine still prevail. Power relationships are in a state of flux. Order has

7 Charles P. Kindleberger, *The World in Depression* (Berkeley, Calif., 1986).

yet to be brought out of confusion. Peace has yet to be secured. And how much this is accomplished will depend very much upon the American people.

Most of the other countries of the world find themselves exhausted economically, financially and physically. If the world is to get on its feet, if the production facilities of the world are to be restored, if the democratic processes in many countries are to resume their functioning, a strong lead and definite assistance from the United States will be necessary.[8]

This involved some transfer of monetary sovereignty in which politically unpopular measures were transferred out of the realm of practical national politics. It is important to note at the same time that the drive for the liberalization of world trade reflected the altered stance of the United States in comparison with the 1920s and a new economic internationalism.

Kindleberger and his long-time friend and colleague, Taylor Ostrander, explain this proposition in detail when they show the U.S. contribution to the dramatic German currency reform of 1948 (Chapter 7). A German reform alone would not have worked. At least in part, this was for political as well as economic reasons: As Knut Borchardt also underlined in a comment on Ostrander and Kindleberger's presentation, the U.S. involvement had the function of being a lightning rod, taking political disapprobation away from as yet weak and uncertain (and thus in modern parlance credibility-deficient) German political institutions.

Jakob Tanner (Chapter 6) shows how the neutral countries of World War II – in particular Switzerland – were worried from the outset about the Americanization of the new postwar international economic order and its implications for the security of small states. Clearly, it was not just small neutrals that felt the pressures and constraints. The security aspects of the new postwar order are also the major feature of the essay by Werner Abelshauser (Chapter 8). Participation in the U.S.-dominated world economic order was a price that had to be paid for security protection, and in the 1960s, as the Bretton Woods system became more and more vulnerable, the U.S. authorities used their security leverage more and more explicitly to win European (and also Japanese) acquiescence in their management of the economic and financial system.

But the new order went beyond calculations about U.S. interest and U.S. security arrangements. There was also a new intellectual consensus, in large part created (as well as eloquently represented) by the Cambridge economist John Maynard Keynes. Keynes's most recent biographer, Robert Skidelsky

---

8 See the text in *Princeton Alumni Weekly*, Feb. 28, 1947, 13. See also Helger Berger and Albrecht Ritschl, "Germany and the Political Economy of the Marshall Plan: A Re-revisionist View," in Barry Eichengreen, ed., *Europe's Postwar Recovery* (Cambridge, 1995), 210.

(Chapter 5), contributes an essay on the extent to which Keynes had experienced a sort of intellectual conversion from the economic nationalism of which he had been an advocate in the 1930s (notable in the famous article on national self-sufficiency printed in the *Nation* and in the *Yale Review*) to the internationalism of Bretton Woods. Skidelsky made a powerful case that the Keynes of Bretton Woods was still driven by a very distinct national, British, and anti-American vision. The central issue for him was finding a mechanism not for the imposition of adjustment on deficit countries (that had been the task and the achievement of the interwar League of Nations), but for forcing the surplus countries to adjust. That had been the major unresolved issue of the later 1920s, and Keynes saw the wartime and probable postwar strength of the U.S. economy with consequent alarm. (Keynes's other recent biographer, Donald Moggridge, was the commentator on this paper in the conference.)

The legacy of these debates is still with us. The issues that were controversial in the wartime debates about the ideal postwar order are still problematical. The distribution of adjustment costs by institutional diktat has long been a critical element in the work of the international community. It appears in regional variants of an international monetary order, as in the case of the evolution of the European Monetary System. Is high-minded internationalism just a cover for national interests – American in the case of the Bretton Woods system and British in the case of the interwar League of Nations? Indeed, there are remarkable continuities between the League and the postwar world, as Louis Pauly (Chapter 10) makes clear in a disturbing and controversial essay (in the discussion at the conference, it elicited a fierce rebuttal from one of the most influential figures in the history of the International Monetary Fund, the former director of the Research Department and later Executive Director Jacques Polak). One of the most remarkable analogies arises out of the fundamental character of the involvement of international institutions in the domestic political complexes that are inevitably produced by debates about appropriate strategies of economic stabilization. On the one hand, the international institutions have a lightning rod function, in which they take away the blame for unpopular decisions. On the other hand, in democratic politics, responsibility and accountability play a decisive role.

These issues have recently assumed a new importance. In the 1990s, views of the appropriate role of the International Monetary Fund (IMF) and other international institutions changed dramatically. In large part, this was the consequence of reflections on the collapse of communism and on the links between political and economic reform. In the 1980s, many political scientists had believed that economic reform was more easily achieved by authoritarian regimes. The experience of Central Europe in particular completely reversed the understanding of the link between economic liberalization and political democratization. In the new picture, only countries in which there was a government sustained by a deep reserve of legitimacy would be able to bear the pains associated with adjustment.

This change had repercussions for the concept of policy conditionality that had previously been at the center of attempts to impose order from the outside of national politics. If there was less room for a benevolent dictator in imposing economic reform, this would also mean a questioning of the traditional role assigned to the IMF. Instead the question of "ownership" became central.

The collapse of the communist economies, or (in the case of China) their transformation into market economies was the last stage in the creation of the new consensus about economic policy, frequently but misleadingly referred to as the "Washington consensus." The consequence has been an increasing homogeneity of political outlook as well as of the economic order. Indeed, one key insight is that the two are linked: that economic efficiency depends on a functioning civil society, on the rule of law, and on respect for private property.

The post–Cold War world has a quite different politics: no longer a line-up of East versus West in which pro-Western regimes automatically obtain support regardless of levels of efficiency and competence and probity, but rather a much more interventionist stance by the international community in which the logic that associates economic and political change is taken much more seriously. The result has been the forcing of a much quicker pace of economic reform in some states (such as Egypt, for example, which until the early 1990s largely resisted attempts to liberalize); the disintegration of the political order in others (the collapse and defeat of Mobutu's Zaire); and descent into the status of international pariah for others (Nigeria after the execution of Ken Saro-Wiwa). The striking change in this area is that there is no longer an acceptance of domestic political inefficiency, corruption, and oppression.

The most visible product of the new political environment is the concern of the Bretton Woods institutions with "governance." In August 1997, a new set of guidance notes of the IMF's Executive Board instructed the staff that in policy advice the IMF "has assisted its member countries in creating systems that limit the scope for ad hoc decision making, for rent seeking, for undesirable preferential treatment of individuals or organizations." The IMF suggested that "it is legitimate to seek information about the political situation in member countries as an essential element in judging the prospects for policy implementation."

The new political outlook had already been reflected in a number of very high-profile decisions in 1996–7. There are four completely new areas, in each of which conditionality has become highly contentious. First, military spending had never been a topic of explicit discussion in the era of the Cold War. In *World Economic Outlook* reports, starting in 1993, it is discussed as a major problem of misallocation of resources. Now, in a number of cases, notably Pakistan and Romania, it became a quite central element in IMF discussions. Second, corruption is now explicitly addressed, not just in Africa but also in the case of Indonesia. Third, so also is democracy, although (unlike the European Bank for Reconstruction and Development) there is no reference to democracy in the statutes (the Bretton Woods Articles of Agreement). Serbia was barred from the IMF on the basis of such a political argument. In the case of Croatia, in July 1997, the IMF withheld the release of a $40 million tranche of structural assistance for privatization, not because of any direct problems with the privatization program but because of "the unsatisfactory state of democracy in Croatia." Fourth, especially in response to the Asian crisis, a critique developed of a feature that had previously been regarded as a linchpin of Asia's economic success. "Trust" and "strong informal networks" were now relabeled and condemned as "crony capitalism." This criticism was linked to the attack on corruption, and "a stable and transparent regulatory environment for private sector activity" was laid out as the solution.[9]

There had been some links with human rights issues in the past – in Poland, whose membership application was held up in the 1980s after the imposition of martial law and the internment of political dissenters; or, more discreetly and subtly, in South Africa in the 1980s where apartheid was attacked as an inefficient labor practice. But the scale of the discussion of political issues in the mid- and late 1990s was quite novel. The gradual extension of the IMF into politics was an immediate result of the new consensus about economic practice and of a new world political order that it has helped to produce. But it reflects something more profound – a realization increasingly shared throughout the world that the world economy, and world institutions, can be a better guarantee of rights and of prosperity than some governments, which may be corrupt and rent-seeking and militaristic.

---

9 Michel Camdessus, "The IMF and Good Governance," address given at Transparency International, Paris, Jan. 21, 1998.

There are many obvious problems with the new position. One of the most fundamental is that the international monetary system is still an arena of national interests. Paul Volcker described IMF economic programs in a neat way: "When the Fund consults with a poor and weak country, the country gets in line. When it consults with a big and strong country, the Fund gets in line. When the big countries are in conflict, the Fund gets out of the line of fire."[10] The same lessons apply to the modern larger sense of a joint political and economic package.

Dealing with military expenditure, corruption, and undemocratic practices is easier for international institutions in the cases of small countries such as Croatia or Romania, or even in isolated states such as Pakistan or Nigeria. But it is likely to be hard and controversial in large states with substantial military and economic potential, for instance, in Russia or China. In other cases, it will be interpreted as a blatant attempt to impose Western values in the hope of restraining or even crippling potential competitors (the criticism frequently voiced by Mahathir Mahomad).

Second, there is the question of institutional capacity for implementation. Some recent programs and statements also go into the question of economic organization: the dismantling of cartels, the improvement of accounting practices, and banking supervision. It is easy to see the macroeconomic effects of the organizational or structural flaws criticized by the IMF. On the other hand, correcting them takes the IMF into completely new areas, in which it has no previous expertise. It is clearly experienced in fiscal affairs, and in advising on central bank policy, but not in wide-ranging reforms of the financial sector and certainly not in accountancy. Many critics will wonder whether the specification and implementation of such advice is not better left to other institutions, or to the concerned firms themselves.

Third, and most fundamentally, this process of adding new expectations will create a dangerous momentum of its own. Part of the package discussed by the U.S. Congress for an IMF quota increase in 1998–9 involved the integration of environmental and labor standard issues in IMF programs. Such demands reflect an expectations trap. The more the IMF is seen to extend its mandate, the more it will be expected to do; and inevitably also the less it will be able to live up to the demands. The problem came into much sharper focus during the Asian crisis of 1997–8, when both the right and the left (including the moderate right and left, not simply extreme positions) focused attention on alleged inadequacies of the international financial institutions.

---

10 Paul A. Volcker and Toyoo Gyohten, *Changing Fortunes: The World's Money and the Threat to American Leadership* (New York, 1992), 143.

The consequence of this perception of failure is already clear in the mounting skepticism even in the mainstream of political life, about the continued viability of the IMF. In order to counter such opposition, it will need to resist institutional overstretch: to ensure that its mandate is limited, clearly defined, and subject to an assessment of results. In 2000, the report of the congressional commission (Meltzer commission) on international financial institutions, the speeches of U.S. Treasury Secretary Larry Summers, and the first actions of the new Managing Director of the IMF, Horst Köhler, indicated that there would probably be a return of the IMF to its "core mission."

The international architecture of some previous period, notably the gold standard, may have appeared in retrospect – especially in the midst of the monetary turbulence of the 1930s or the 1970s – as a kind of ideal that should be emulated or recreated. But it was really a product of the development of nineteenth-century nation-states, with nationalism concealed from the eyes of the careless observer behind a veil of internationalism. Its making was not the achievement of visionary architects but a product of national rivalry. In the interwar period, national rivalry worked in a deeply destructive way. The task in the postwar period, in the upward movement of the U trajectory toward greater international economic integration, was not the suppression of national demands and interests but the devising of an institutional mechanism that could mediate them. The result, an economic environment in which growth helped to produce political stability and legitimacy, made that mediation more efficient. Modern supporters of a new architecture may be well advised to ponder these lessons before they start telling us about the necessity of a complete reinvention or recasting of the international monetary system.

1

Caveat Emptor

Coping with Sovereign Risk Under the International Gold Standard, 1871–1913

MARC FLANDREAU

Caveat emptor. To those who forget the maxim, each new financial crisis brings an opportunity to relearn their lesson. The turmoil that swept Southeast Asian countries in the late 1990s is no exception: Once again, it has produced classic tales about late investors buying out of ignorance. According to some economists, rating agencies should take their share of the blame: They failed to provide appropriate signals to the market through early downgrades and then followed the market mood as it spiraled down.[1] In self-defense, rating agencies emphasize that their grades are not (and have never been) meant to establish any kind of standard on which one could base investment decisions: The availability of formal ratings should not discourage investors from devoting time and effort to get their own opinion. Why look for someone to blame? It is after all in the nature of risk to bring its crop of regrets.

At a deeper level, these recurrent complaints may be seen as illustrating the complexities of the economics of economic intelligence: The supply and demand of information are nested into an institutional setting from which they cannot be separated. This setting in turn provides incentives that contribute to more or less risk-taking on behalf of agents. For instance, the expectation of an eventual bailout by some public body (national or multilateral) reduces investors' incentives to collect data and process it in original ways: Less attention is paid to discussing economic developments

The comments of the conference participants are gratefully acknowledged. The author wishes to thank Roger Nougaret, Conservateur des archives historiques du Crédit Lyonnais, for his kind, patient, and friendly help. Thanks to Lucette Levan-Lemesle and Luc Marco for their information on the Parisian political economists of the nineteenth century, and to participants of the OFCE/EHESS "Convergences en Histoire Economique" Seminar as well as of the Warwick Conference on Globalization for their suggestions. Thanks are also due to Valérie Richard for her help with the manuscript.

1 G. Larrain, H. Reisen, and J. von Maltzan, "Emerging Market Risk and Sovereign Credit Ratings," OECD Development Centre, Technical Paper, no. 124.

in borrowing countries, fewer analyses are supplied, and they are of lesser quality.

Hence, the organization of economic intelligence should be a research topic in its own right. Yet problems of identification line the way. While a theoretical case can be made that the expectation of a rescue amplifies the magnitude of risk-taking, it is an altogether different and more difficult matter to prove it empirically. History on the other hand provides a way to ask that question in reverse: One only needs to look for occurrences when the market mechanism is "bailout free." One such episode is the years before World War I. True, some authors have tried to argue that a measure of central bank cooperation existed between 1890 and 1914 and that it did work, on occasion, as a partial substitute for international lender of last resort facilities.[2] But such schemes (which in any case were not outright bailouts) were very occasional, often failed, and depended on a set of complex factors on which it was dangerous to bank.[3] The concern about moral hazard was a close companion of late nineteenth-century laissez-faire. The boldest proposal for an international mechanism to prevent crises from spreading was met with the belief that irresponsible behavior – not contagion – was the real danger.

Of course, it could still be that, even if they did not anticipate being bailed out by domestic monetary authorities, nineteenth-century investors expected their governments to help them "bail in" foreign debtors. Lending countries used in cases military expedients that mitigated the meaning of "sovereignty." The inclusion in sovereign debt contracts of collateral clauses provided a legal justification for military intervention. International control, as in Turkey and Greece, could ensue.[4] But muscle flexing is not without costs and, to be effective, requires a fair amount of lender coordination. Coordination was far from natural in the explosive political climate of the years before World War I, when global providers of capital were also global rivals.[5] Defaults did take place, and military intervention, when it occurred,

2 Barry Eichengreen and Marc Flandreau, "The Geography of the Gold Standard," in J. Braga de Macedo et al., eds., *Currency Convertibility, the Gold Standard, and Beyond* (London, 1996).
3 Marc Flandreau, "Central Bank Cooperation in Historical Perspective: A Sceptical View," *Economic History Review* (1997).
4 N. Herbault, "Le contrôle international en Egypte, Turquie et Grèce," Congrés International des Valeurs Mobilières, 4 fascicule, no. 166 (1901): 1–51.
5 On these "debt games," see V. Aggarwal, *Debt Games* (Cambridge, 1996). Charles Lipson provides an overview of the interactions between debt crises and international politics before World War I (Charles Lipson, "International and National Debt: Comparing Victorian Britain and Postwar America," in Barry Eichengreen and P. Lindert, eds., *The International Debt Crisis in International Perspective* (Cambridge, Mass., 1989)). The classic reference on the topic remains Herbert Feis, *Europe, The World's Banker, 1870–1914* (New Haven, Conn., 1930).

did not result in complete recovery of lost funds. Banks thus had to watch their steps: In France, an early Crédit agricole went under in 1876 as a result of the Ottoman default. In England, Baring had to pay a high price for its way out of Argentinean losses.

This makes the pre-1914 experience of globalization "without the multilaterals" fascinating. A large number of classic studies have demonstrated that capital did move across borders, either through the agency of financial markets or, increasingly, through direct foreign investment or other arrangements such as "free standing companies."[6] These studies have paid much attention to the geographical distribution of international investment, to its contribution to economic growth, and to the trends and cycles of international finance. Yet the question of determining how investment priorities were set remains obscure. In what is perhaps the only study that has explicitly tackled the issue, Herbert Feis maintained that "politics" had been the overarching factor in allocating (or misallocating) capital.[7] To date, no full-fledged alternative has been provided. We know very little about the nineteenth-century devices to screen potential borrowers, balance risks, and "rate" sovereigns. This may explain the resilience of the popular myth of nineteenth-century investors lured by politicians.[8] Didn't sovereign rating begin only after World War I when U.S. capital arrived in the Old World?[9] To many, this is prima facie evidence of the lack of economic literacy among European bankers before World War I.

This chapter challenges that view. It argues that the type of analyses that are at the heart of formal rating had in fact developed in Europe at least a quarter of a century before World War I. I take a look at one French bank: France was the second largest international investor in the late nineteenth and early twentieth centuries. It specialized in lending to the "risky" regions of the European Continent, such as the Mediterranean or Russia, where public debts were large and sovereign default a potentially huge problem. I focus on the Crédit Lyonnais. The choice, which in view of some recent

---

6 L. H. Jenks, *The Migration of British Capital to 1875* (London, 1927); Albert H. Imlah, *Economic Elements in the Pax Britannica* (Cambridge, Mass., 1958); Rondo Cameron, *France and the Economic Development of Europe, 1800–1914* (Princeton, N.J., 1961); Maurice Lévy-Leboyer, *Les banques européennes et l'industrialisation internationale dans la première moitié du XIXème siècle* (Paris, 1964); Mira Wilkins, *The History of Foreign Investment in the United States to 1914* (Cambridge, Mass., 1989). See also Mira Wilkin's chapter in this book.

7 Feis, *Europe, the World's Banker.*

8 Ignorance and herding behavior play an important role in the boom and bust approaches to international lending. See Charles P. Kindleberger, "International Propagation of Financial Crises: The Experience of 1888–93," in Charles P. Kindleberger, *Keynesianism vs. Monetarism and Other Essays in Financial History* (London, 1985).

9 The first edition of Moody's *Government and Municipals Manual* appeared in 1919.

developments may sound ironic, is not fortuitous: The Lyonnais, a private commercial bank created in 1863, grew patiently and prudently from being a financial underdog to becoming the largest European institution at the turn of the century.[10] At that point, it established itself as a prominent actor in foreign lending, even displacing traditional players of the Rothschild kind from this market to some extent.

The chapter's first lesson is that in the absence of international agencies, private risk analysis played an essential role in bringing about financial integration before World War I. In addition, I show that the lack of official provision of international statistics and rating led the Lyonnais to integrate the collection and analysis of data: Its financial studies unit, the Service des Etudes Financières (SEF), constructed a series that permitted direct comparisons between the macroeconomic health of various borrowers. The second lesson is that the lack of multilateral agencies, while providing incentives for private investment in information gathering, does not necessarily lead to an efficient provision thereof. The externalities in the supply of information can lead to monopolization. In this instance, I show how the Lyonnais sought to become a kind of mood-setter in the Paris market.

The remainder of the chapter is organized as follows: The first section is mostly descriptive. We start at the most microeconomic level and survey the background in which the SEF emerged and developed. The second section focuses on the Lyonnais's methods of assessing public finances and sovereign risk. I show that these methods led to a straightforward way of rating countries in risk categories. The conclusion, finally, discusses the lessons of the nineteenth-century experience.

THE SERVICE DES ETUDES FINANCIÈRES, 1871–1914

The Founding of the SEF: Speculations

The SEF was set up in 1871 on request from Henri Germain, director and creator of Crédit Lyonnais. Its proclaimed objective was to provide facts and figures that would assist investment decisions. Over time, the SEF grew into a large research unit with a reputation.[11] Eugène d'Eichtal, in the short hagiographic obituary he wrote on Germain, makes special

---

10 Jean Bouvier, *Le Crédit Lyonnais, de 1863 à 1882: Les années de formation d'une grande banque de depots*, 2 vols. (Paris, 1961).

11 It was to the SEF that the Bank of France turned when it was asked by the U.S. National Monetary Commission to provide data on the French Monetary System. And it would be to the SEF that French officials would turn when they sought to assess the German reparations after World War I.

reference to the SEF.[12] Its creation, he explained, resulted from the great man's "passion for political economy." I suggest, instead, that one needs to relate the founding of the SEF to the general background of the market for economic information around 1870.[13]

The 1850s and 1860s were years of an "information revolution." This revolution had its technical side, with the installation of the cable between London and the Continent (1852) and later between Europe and America (1866). The cable brought national financial markets closer together, shortened drastically transmission lags from market to market, and reduced cross-border uncertainties. This revolution had, of course, an important economic side: The technical possibilities for channeling funds from market to market improved at the same time that both the supply and demand of funds were growing more competitive. The period after 1840 displayed a massive expansion of the key financial markets as global centers. The capitalization of both London and Paris accelerated, and cumulated securitized foreign lending amounted to a large share of both England and France's GDP.[14] Other industrialized countries, such as Belgium and Switzerland, also contributed to the process, exporting their own capital through the pipes of the leading financial centers.[15] The networking of railways across the Continent and the need to finance new nations in both their military and industrial enterprises also multiplied the number of possible outlets.

For lenders, this called for increased screening capacities. More information was required on more projects. With the growth of the number of markets, geopolitical coverage had to expand. The move that had begun in England with the creation of *The Economist* in 1844 extended to the Continent. *La Semaine financière*, the most comprehensive and well-informed French-language weekly, began in the 1850s in Brussels. The quality of its information was enhanced by a freedom of tone provided by its ability to escape from French political censorship. Progressively, the success of *The Economist* led to a multiplication of continental offspring: In 1873, at about the same time the SEF was launched, Paul Leroy-Beaulieu created *L'Economiste français*. Other clones followed.

The multiplication of sources of economic data also created a need for reference. Financial handbooks listing quoted bonds and collecting official

---

12 Eugène d'Eichtal, *Notice sur la vie et les travaux de M. Henri Germain* (Paris, 1905).

13 Bouvier (1961), p. 289ff. provides a somewhat different narrative of the evolution of the SEF between 1871 and 1873 but concurs with our view of the "information revolution."

14 For instance, cumulated foreign issues in Paris amounted to about 8 billion in 1865 while French Net National product was about 18 billion.

15 Lévy-Leboyer, *Les banque européenes et l'industrialisation internationale.*

information in a systematic way came much in vogue. From 1863, for instance, *The Economist* started issuing the *Investor's Monthly Manual*.[16] In France, Alphonse Courtois published the first edition of his *Manuel des fonds publics et des sociétés par actions* in 1856.[17] The volume described systematically all public and private bonds listed in Paris. The book was a hit and would be republished several times. It would later have an official competitor, the *Annuaire officiel des agents de change* issued by the association of Parisian brokers.

Such publications, however, were mere compilations of official pamphlets that borrowing institutions circulated when new loans were floated. The need to provide background information relating to the general macroeconomic, institutional, and political outlook thus remained. Macmillan seized the opportunity in the 1860s, when it started issuing *The Statesman's Yearbook*. Another slightly later attempt at improving the statistical background was that of the Société Internationale de Statistique, an international network of statisticians created in the 1880s that held conferences every four years. The meetings, which drew both official and independent statisticians, sought to define statistical "best practices." Proceedings were published. In some cases, the Société Internationale also lobbied to obtain changes in the way official returns were either collected or presented.[18] However, political resistance turned the odds against the feasibility of such "multilateral" endeavors, suggesting that more solitary investigations were better equipped to succeed. This may explain the large supply of individual statistical compilations, impressive by modern standards yet often redundant, and among which Michael G. Mulhall's stand out prominently.[19]

In contrast, the expansion in the competition for foreign credit implied that borrowers had growing incentives to become more transparent. Bilateral relations were increasingly replaced by broader multilateral underwriting syndicates that then turned to a large crowd of customers. This meant that borrowing governments could shop around for lower prices. But this also meant that they had to find some way to communicate with the rich public of the lending countries. The practice thus developed among borrowing governments to publish, on an annual basis, detailed financial accounts. Whereas in Western Europe, transparency of public accounts had

16 See also W. T. C. King, *History of the London Discount Market* (London, 1936), 266.
17 Alphonse Courtois, *Manuel des fonds publics et des sociétés par actions*, 8th ed. (Paris, 1883).
18 Lucette Levan-Lemesle, "L'enseignement de l'économie politique en France 1860–1939," 6 vols., Ph.D. diss., University of Paris I, Panthéon-Sorbonne, 1995.
19 Michael G. Mulhall, *Industries and Wealth of Nations* (London, 1896); Michael G. Mulhall, *The Dictionary of Statistics*, 4th ed. (London, 1909).

been a companion of the rise of parliamentarism (the lenders to national governments were the domestic bourgeoisie), financial accountability developed in other countries with international lending. Fiscal returns were often bilingual: Russian accounts were published in Russian and French, the Hungarian ones also used French, while Japanese returns (after 1900) used both English and French. Thus, every year from the 1860s and 1870s onward, a huge crop of government documents flooded the marketplace.

This information "overflow" was both a challenge and an opportunity: If exploited intelligently, information could give an edge to newcomers. For years, international finance had been the private hunting ground of the traditional investment bankers. The Haute banque, with its high-profile customers and correspondents, collected money and information almost in the same move. By its extensive political and economic networks, the Haute banque had a first-hand knowledge of the risks involved and, through its political clout, even a degree of command on the risks themselves.[20] The limited extent of democracy in several borrowing countries also implied that fewer levels of government were involved. Personal contacts had a premium over "macroeconomic" analysis. This sort of intelligence clearly outsmarted any attempt at putting together figures that in most cases just did not exist. But the expanding supply of statistical returns meant that the time of bankers who kept your account in the back of their mind was passing. It is thus no wonder that the SEF was created in the middle of the early 1870s boom in foreign lending. As a newcomer on the financial scene, the Lyonnais did not have as strong political connections as the establishment. Being an outsider, it was excluded from the safest bets and had to take calculated risks.

The First Years of the Service, 1871–1889

The link between the expansion of financial press and the creation of the SEF is a direct one: While Desseilligny (a board member) was responsible for general supervision, Courtois (the author of the famous *Manuel des fonds publics et des sociétés par actions* to which I referred earlier) was appointed head of the service. An archetypal self-taught financial journalist, Courtois had, according to some sources, worked for the Lyonnais since the 1860s.[21] He was well acquainted with financial techniques and had authored a famous

20 Karl Polanyi, *The Great Transformation* (Boston, 1944); Bertrand Gille, *Les Rothschild*, 2 vols. (Geneva, 1967).

21 See *Dictionnaire de biographie française*, 9:1036. G. Vapereau, *Dictionnaire universel des contemporains*, 6th ed. (Paris, 1893), 386, concurs, albeit in looser terms. We could not check the accuracy of this information. Documents from the Crédit Lyonnais written at the time of the creation of the SEF refer to Courtois as a "publiciste," suggesting that he was really a journalist at the time.

Traité des opérations de bourse (1855). He had also been a pioneer in data collection: His *Tableaux des cours des principales valeurs* provided time series for bonds and stocks on the Paris bourse since 1797.[22] An opponent of government intervention and a member since 1851 of the Société Economique Politique, the French laissez-faire lobby, he had argued forcefully in his books that governments should not tamper with the stock market. In short, the Lyonnais had appointed a specialist of the French Bourse well acquainted with the tout Paris of economics.

The correspondence surrounding the creation of the SEF suggests that the whole process took place under much pressure from the top management. Abundant space and resources were devoted to the project. Two kinds of information were sought. First, Germain wanted the SEF to provide "insider" information that would fuel profitable trading. Second, he wanted it to perform "modern" economic analysis, which derives value from the intelligent use of publicly available information. This multiplicity of purposes was reflected in duality of names: The SEF was alternatively referred to as the "information office" (*bureau des renseignements*) or the "research bureau" (*bureau des etudes*). This caused much confusion for both Courtois and later historians.[23] Although both roles initially coexisted, the latter would gradually dominate.

The search for insider information involved spying on other banks and governments: The service hired foreign "agents" (in French, *correspondants*) working in competing finance houses. One of the first agents in Vienna was an employee at Rothschild's. Agents were paid for their tips, and in some cases valuable information was given in return. To maximize the flow of information and avoid the risk of being deceived by its own correspondents, the Lyonnais arranged redundancies: Two agents were hired in a single market, without their knowing.[24] Of course, insider information was not limited to foreign markets: Some SEF employees in Paris (*employés sédentaires* or resident employees) were hired because they were thought to be "well

---

22 Alphonse Courtois, *Tableaux des cours des principales valeurs négociées et cotées en bourse des effets publics de Paris* (Lyon, 1873).

23 This tension is, in my opinion, the origin of the alleged formal distinction which Bouvier is thought to have identified between "renseignements" and "etudes" (Bouvier [1963]). Bouvier's claim is swept away by a letter from Courtois, who lost patience: "We are called Etudes financières!" (letter of Oct. 13, 1871, Archives historique du Crédit Lyonnais, Historique DEEF (hereafter Historiques DEEF)). Clearly, the "bureau des renseignements" was a subsection of Service des Etudes Financières, not a separate unit. This interpretation is fostered by the eventual use of the expression *bureaux* as a substitute for SEF *sections* (DEEF 62694).

24 Key financial centers included New York, Rio de Janeiro, Buenos Aires, Berlin, Frankfurt, Vienna, Saint Petersburg, Constantinople, Florence, Madrid, Lisbon, Brussels, Alexandria. The Lyonnais had a branch in London.

acquainted" or for their abilities "at finding [their] ways in ministries."[25] To conduct its economic studies, the SEF had to collect statistics. For this, it was equipped right away with a reference library that started purchasing books, newspapers, periodicals, and official reports. The library was meant to be comprehensive. This was to some extent similar to what the Library and Record Department of the Council of the Corporation of Foreign Bond Holders was doing at about the same time, although the library of the Lyonnais (which was substantially larger than CFB's) was meant for private use only.[26]

The output of the SEF was of two kinds. First, the service had to produce a daily "bulletin." The bulletin contained financial information of general interest made out of clippings from the international press. The daily bulletin's circulation was restricted to top management use: Only the heads of both the Paris and Lyons offices and of the main branches received it. Second, and more importantly, the service had to produce specific reports made on request from the executive office. Reports could cover a wide variety of topics, ranging from the prospects of PLM railways to Austrian finances.

Courtois had been asked to find the appropriate people. His correspondence is an echo of the obstacles he encountered. In 1871, political economy (not to mention applied macroeconomics) was not widely taught in France.[27] Courtois hired people from the Bourse (stock exchange) or the financial press. The results were disappointing.[28] Germain suggested recruiting from the offices of the Ministry of Finance, where one could find "hard working, intelligent, and moreover low paid, young men."[29] Germain must have been referring to services such as the Bureau de statistique et de législation comparée, which statistician Alfred de Foville headed since 1867.[30] But potential employees did not turn out to be as bright as Germain had hoped.[31] Courtois then sought to recruit economists through recommendations from members of the Société d'Economie Politique, of which he was a member. He used social events such as the dinner of the society to

25 Letter of Nov. 3, 1871.   26 See the CFB, Annual Report, 1899.
27 The only business school in Paris, the Ecole Supérieure de Commerce de Paris was described by one of its former graduates as being at the time a "school where there were indeed a few lectures on trade, but whose main occupation was to teach French to young men from Latin America, who came to study these things which one learns so well in Paris" (Levan-Lemesle, "L'enseignement de l'économie politique," vol. 2, chap. 10).
28 Archives historiques du Crédit Lyonnais, 62AH 20, Letter from Mazerat to Letourneur.
29 Letter of Oct. 4, 1871.
30 Levan-Lemesle, "L'enseignement de l'économie politique."
31 One potential candidate who was approached turned out to be a typical "rond-de-cuir" (lazy bureaucrat): He asked whether he could work at home.

carry on his investigation and paid personal visits to some economists, again, with limited success.[32] He then turned to second-best solutions. Reasonably appropriate applicants, whose background showed their adaptability, could be tried. One of the first employees was a graduate from Saint Cyr (the French Military Academy) who had left the army and had become a merchant, then a broker, in various towns. This ensured that he was both numerate and flexible; the rest would have to be learned on site.

Looking through the Lyonnais files, one gets the feeling that the search was also impaired by the bank's own position. At that time, the Lyonnais was still a relatively recent institution and a career there implied a measure of risk taking. As a matter of fact, one civil servant from top government engineer schools which the Lyonnais was lucky to hire turned out to be a second-order type whom the administration was happy to part with.[33] The difficulty of actually attracting people is also evident from Germain's suggestion to recruit females.[34] It is probable that Germain had realized that top male graduates would not consider work at the SEF sufficiently attractive. Yet even this did not succeed.

To what extent did these obstacles hamper the initial development of the SEF? From its projected twelve employees in 1871, the staff rose to about twenty in 1881. This was quite large by the standards of the time, but in a sense fell rather short of the original ambitions. Moreover, the size of the staff did not increase much during the first twenty years. While it kept accumulating books, statistics, and studies, the SEF did not realize the grand scheme that had been initially envisioned. Ultimately, it would take the development of the teaching of economics in France, the rise of Lyonnais as a major bank, and the international banking crisis that climaxed in 1890 for the SEF to meet its initial goals.

The Rise of the SEF, 1889–1914

During the board meeting of November 5, 1889, Germain announced that he wanted to increase the size of the SEF. "Time has come," he said, "to give to the operations of the SEF maximum scope and efficiency."[35] René

---

32 Showing up at Cernuschi's mansion, he was told that the famous bimetallist was touring silver standard Asia.

33 Information provided by Cécile Omnes, "La gestion du personnel au credit Lyonnais (1863–1939)," 2 vols., Ph.D. diss., University of Paris I, 1997.

34 Germain encouraged Courtois to hire Félicité Guillaumin. Félicité, twenty-five at the time, was the elder of two daughters of the famous publisher of *Political Economy*.

35 Minutes of the Conseil d'administration, Nov. 5, 1889.

Brice, a member of the council of administration, was asked to head the service. He had no special skills in political economy: His appointment really reflected the increased control which Germain took at that point over the SEF, and, from that date on, the service expanded.

One factor explaining this evolution was the removal of bottlenecks on the supply of human capital. The Lyonnais's initial dissatisfaction with the general background of graduates had been a widely shared feeling in French commercial circles. The defeat of 1871 and the ensuing concern about economic decline provided the impetus for the creation of a number of institutions devoted to the teaching of business and economics.[36] At the Ecole Libre des Sciences Politiques, which was set up in 1871, Leroy-Beaulieu initiated a course on public finances in 1872. Although Leroy-Beaulieu stopped teaching in 1880, the number of courses in "macroeconomics" (political economy, money, finance) kept increasing. In 1883, these courses were organized within a formal curriculum in economics and finance – the "section économique et financière." In 1891, students of this program could major in either private or public finance. Those two majors became separate curricula in 1909–10. Lecturers at Ecole Libre (or "Sciences-Po" as it was already known at the time) were recruited from among the top echelon of statistics and economics.[37]

The Paris business school, known as Hautes Etudes Commerciales or HEC, was created in 1881. Garnier (1881–3) and, later, Courcelle-Seneuil (1883–8), both leaders of the French lobby for political economy, taught there. According to Levan-Lemesle, when Octave Noël took over the course in 1888, he gave it a practical twist that was most welcome.[38] Noël was a prolific writer who had published extensively on railways, money, and central banking. His lectures were intended to make the case for laissez-faire on the basis of practical examples. For instance, in an 1888 book, Noël explored the economic and institutional record of a number of European central banks in an attempt to show the advantages of central bank independence from government intervention – a view that would later become the conventional wisdom during the Belle Epoque.[39] This approach reflected Noël's special concern about the relevance of his teaching for the four hundred students he taught each year.

36 Levan-Lemesle, "L'enseignement de l'économie politique."
37 They included Levasseur, Juglar, Foville, Aupetit (a student of Walras), and Cheysson (a founder of modern econometrics). See Levan-Lemesle, "L'enseignement de l'économie politique."
38 Levan-Lemesle, "L'enseignement de l'économie politique," 472.
39 Octave Noël, *Les banques d'émission en Europe* (Paris, 1888). Marc Flandreau, Jacques le Cacheux, and Frédéric Zumer, "Stability Without a Pact? Lessons from the European Gold Standard," *Economic Policy* (1998): 27.

Taken together, graduates from HEC and Sciences-Po's "section économique et financière" represented a total of about five hundred students with degrees in economics. Moreover, the rising prestige of Crédit Lyonnais (it was by now no longer an eight-year-old outsider as in 1871, but an over twenty-five-year-old bank that often led major syndicates and had successfully resisted the 1881 stock market crash in Paris) had implications on its ability to attract first-class graduates from all schools. In addition to economists from HEC or Sciences-Po, the Lyonnais hired engineers from Ponts et Chaussées, Mines, Arts et Métiers, Polytechnique. This was especially important given that investment opportunities generally included a technical aspect for which "pure" economists were inadequate.

Whereas the availability of graduates with the appropriate background was probably a necessary condition for the growth of the SEF, it nevertheless did not prompt the November 1889 decision to expand. Rather, Germain's decision must be related to the increasing risks in international banking that developed as a result of the lending spree of the late 1880s.[40] The escalating tensions precipitated the collapse of Comptoir d'escompte in 1889 and of Baring in 1890. The Banque de Paris et des Pays-Bas recorded heavy losses in Argentinean railways in 1890–1 and, in general, many banks suffered. Contagion ensued and the bonds of weaker governments depreciated. The exchange rates of a number of South American and Mediterranean countries declined. Several suspensions of interest payments followed. In this context, and given the Lyonnais's compulsive concern about liquidity and mismatches (an attitude that was Germain's trademark), the decision to expand the SEF seems quite understandable. The Lyonnais had probably realized that those who would survive would be the most careful students of international finance.

Recruiting thus resumed after 1890. The move, first gradual (there were still twenty employees in 1893), quickly accelerated: Eighty people worked in the service at the turn of the century. Increased budgets followed: Before 1889 the annual budget of the service had oscillated between 100,000 and 200,000 francs.[41] Returns for the period 1890–1905 show a take-off: The SEF's expenses trebled over the 1890s.[42] Drastic increases brought budgets near 800,000 francs per year after 1900. Indeed, budgets were mostly driven by trends in the work force (Figure 1.1): General office expenses, despite the 1890 introduction of the typewriter as well as of a number of computing

40 Kindleberger, "International Propagation of Financial Crises."
41 Bouvier, *Le Crédit Lyonnais*, 294.
42 Archives du Crédit Lyonnais, DEEF, Bd des Italiens.

Figure 1.1. SEF expenses (French francs, left scale) and number of employees (right scale).
Source: Archives DEEF, "Boulevard des Italiens," sans cote.

machines and massive purchases of books for the library, amounted to little
in comparison to employees' earnings.[43]

The increase in the number of SEF employees also outpaced the growth
of labor inputs for the bank at large. The gross wage of the SEF represented
about 1.5 percent of the total wage burden in 1894.[44] This proportion
almost doubled, rising to 2.5 percent in 1900. Similarly, the number of
SEF employees rose during the same period from 0.5 percent of the overall Lyonnais work force to about 0.8 percent. The average wage in the
SEF (which came to about 6,300 francs per year) was roughly three times
higher than the average at the Lyonnais (about 2,100 francs per year). This
reflected the greater share of highly skilled employees in the service. The
share of graduates was somewhere between 40 percent and 60 percent,
while at the same time these represented only 10 percent of the Lyonnais
at large.[45] After 1905, however, the growth of the service stalled. Budgets
and probably staff stopped expanding. Yet with about a hundred employees and an annual budget between 500,000 and 600,000 francs, the SEF

43 Nonwage costs were limited to journal or periodical subscriptions, purchase of books, paper, pencils,
and travel expenses for missions. A breakdown of these expenses is found in Archives du Crédit
Lyonnais, DEEF, sans cote, Bd des Italiens.
44 See author's computation on the basis of the SEF archives and Omnes, "La gestion du personnel au
crédit Lyonnais."
45 For the Lyonnais at large, the estimate is provided by Omnes. For the SEF, the estimation is made as follows: Kaufman claims that there were before the war about fifty white collar employees (economists,
lawyers, accountants) working in the service. Given the figures we have for the overall SEF work
force, this implies that there were about as many clerks without university degrees. E. Kaufman, *La
banque en France* (Paris, 1914).

stood on the eve of the war unparalleled by contemporary or even modern standards.[46]

The growth of the SEF also led to a rationalization of its organization. During the 1890s, work was gradually divided among a number of research groups called "sections." Each section was headed by a *chef de section* who worked under the authority of the *directeur du Service des Etudes* (head of the SEF). Twelve formal sections emerged. Among the administrative sections, one finds the *section du bulletin*, which collected clippings from the press and edited the daily house magazine that was circulated to the managers. The *section des notes* wrote briefs to answer the queries of individual customers or official bodies (for example, ministries). The total number of replies generated per annum rose from 5,710 in 1893 to 11,297 in 1896, from 17,110 in 1899 to 20,057 in 1902, with a growing portion going to public administrations.[47] The *section des notes* could rely on the help of the *section des archives*, which kept and stored records, as well as of the *section du repertoire*, which maintained a huge database of facts and figures on companies, banks, and so forth.[48] Secretarial aid was provided by the *section de copie*, which typed memoranda, drew charts, and performed other such tasks.

Moreover, there were five research sections. These sections had the largest staffs and were fully separate from the rest of the bank. They were never directly involved in investment decisions, and their reports could not be communicated to other departments without management approval.[49] One section dealt with industries and mines (*section des mines et de l'industrie*), one with railways and navigation (*section des transports*), one with banks (*section des banques*), and one with public finances (*section des fonds d'états*).[50] In addition, the *section de statistique* collected macroeconomic data (for example, on agricultural and industrial products, money, and population). Over time, the *section de statistique* also developed expertise on fiscal issues, which gave birth after World War I to separate *section de législation fiscale*. Finally, two sections provided technical support: The *section des cotes* recorded exchange

---

46 For budgets, Kaufmann quotes even higher figures (between 600,000 and 800,000) but it is not clear to what period he refers. The slowdown in the growth of the SEF was both absolute and relative. By 1913, the SEF had returned to about 1.5 percent of total wages and 0.5 percent of the Lyonnais total work force. Kaufman, *La banque en France*.

47 3,554 in 1901, 6,875 in 1902. Archives du Crédit Lyonnais, DEEF, sans cote, Bd des Italiens. In a later document of July 10, 1916, the section des notes is called "section de renseignement" (DEEF 62694).

48 We are told (Archives du Crédit Lyonnais DEEF 62694) that in 1904 the *répertoire* contained 117,000 referenced items; 243 volumes listed information on governments, municipals, and 51,000 joint stock companies. The *répertoire* has been lost.

49 Archives du Crédit Lyonnais, DEEF 62694. This is reminiscent of the "Chinese wall" that exists between commercial and research departments in modern banks.

50 See also Kaufman, *La banque en France*, who finds only 8 sections.

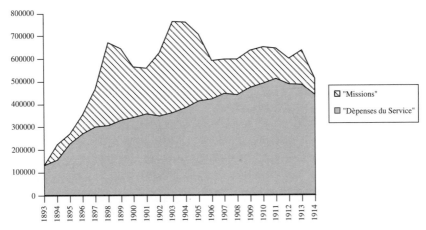

Figure 1.2. SEF expenses (French francs): Paris and Missions. *Source: Archives DEEF, "Boue-vard des Italiens," sans cote.*

rates and stock prices; the *section des calculs financiers* used or constructed logarithmic tables to make actuarial computations.[51]

The SEF's operations were not limited to the Paris facilities. The creation of agencies or branches in leading financial centers provided the Lyonnais with a ready infrastructure for collecting and double-checking information. The former policy of paying for tips was progressively abandoned, or at least did not feature as prominently as in the past. Offices were opened within the Lyonnais's foreign branches. In 1905, there were permanent representatives in Berlin, Johannesburg, London, New York, and Saint Petersburg. These outposts were run by civil engineers from the SEF who conducted audits of local companies.[52] In Saint Petersburg, for instance, there was a *bureau de l'ingénieur chargé des études industrielles et financiers* (office of the engineer in charge of industrial and financial studies).[53] In general, foreign facilities also served as mediators between the SEF and local officials, bankers, and entrepreneurs. A fascinating letter of 1898 from the Lisbon branch, for instance, recalls the visit of a Portuguese official who was offered a position in the Ministry of Finance and wanted to look at the Lyonnais figures on Portugal before accepting the position.[54] Finally, extensive expeditions were sent abroad to prospective markets. These included Australia, China, Mexico, South America, and the Danubian states. Most of these missions took place between 1897 and 1905 and feature prominently in SEF expenses (Figure 1.2).

51 DEEF 62694.   52 DEEF 62694.
53 Historique DEEF.
54 Archives du Crédit Lyonnais, "Visite de M. Figueira."

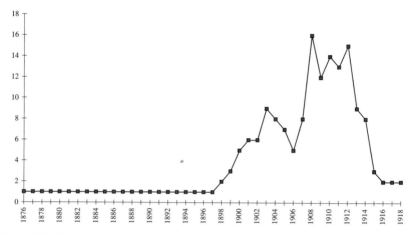

Figure 1.3. Number of employees in the *Section des Fonds d'Etats. Source: Author's computation, Archives du Crédit Lyonnais, Historique DEEF.*

The Public Debts Unit

We have quite detailed records on the personnel from *section des fonds d'états*, which formalized as a specific unit in the late 1890s.[55] From 1896, the number of *chargés d'études* monitoring sovereign debts increased steadily. A first surge took place between 1899 and 1906, when the section reached nine *chargés d'études*. This puts the section at 20 percent of the SEF (including clerks and *auxiliaires*). A second surge occurred after 1905. Between 1908 and 1912, there were twelve to sixteen *chargés d'études* in the section, or a total of about thirty employees, one-third of the SEF. This evolution ran counter the general trend of the SEF in the ten years preceding the war, which was one of relative stagnation: The prewar growth of the section thus took place at the expense of other sections.[56] This suggests tremendous activity in *section des fonds d'etats*.[57] The movement stalled in 1912 (see Figure 1.3).[58] The interruption of French foreign lending with the outbreak of World War I was a final blow to the section that was nonetheless revived after the war with the resumption of international capital flows.

---

55 "Fonds d'états, composition de la section," Historique DEEF, Archives du Crédit Lyonnais.
56 Mostly from the section de statistique, the section des banques, and the section du bulletin.
57 The number of governments (local and central) covered rose from 182 in 1905 to 206 in 1907. At that time, there were 2,519 tables, 436 notes, 30 maps, 2,182 budgetary returns, and 817 memoranda on individual loans. DEEF 62694.
58 This reduction took place to the benefit of the rest of the SEF. There were eight departures to other sections between 1910 and 1914 against four arrivals from other sections. See DEEF, "Fonds d'états, composition de la section."

All *chargés d'études* from the *section de fonds d'etats* came from either HEC or Sciences-Po. The right candidates had strong skills in accounting, high performance at school, and a command of foreign languages. Fonds d'Etats produced a kind of elite. One, Dujardin, a major (prize winner) from HEC later became head of the Paris offices. Another, Escarra became head of the SEF and later CEO of Crédit Lyonnais. Most departures from the *section de fonds d'états* on which we have information were really promotions. Those who left the Lyonnais received attractive offers to head or create small research departments in other financial institutions. One, Hennequin, a graduate from HEC who had worked for the *section des fonds d'états* between 1900 and 1911, became chief economist at the Banque française de commerce et d'industrie. One, Laroche, became *chef des études* at the Banque de la Seine. One, Droz, moved to Union parisienne. Over time, the SEF had been able to overcome the initial human capital shortages to the extent that it could now export employees it had trained.

The Glory and the Power: SEF Propaganda During the Belle Epoque

The Belle Epoque was the heyday of the SEF. With its impressive library of more than 30,000 volumes, its 45,000 files on countries, industries, railways, and banks, its catalog of firm-specific data, and its hundreds of employees, it clearly surpassed anything that existed at the time, either in France or abroad. Kaufman argued that in France only the Comptoir national d'escompte had a somewhat analogous service.[59] But this service, created only a few years before World War I, was of much more limited scope. As for Europe, Kaufman believed, no other bank, British, German, or other, could stand comparison.[60]

Having heavily and steadily invested in the SEF, the Lyonnais was fully aware of its superiority.[61] This unique position had many advantages that could be exploited in various ways. One possibility would have been to sell its "ratings" to the market place. In effect, however, the bank never abandoned

---

59 Kaufman, *La banque en France*.
60 Kaufman, *La banque en France*, 353. According to my colleague Richard Roberts, the Lyonnais's example was also unparalleled in the UK before the war. Knut Borchardt told me during the Princeton conference that he could not think of a German equivalent.
61 The scathing description of the Bank of France research department made by an employee from the SEF in 1894 is one example. The Lyonnais ridiculed the meager resources, three-employee staff, and six square meters of the bureau des études économiques. Des Essarts, the chief economist, was reportedly "completely left to himself, working at random, without any method, any guide, any compass." He had been hired as a reward for the "numerous services" he had rendered to the Bank of France, not for his skills. His role was merely to produce, "once or twice per year, the situation of the reserve of Banks of Issue," Archives du Crédit Lyonnais Historique DEEF.

a strict policy of secrecy: It never disclosed more than limited parts of its reports. It is striking that, although contemporary economists were aware of the existence of the service, they apparently never received access to the figures it collected, nor to the precise way the SEF combined them.[62]

There were two mutually reinforcing advantages for this policy. The first had to do with the notes that the SEF wrote for customers. Without disclosing complete returns, the Lyonnais could provide depositors with topical memoranda on specific issues. This was a way to attract more depositors and increase market share. Second, the expertise of the SEF could become a resource to foster the bank's influence as a market mood setter. The Lyonnais thus took great care to make sure the general public realized that the bank had access to valuable information. Prestigious foreign guests were thus invariably brought to the SEF when they visited the Lyonnais.

One high point of this campaign was the April 1904 visit that the Lyonnais organized for the international press. The occasion was to show the bank's new facilities on the Boulevard des Italiens. A crowd of journalists gathered at the SEF, and during the following days, long articles appeared in the French, English, Spanish, German, Italian, and American press.[63] From the striking similarities between the various articles, it is obvious that the Lyonnais had provided journalists with a document on which they could canvass, perhaps monetary incentives as well. The articles praised the SEF in forceful words. For instance, A. Johnson, from the *New York Herald*, wrote:

From a financial point of view [the SEF] is a "veritable practical university." I have never heard of a similar organization either in France or abroad. Figures taken from official documents, accounts of sovereign states and reports of limited liability companies are tabulated methodically by employees chosen in the majority of cases from prize winners at the Polytechnic, the Ecole Centrale, the Ecole des Mines, and the Ecole des Hautes Etudes Commerciales. The most rigid impartiality presides at the making up of these tabulated records, without the employees, who do not know about the conclusion of the affairs studied by the bank, having other care than the finding out of the truth. The clientele of the Crédit Lyonnais is greatly benefited by this department, which acts as its secretary, and which, upon a request to that effect, addressed to the branch office with which the client transacts business, will go through all the documents published upon any commercial, industrial or other affair.[64]

62 Historique DEEF. With the departure of a number of SEF economists to other banks around 1910, it is probable that the Lyonnais's methods became widely known. But by the time this took place, the huge volume of past studies was the bank's best protection. There were probably cases where specific individuals were shown original returns. One such instance was the conversion of Luzzatti to favorable views toward Russian finances, a conversion which reportedly occurred after an extensive stay at the SEF (see L'Economista d'Italia, 1908, n.d. clipping found in DEEF 73316/1).
63 Une journée au Crédit Lyonnais. Paris, 1904.
64 *New York Herald*, European ed., Paris, Saturday, Apr. 23, 1904.

Virtually identical accounts with carbon copy wording (including the reference to the "practical university" which also features in Germain's obituary) were found in other newspapers.[65] They reflected the attempt at presenting the Lyonnais as a standard of informational reliability. The claim was everywhere the same: The Lyonnais had paid a high price to have a huge database that you could not bank against. So you were better advised to bank with the Lyonnais. As one French journalist wrote: "We got the message: the Lyonnais is well informed."[66]

SOVEREIGN "RATING" AT THE LYONNAIS

Fiscal Concerns, Statistical Doubts, and the Making of a Framework of Analysis

Whereas the need to attract foreign capital had created pressures on borrowers to release financial information, efforts at increasing formal resemblance between national returns remained nonetheless inconclusive: The definition of "revenue" and "expenditure," the units in which outstanding debts were denominated, or even the comprehensiveness of public accounts varied significantly among countries. This was not always disingenuous, but in some cases, concerns about the implications of deficits on borrowing costs led governments to creative accounting: As one Portuguese official confessed to the Crédit Lyonnais in 1898, the annual abstract of Portuguese finances was "filled with intended errors."[67]

One reason for this was the lack of national (let alone international) consensus on the appropriate framework. This problem was widely recognized at the time, because fierce battles were fought over figures in almost every country.[68] Such disputes were not clear-cut bouts that pitted fudging governments against benevolent opponents. Rather, information was retained, released, corrupted, and criticized according to the interests of the various

---

65 Whole parts of the *Herald* article can be found in the *Daily Telegraph* dated May 2, under a different name. D'Eichtal, *Notice sur la vie et les travaux.*

66 Crédit Lyonnais, *Une visite au credit lyonnais, ses nouvelles installations, opinion de la presse étrangère* (Paris, 1904).

67 Archives du Crédit Lyonnais, "Visite de M. Figueira," AH.

68 See the various issues of *The Statesman's Yearbook* or the *Bulletin de la Société Internationale de Statistique* (1886–). In fact the contemporaries' reluctance to swallow official figures is in contrast with the gullibility that rating agencies would display during the interwar period. In its general introduction, *Moody's Government and Municipal Manual,* 1926 ed., plainly stated: "The information furnished on foreign governments and their securities is derived from original sources [i.e., official documents]. We have taken great pains to gather facts and figures directly from the governments and municipalities of the whole world. And the prompt and very satisfactory replies were indeed most gratifying." One may doubt that statistical honesty had much changed over the war to warrant such trust.

groups involved. The press (domestic and foreign) was often bought. Perhaps the most famous illustration of this was the debates within the Russian Imperial Council in the late 1890s and early 1900s, where statistical accuracy became a political issue.[69] The Russian case was not exceptional. As SEF economists concluded: "If one were to judge from the disputes surrounding the yearly vote of the budget, it would seem that it is absolutely impossible to assess the financial situation of any given state with enough precision. Except in rare instances, those who participate in those discussions do not seem to be prepared to agree on the calculus that serve as a basis of their discussion. Concerned more than anything else with the need to free themselves from any kind of controls, they oppose unfounded rebuttal to unfounded assertions, and if by chance, debate develops, the general tone of the discussion quickly deteriorates without bringing any clarity."[70]

This situation was discouraging in view of the kind of systematic quantified comparisons that investors were looking for. Yet one could dream of a "rationalist" alternative, which would require designing a framework in which itemized public accounts could be split and then reconstructed. This framework, by fixing the methodological problems, would in turn help to focus more specifically on accuracy. Such was the ambitious route that the Lyonnais adopted. It is possible to identify the main stages in the development of the Lyonnais's method. Economists had long been aware of the relations between public finances and the price of debt instruments. For instance, in his *Traité des opérations de bourse*, Courtois claimed that the financial situation of a given government determined the likelihood of an increase in its demand for funds. The greater that probability, the lower the price of its bonds.[71]

These views were echoed by those of Germain, who displayed an early interest in the empirical assessment of the way public finances would behave in the wake of given shocks. In 1871, he asked SEF economists to perform some "stress analyses" in their fiscal reports in order to determine, for instance, how public finances would react to a one-time increase in spending: Given the inertia of some expenses (such as interest service), he reasoned,

69 The more recent controversies between Theodore H. Von Laue ["The High Cost and the Gamble of the Witte System: A Chapter in the Industrialization of Russia," *The Journal of Economic History* 13 (1953): 424–48] and Arcadius Kahan ["Government Policies and the Industrialization of Russia," *The Journal of Economic History* 27 (1967): 460–77] illustrate how partisan views on the topic have transpired until more recent debates.

70 Etudes financières, "Comment faut-il?" p. 1, Historique DEEF.

71 Alphonse Courtois, *Traité des operations de bourse, un Manuel des fonds publics français et étrangers et des actions et obligations de sociétés françaises et étrangères négociés à Paris, précédé d'une appréciation des opérations de bourses dites de jeu, et des rapports de la bourse avec le crédit public et les finances de l'État* (Paris, 1855).

one could get an idea of the amount of free resources that would be available. He further argued that this could be used to extrapolate the borrowing capacity of any government given alternative scenarios on the evolution of its revenues.[72] Such analyses, however, remained fairly rudimentary, at least until the early 1890s.[73]

The crisis of 1890 was a watershed. In 1891, as the Argentinean crisis was spreading, Germain received several reports among which were memoranda on Spain, Portugal, and Italy, with whom the Lyonnais had business relations and whose bonds had been seriously shaken. Germain was perceptibly anxious about financial developments in these nations, and he wanted to better understand each country's macroeconomic prospects. In particular, he wanted to disentangle permanent weaknesses from transitory difficulties and to understand whether there were structural differences between the countries under study. This led him to write a detailed technical memorandum.[74]

Germain's blueprint for public finance research combined four main directions. First was the concern about accuracy. All government accounts (general and special) had to be investigated in detail. To track inconsistencies, Germain recommended constructing separate "capital" and "operating" accounts, and to decide whether they matched: Variations in public indebtedness had to be mirrored into government deficits. Government borrowing accounts, he emphasized, should include short-term obligations on top of the long-term debt. These included government bills, overdrafts from both private and "central" banking institutions, and foreign loans. The importance of short-term debt was of special concern because it could be more easily concealed. Moreover, short-term debts, facing a rollover risk, were inherently riskier.

The second direction was to use a "historical approach" that would serve "to characterize with more certainty the country's performance."[75] A country's tendency to run persistent deficits could escape the scrutiny of an observer focusing on short frequencies but would come to the crudest light when extended time periods would be considered. The historical approach also served as a guide to extrapolate current trends, as it would give some clues on what should be considered as "permanent" versus "transitory." Finally, the historical approach permitted checking the consistency of returns, revealed hidden items, and provided indications on each country's

---

72 Letter dated October 19, 1871, Archives du Crédit Lyonnais AH 9–58.
73 Henri Germain, *La situation financière de la France en 1886* (Paris, 1886).
74 Historique DEEF. The idea of ascertaining "scientifically" the economic situation of economic entities was emerging at the time. E. Cheysson, "La statistique géométrique ou méthode pour la solution des problèmes commerciaux et industriels," in *Oeuvres Choisies* (Paris, 1887/1991), vol. 1.
75 Henri Germain, 1891, note "Finances portugaises," Historique DEEF.

propensity to turn to short-term debt in case of fiscal needs. In practice, Germain asked for a twenty-year period.[76]

Third was the concern about the dynamics of government assets. Germain advised that one should provide a breakdown of government revenue between "taxes" and "income from government assets" (railways, forests, state monopolies, state properties, and so forth) in order to underline the element of enterprise in the fiscal machinery. Similarly, spending should have to be differentiated to highlight its nature. Government investment was not the same as consumption. The former would eventually bring an increase in government revenue. This view was quite pervasive at the time: The nature of government spending was a frequent theme of the annual reports of the Council of Foreign Bondholders (from 1873). Similarly, Mulhall's estimates of public debts sought to disentangle "consumption debt," from "railway debt," although his estimates only focused on railways.[77]

The last direction was to require that the new accounts be tabulated along with background information regarding the country under study: imports, exports, exchange rates, interest rates, and population. Space was saved for comments; this could be used to mention specific events with fiscal relevance. Germain asked that three studies be made right away according to the new principles. The first would focus on Russia, the second on France, and the third on Italy. Dozens of others would follow. Whereas a substantial share of these studies have been lost, those surviving are rather impressive: huge spreadsheets, spanning three feet by five feet with extra columns pasted or pinned, listed for time periods of about fifteen to twenty years scores of statistical series.

"Une méthode rationnelle"

The actual method that the SEF developed was a response both to Germain's requests and to the practical challenges encountered along the way. In line with Germain's emphasis on the entrepreneurial functions of the state, the SEF tables were organized around "revenues and expenditure accounts," on

76 Germain's memorandum, 1891, historique DEEF. This lag, not accidentally, coincided with the creation of the SEF.
77 Mulhall, *Industries and Wealth of Nations*, 54. In a recent article, Trish Kelly found that in the 1890s, the nature of government spending had favorable consequences on sovereign debtors' willingness to pay (Trish Kelly, "Ability and Willingness to Pay in the Age of Pax Britannica, 1890–1914," *Explorations in Economic History* 35, no. 1 [1998]: 31–58). The difference between investment finance and consumption finance was also emphasized by Albert Fishlow in "International Capital Flows: Lessons from the 1890s and 1980s," *International Organization* (1985).

the one hand, and states' "balance sheets," on the other. These accounts were constructed though an investigation of all government records, which involved careful corrections.

The next step was the construction of what the SEF called *comptes d'ordre*. In an attempt to measure the net income from specific taxes as well as the net cost of given expenditures, these recorded either expenditures implied by revenue collection or revenues associated with given expenses. On the revenue side, one had, for instance, to pay the taxman: The net return from taxation was the difference between taxes and tax collection expenses. On the spending side, a government that subsidized education could nonetheless collect some tuition fee that partly covered expenses – net subsidies to education were the difference between the two items. *Comptes d'ordre* were handled with special care when it came to state business. National accounting techniques created spurious fluctuations in official revenue and expenditures: One example was the Spanish tobacco monopoly, which, until 1887, was state run. Spending on personnel and the like was thus recorded among government expenditures, and gross income was recorded on the revenue side. The resulting net profit until 1887 was an annual income of about 70 million peseta. In 1887, however, the Spanish government farmed out its monopoly. The franchised company had to pay a 90-million peseta annual duty. These 90 million became the only item recorded on the revenue side. This represented a 20-million improvement on net revenues, but also implied that total government income was reduced. If one wanted to assess the "normal income" of the Spanish government, the Lyonnais reasoned, one would have to correct the pre-1887 returns in order to purge both the income and expenditure side from gross expenses. This way returns would display a 20-million increase in government revenue in 1887. By contrast, measures based on gross revenue would display a spurious weakening of government income.

The Lyonnais method had the effect of making accounts leaner: Revised revenues and expenditures (called *recettes et dépenses normales*) were constructed by netting out items. This implied a seemingly smaller burden of government in economic activity and was thus in contrast with the more familiar concept of government share in the economy, where aggregate income and expenditures are compared to national products.[78] In fact, this comparison with modern practices underlines the Lyonnais's view of states

---

78 See, e.g., L. Schuknecht and V. Tanzi, "The Growth of Government and the Reform of the State in Industrial Countries," IMF Working Paper, WP/95/130, Dec. 1995.

as investors and its corollary concern about efficiency, as opposed to the Keynesian view of states as spenders and the corollary concern about weight. The *comptes d'ordre* allowed one to focus on the net income from government activities, thus getting closer to a concept of comparative profitability.[79] As a lender to governments, the Lyonnais wanted to trace what governments had done with private monies.

Moreover, *comptes d'ordre* were an intermediary step in the construction of state balance sheets, which compared public debts and public assets. Indeed, while constructing debt estimates merely required care and patience, the asset side involved much greater challenges. Official assets accounts were poorly maintained if at all. Only some countries such as Scandinavia, Switzerland, and a number of German states published such returns.[80] Existing accounts overlooked amortization, recorded assets at their nominal purchasing price, and gave a positive price to loss-making enterprises.[81]

Comptes d'ordre, by contrast, provided a way to circumvent these shortcomings: The itemized accounts of government activities yielded a direct measure of "dividends" (net of maintenance, reparation, and so forth) from public assets. One way to look at net indebtedness was thus to capitalize net dividends at an interest rate equal to the government marginal borrowing rate. A 100-franc debt bearing a 5 percent interest and issued to finance the construction of a railway whose net return was 4 francs per year implied a corresponding asset of 80 francs – a 20-franc net debt. Another way to look at net indebtedness was to focus on flows. The SEF suggested comparing state dividends to the annual flow of interest payments on the public debt. As the SEF reckoned, each way to assess net indebtedness had weaknesses of its own. The stock approach raised the question of which interest rate should be used to capitalize dividends; it compared a known expense to an uncertain income. On the other hand, the flow approach was unable to handle non-interest-bearing assets or debts: Two governments that were similar in all respects but an interest-free debt (for example, an overdraft at the central bank) would feature in a similar way in the flow approach and yet would be in a different situation. Taken together, however, these measures were much superior to anything existing at the time and could in addition allow more rigorous comparisons of real indebtedness.

---

79 For instance, it was well known that the corrupted Russian Internal Revenue Service brought a lower return than other nations' revenue services. See Jean de Block, *Les finances de la Russie au XIXe siècle*, 2 vols. (Paris, 1899).
80 See *The Statesman's Yearbook*, various issues.
81 Mulhall's net debt estimates were flawed by this very problem. Mulhall, *Industries and Wealth of Nations*.

Toward Quasi-Cardinal "Ratings"

The measures of net indebtedness that the SEF constructed opened the door to recommendations for investment strategy. The trick was to find a denominator to which indebtedness could be compared in order to provide a measure of "debt sustainability." The hierarchy of risk that would emerge from this could then be compared to hierarchies of prices and signal profitable portfolio reallocations. Modern approaches to sovereign debt sustainability typically use the ratio of public debts to national income, measures of openness, and so forth. Nineteenth-century economists believed in stocks more than in flows, and the consensus view was that national wealth, not national income, was what mattered. Public obligations would have to be serviced out of taxing private agents: A sovereign's ability to pay was thus best measured by comparing its current stock of debt to the present value of private wealth owned by the agents it could tax.

This conceptual clarity contrasted sharply with a dearth of data. One exception was Mulhall, who computed wealth estimates for 1895 and provided pointwise debt-to-wealth ratios for Europe, the United States, Canada, and Australia (Figure 1.4). However, Mulhall's estimates had serious limitations. He used fixed coefficients (calibrated on the basis of estimates for countries for which he had returns) to capitalize national earnings: Land was capitalized at 30 times the annual agricultural production, houses at 16.5 times the

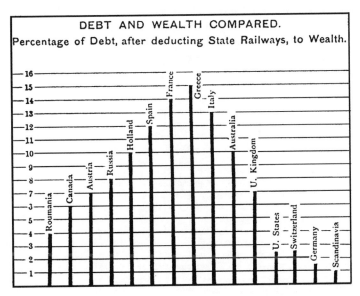

Figure 1.4. Mulhall's debt-to-wealth ratios. *Source:* Mulhall (1896), p. 55.

gross rental, and so forth.[82] Contemporaries were critical, especially when it came to late developers whose economic structure was likely to differ from the countries upon which coefficients had been calibrated. Tito Canovai, a leading Italian economist, thought that Mulhall's figures "lacked scientific basis."[83] The whole issue was further complicated by matters of national pride, as well as by international politics: Because political alliances had a financial side, official statisticians were under much pressure. On top of it all, Mulhall's returns were only comprehensive for 1895 and were never updated: The 1909 edition of Mulhall's *Dictionary of Statistics* still relied on estimates for 1895.[84]

Contemporaries thus used proxies that would serve to monitor financial evolutions over shorter frequencies. National income figures were as scarce as wealth estimates. A frequent denominator was population: *Faute de mieux*, this was seen as a crude substitute for wealth.[85] Such ratios, however, were not computed out of candor: Readers were immediately warned against the deficiencies of such measurement. Different levels of economic development meant very different income per head. For instance, dividing both Russia's and Britain's debts by their respective populations gave a fictitious advantage to the former.[86] Poor countries such as India or China had the largest populations.

Like everybody else, the SEF thus had to rely on its own tools. But contrary to others, its way of reorganizing government accounts yielded an almost straightforward way to compare debt burdens. The flow approach to net indebtedness led to a natural choice of the denominator: Dividing the annual flow of interest payments net of dividends from government assets, by "normal revenues" (that is, the SEF-corrected gross government revenues

82 Ibid.
83 Tito Canovai, "Del Problema Finanziaro in Italia," *Nuova Antologia*, 4th ser., 78 (1898): 344.
84 These dilemmas proved quite resilient: They were still present a quarter century later when formal sovereign rating developed. For instance, the 1926 introduction of *Moody's Government and Municipal Manual* sought to provide debt-to-wealth tables in order to document comparative debt burdens: "The best single index to the credit or standing of foreign governments undoubtedly is the wealth per capita. . . . In the past unfortunately, estimates of wealth have been too much biased by national prejudice. Even learned economists have placed high estimates upon the wealth of their own and related peoples, and low estimates upon that of unrelated and disliked peoples. Besides this, even now, there is a great dearth of data regarding both total wealth and per capita wealth" (*Moody's Government and Municipals Manual*, 1926 ed., xiii).
85 See, for example: R. Dudley Baxter, *National Debts* (London, 1871); NAME Canovai, "Del Problema Finannziario in Italia," *Nuova Antologia*, 4th ser., 78, 340–52; Ottomar Haupt, Arbitrages et parités (Paris, 1894); Edmond-Amédée Théry, *Europe et Etats-Unis d'Amerique* (Paris, 1899).
86 The use of population as a proxy for GDP was customary up to the 1870s, for instance in international treaties. It had the advantage of being a well-known figure, and thus one which it was easy to agree upon. When the Latin union was created in 1865, for instance, national quotas for issued of debased coins were expressed in percentage of the population.

minus *dépenses d'ordre*) produced an index of sustainability. Indeed, this ratio measured the proportion of government income that was earmarked for debt servicing: The smaller this ratio, the less likely was the government to meet servicing problems. In turn, this could be thought of as an index of "sovereign riskiness."

Rating agencies are explicitly concerned with providing assessments of sovereign risks. As a result, their output is highly formalized. Grades are given to each country, and the significance of each grade is explained. But because the SEF analyses were homemade and home-consumed, they did not need to be summarized through explicit grades. This, of course, is an obstacle for modern researchers. Yet in one instance, the SEF did provide a formal classification of countries: We found three spreadsheets, constructed in 1898, which ranked foreign sovereigns in three groups.[87] Each document displayed a list of countries belonging to a given "risk group" and provided an estimate of the ratio of net interest service to "normal revenues" in 1897–8 (plus a reference to the level of that ratio ten years earlier). The first list included countries "whose financial management is of first order" ("Pays dont la gestion financière est de premier ordre" in Lyonnais's words).[88] The second group included intermediary nations, whose "financial management is of second order." Finally, a third list included nations "of third order."[89] The lists also included brief comments on each country and an indication of whether a default or repudiation had occurred in the recent past.

These tables were not comprehensive, and the exercise was never made again.[90] Yet they can help us to demonstrate that the SEF's measure of debt sustainability loomed large in shaping its perceptions of sovereign risks. Consider that the SEF operated on the basis of some implicit function (the Lyonnais formula), which related each given country's diagnostic statistics (for example, the ratio of net interest service to normal revenues) to a score.

---

87 DEEF, 72879/1, "Généralités, 6, Classification des Etats d'après les résultats de leur gestion financière." The tables included, along with pure sovereigns, a number of borrowers that belonged to federal or confederated states countries (Prussia, the Swiss cantons), and colonies (the British and Dutch Indies).

88 Moreover, the SEF hinted that the way countries were listed in the category had to be interpreted as formal intra-category ratings: Some cursory comments explained the position of a given country in the list of well-behaved countries. No intra-group ratings were provided for the second and third categories.

89 Extensive footnotes described first- and second-order countries in some detail. Third-order countries, by contrast, did not receive any mention, apart from records of the net interest service before and after the default.

90 It is not fully clear what led the SEF to include or exclude given borrowers from the list. Note that in terms of volume the list included most of the outstanding bonds, although some substantial sovereigns, such as Mexico or France, were excluded. Data limitation cannot explain this, as the SEF had files on virtually every country.

Table 1.1. *Estimating the Lyonnais grading formula:*
$$q_i = \alpha_0 + \alpha_1 \cdot I_i + \alpha_2 \cdot Fault_i + \omega_i$$

Parameter	Estimate	Standard-Error	t-statistic
α_0	−3.06*	0.69	−4.42
α_1	0.21*	0.046	4.58
α_2	13.57*	1.23	11.03
$\sqrt{q_1}$	2.37*	0.35	6.69

n-obs = 24; standard errors computed from analytic first and second deriva-
tives (Eicker-White).
* : significant at 5%. q_1 = 5.6.

Table 1.2. *The Lyonnais risk tables*

Group 1: Pays dont les finances sont de premier ordre	Group 2: Pays dont les finances sont de second ordre	Group 3: Pays dont les finances sont de troisième ordre
Germany (imperial gov.), United Kingdom, United States (federal gov.), Russia, Sweden, Finland, Denmark, Belgium, Norway, Transvaal, Switzerland (federal gov.)	Holland, Egypt, Japan, Austria, Hungary, Romania, Italy, [Chile, Dutch Indies, British India]	Brazil, Argentina, Spain, Portugal, Greece, Serbia, [Bulgaria, 'Roumélie']

Note: No figures reported for countries within brackets. These countries were excluded from the regression.
Source: Archives du Crédit Lyonnais, DEEF 72879/1.

Depending on the score that a given country obtains, the SEF then decided
to put it either in the first (low risk), second (average risk), or third (high risk)
group. The Lyonnais formula is unknown to the modern researcher, and the
score is unobservable, but we do observe the final allocation. Assuming that
the Lyonnais formula was linear, it is possible to implement an econometric
technique (described in the appendix) that yields both the parameters of the
Lyonnais formula and the thresholds at which countries switched from one
category to the other one.

The explanatory variables that we use are the SEF's estimates of the net
burden of interest service as a share of normal revenue and a "dummy"
variable that captures the recent occurrence of sovereign default. Defaults
or debt repudiations, while they lowered the interest service, also signaled
a higher risk, and this balanced the seemingly "good" performance which
interest service alone implied. Results are presented in Table 1.1 (groups
of countries are listed in Table 1.2). Figure 1.5 displays the estimated score

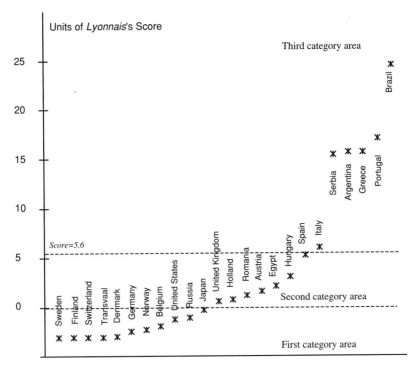

Figure 1.5. The Lyonnais's scoring formula: predicted grades and implied category. *Source: Author's computations.*

(a low score means a low risk). Countries whose scores are less than zero were put in the top category (group I). Countries between zero and 5.6 were put in the intermediate category (group II). Finally, countries whose score is above 5.6 are put in the high-risk group (group III). The best scores (equal to α_0 or -3.06) were obtained by countries with essentially no net interest service and no recent default: Sweden, Finland, Switzerland (Federal state), Denmark, and the Transvaal. In general, category I includes countries with a low net-debt service and no payment problems. One such country was Russia, which was featured within group I. This resulted from Russia's policies of public investment: The large involvement of the Russian state in the domestic economy implied that substantial net dividends accrued to the government. These compensated the annual flow of interest payments, bringing it (as a share of government income) below 10 percent. No default countries, on the other hand, were downgraded to the second category when they reached a net interest service around 15 percent of normal revenues. This was true in the case of Holland, a nation with otherwise sound

finances. The switch to the third category occurred when the interest service moved beyond 40 percent (again, with no default).[91] Recent defaults,
finally, automatically put a country (whatever its interest service burden) in
the third category.

One way to assess the performance of the model is to examine its ability
to replicate the Lyonnais's actual groupings as presented in Table 1.2: Most
countries (20 out of 24, or 83 percent) are adequately allocated by the model.
Misallocated countries obtain scores that are borderline and thus in fact very
close to the group where they "should" have been put. The model, despite
its simplicity, is extremely close to perfection, suggesting that the explicit
scoring formula that we have reconstructed is a very good approximation of
the Lyonnais's perceptions of sovereign risks. The important conclusion is
obviously that the SEF's sustainability measures played an overarching role
in deciding relative risks.[92]

However, the small discrepancies between the Lyonnais's predicted scores
and the observed allocation of sovereign debtors suggest some qualifications
regarding the attitude of the SEF toward its own measures. First, it seems
that the ratings had not been constructed in a mechanistic way. A naive
implementation of the net debt burden measure, for instance, would have
implied putting the United Kingdom in the second category. Yet it is obvious that the "richest and most developed economy in the world" – as
was written on the margin of the document – had to be put in the lowest
risk category despite a net interest service at 16.8 percent of revenues.[93]
Similarly, the inverted ordering of Spain and Italy (respectively, just below
and above the switching line, and yet placed by SEF economists in the
third and second category) reveals an awareness of current developments.
Italy, while being the most heavily burdened European nation, had stabilized its public debt by 1898 and reorganized its fiscal process, without
default, thus paving the way for a successful debt conversion a few years

91 Interestingly, this echoes a mention in the SEF's files that "no trouble has been observed in countries whose net interest service was below 40 percent" (Archives Crédit Lyonnais, Historique
DEEF).
92 It is in fact very hard to improve on the model given the almost perfect allocation provided by the
net debt service measure alone. Adding additional explanatory variables, such as a dummy for each
misallocated country or a measure of deficits, creates a situation which is equivalent to the well-
known "complete separation" problem in a binary probit model. Provided that the extra variables
are able to capture the little variance that's left out in the original model, the data fits the new model
perfectly. In this case, the coefficients want to become infinitely large although preserving their
relative magnitude.
93 The same would probably also hold for France, which was not included in the risk tables but which
would have probably featured in group one despite a net flow of interest service of 39.4 percent
in 1887 and 30.4 percent in 1897 (see "Etude de la situation financière de la France," 42, table
"Comparaison du produit net de l'actif de l'Etat et du service de la dette").

later.[94] Spain, in contrast, was in 1898 in the midst of a military conflict that could push it to the verge of bankruptcy (as a matter of fact, a note on the margin of the document recognized that partial repudiation was an option). Finally, the allocation of Japan to the second category – despite a debt burden that should have had it mechanistically in the first one – might have been related to the monetary system of the country: Indeed, SEF economists argued that while stabilization on the gold standard was under way in Japan, the nature of the monetary regime was not yet fully established.[95]

Thus, a number of factors balanced the lessons from the SEF's sustainability measure. As emphasized in the 1903 memorandum, the SEF fulfilled a "purely scientific" role and had no ability to determine the incidence of some complex facts on creditworthiness.[96] The SEF's task rested mainly in providing information to the Conseil d'Administration, where responsibilities remained. This may explain why formal "ratings" were never performed again after 1898. Instead, SEF country studies came to be accompanied by a number of qualitative notes, economic, political, or financial.[97] Such were the elements that, along with the more general policy orientations of the bank, drove investment decisions. Yet it remains that the statistical exercises performed by the Lyonnais were undoubtedly, by their clarity and "objectivity," an essential piece of information and thus an essential aspect of decision making. It is possible to claim, on the basis of existing evidence, that they loomed large in orienting the direction of French foreign investments: How to resist relating the surprisingly good grade obtained by Russia, or the excellent mark which Scandinavia received, to the well-known attraction that these countries' public debts had on French monies, especially from the 1890s? Although more evidence and further research are needed, we believe that our finding is a first hint that, contrary to the conventional wisdom, economics, not politics, was a key factor in allocating

---

94 Canovai, "Del Problema Finanziaro in Italia."
95 See Eichengreen and Flandreau, "Geography of the Gold Standard."
96 "Note sur la méthode," 12.
97 These included a list of comments on macroeconomic outlook, a general assessment of financial policy, information on specific questions (monetary or fiscal reforms, and so forth), a note on the evolution of the public debt, a note on the political regime and bureaucracy, and a political chronology since 1875. Interestingly, this is exactly the type of information on which credit agencies would rely twenty years later. *Moody's Government and Municipal Manual*, 1929 ed., recommended to enquire on "Geography, ethnology [by which it meant "culture"], history, type and stability of government, actual and potential wealth, enterprise, international position [creditor vs. debtor and underlying trend], fiscal, monetary and banking systems, government budget, taxation and debt, and finally an assessment of the "vitality of civilization." "A knowledge of all the foregoing subjects," Moody's concluded, "will enable the investor to determine intelligently the question of credit in a broad, general way."

French exports of capital. At least, we hope to have convinced readers that the Lyonnais's sustainability accounts, for what they were worth, made a decisive contribution in shaping the opinion of French financiers regarding foreign investment opportunities.

CONCLUSIONS: MARKET OPINION AND WILLINGNESS TO LEND

This chapter has described the evolution of the Crédit Lyonnais sovereign risk analysis department, the *section des fonds d'etat*, a subunit of the SEF, the Lyonnais's research department, over the period from 1871 to 1914. I described how the SEF grew into a large research center with numerous and ample means. I also studied the making of its "ratings" system. Several lessons can be drawn. First and foremost, this episode sheds light on how late nineteenth-century investors reacted to the absence of official data, formal ratings, and international bailouts. Both the enlargement of the SEF and the design of a systematic framework of financial analysis were prompted by the collapses of the Comptoir d'escompte and Baring. The process accelerated during the severe international financial crisis of the early 1890s, when the Lyonnais realized that it needed to determine which, among the various sovereigns of the gold standard periphery, deserved support. The decision to internalize a number of methods for monitoring sovereign risk is thus evidence of the key contribution of the market mechanism to pre–World War I "globalization."

A second lesson is the considerable importance of investors' perceptions in shaping the market mechanism itself. While a large literature has studied the determinants of debtors' willingness to pay, I found that cognitive aspects of the assessment of public finances played a crucial role for what I suggest calling investors' willingness to lend. In particular, I demonstrated that the favor in which investment finance (as opposed to consumption finance) was held proved decisive in comparing sovereign risks. This belief was pushed to its logical conclusion in the SEF's measure of debt sustainability, which discounted from interest service the net dividends from government "assets" and was responsible for a grading formula that most characteristically featured Russia as a "blue chip" country. Because most loans to the Russian government were used for industrial investments and because these investments provided a revenue, Russia's "indebtedness" remained moderate in the eyes of Crédit Lyonnais economists. This finding is obviously important in view of the well-known attraction that Russia had for French capital. Inasmuch as the SEF's ratings mattered (and I suggested they did), they provide a strong case for arguing that economics, not politics, drove French capital in Saint Petersburg.

Finally, my last conclusion has to do with the economics of financial information. I began this chapter with a reference to the challenges of sovereign risk assessment by rating agencies. My discussion of nineteenth-century experience suggests that privately collected information is not without faults. Indeed, the SEF was not a research department picked at random in a large population of competitors. It was not an individual voice in a broad market of opinions. Rather, the SEF was the research unit of one bank that took a prominent position in French and international finance. While the Lyonnais's willingness to retain its credibility certainly encouraged it to do its homework, it is likely that this also led other banks to pay much less attention. The absence of other serious domestic competing opinion and the secretive attitude that the Lyonnais took toward the SEF output probably induced other banks to get on board of Lyonnais-led syndicates without due caution. The issue is thus not to question the sincerity of the SEF – it genuinely believed in its reports. But finance is a game where one makes money because one's view becomes the market view, not because one is right: The externalities of being a market leader cannot be ignored.

APPENDIX: ESTIMATING THE LYONNAIS GRADING FORMULA

We use a three states ordered probit model. The intuition is the following: The SEF was observing a vector of (exogenous) variables (X) which it then sought to relate to a given country "score" (q). The score (known in qualitative variables econometrics as a "latent variable") is not observable, but we assume that it was a linear function (vector α) of the exogenous observations. ω is an error term. We have:

$$q = X\alpha + \omega$$

There are three "states" (risk categories) available. They are mutually exclusive. Category 1 is the group of countries whose financial management is of first order, and so on. Let's call y the state variable. We have:

$$y = 1, 2, 3$$

If the score obtained by multiplying the performance variables by their corresponding weight is below 0, the country under study will be assigned to category I (first-order country). If the score obtained is between 0 and q_1, the country will be assigned to category II (second-order country).

Finally, if the score is above q_1, the country will be assigned to category III (third-order country):

$$y = 1 \quad for \quad q \leq 0 \quad i.e. \quad \omega \leq -X\alpha$$
$$y = 2 \quad for \quad 0 < q \leq q_1 \quad i.e. \quad -X\alpha < \omega \leq q_1 - X\alpha$$
$$y = 2 \quad for \quad q_1 < q \quad i.e. \quad q_1 - X\alpha < \omega$$

The exogenous variables are: I_i (the net burden of interest service as a share of Lyonnais measured revenues) and $Fault_i$ (which takes value 1 if a default has recently occurred and zero otherwise). We have the Lyonnais grading formula:

$$q_i = \alpha + \alpha_1 I_i + \alpha_2 \, Fault_i + \omega_i$$

The estimation procedure uses the maximum likelihood formula, assuming that ω_i are i.i.d. Results are shown in Table 1.1.

2

Conduits for Long-Term Foreign Investment in the Gold Standard Era

MIRA WILKINS

The literature on foreign investment during the Gold Standard Era is formidable, reflecting the importance of the subject.[1] I define the Gold Standard Era as roughly the years from 1880 to 1914. For this period, there exists a consensus that the amount of capital that moved over national borders was substantial. Table 2.1 provides a 1914 balance sheet – indicating, by country, the principal sources and principal recipients of capital. The capital flowed from private savings (from the private sector) in source-of-capital

In preparing this chapter, I owe a great debt to many individuals, including, Michael Bordo, the late Rondo Cameron, Alfred Chandler, Tony Corley, Lance Davis, John Dunning, Marc Flandreau, Jean-François Hennart, Harold James, Geoffrey Jones, Robert Lipsey, Ranald Michie, Larry Neal, Michael Twomey, Guus Veenendaal, and the late Raymond Vernon. In addition, in connection with a 1997 trip to Australia and New Zealand, I have had valuable conversations with Simon Ville, David Merrett, Stephen Nicholas, Diane Hutchinson, and Gordon Boyd. My student, Giyas Gokkent, was a good listener and helped me clarify a number of points.
1 A sample of this literature, in alphabetical order, includes Arthur Bloomfield, *Patterns of Fluctuation in International Finance before 1914* (Princeton, N.J., 1968); A. K. Cairncross, *Home and Foreign Investment, 1870–1913* (London, 1953); Rondo Cameron, *France and the Economic Development of Europe, 1800–1914* (Princeton, N.J., 1961); Rondo Cameron and V. I. Bovykin, eds., *International Banking, 1870–1914* (New York, 1991); P. L. Cottrell, *British Overseas Investment in the Nineteenth Century* (London, 1975); Lance E. Davis and Robert E. Gallman, *Evolving Financial Markets and International Capital Flows: Britain, the Americas and Australia, 1865–1914* (Cambridge, 2001); Michael Edelstein, *Overseas Investment in the Age of High Imperialism: The United Kingdom, 1850–1914* (New York, 1982); Charles Feinstein, "Britain's Overseas Investments in 1913," *Economic History Review* 2d ser., 43 (May 1990): 288–95; Herbert Feis, *Europe the World's Banker, 1870–1914* (New Haven, Conn., 1930); Albert Fishlow, "Lessons from the Past: Capital Markets during the 19th Century and the Interwar Period," *International Organization* 39 (summer 1985): 383–439; A. R. Hall, ed., *The Export of Capital from Britain, 1870–1914* (London, 1968); C. K. Hobson, *The Export of Capital* (London, 1914); A. G. Kenwood and A. L. Lougheed, *The Growth of the International Economy, 1820–1990* (London, 1992), chap. 2; Charles P. Kindleberger, *A Financial History of Western Europe*, 2d ed. (New York, 1993), chap. 12; Cleona Lewis, *America's Stake in International Investments* (Washington, D.C., 1938); Mira Wilkins, ed., *British Overseas Investments, 1907–1948* (New York, 1977); Mira Wilkins, *The Emergence of Multinational Enterprise: American Business Abroad from the Colonial Era to 1914* (Cambridge, Mass., 1970); Mira Wilkins, *The History of Foreign Investment in the United States to 1914* (Cambridge, Mass., 1989); Mira Wilkins and Harm Schröter, eds., *The Free-Standing Company in the World Economy, 1830–1996* (Oxford, 1998).

Table 2.1. *A 1914 balance sheet*

Principal Sources of Capital		Principal Recipients of Capital	
Home Country	Level (in billion U.S. dollars)	Host Country	Level (in billion U.S. dollars)
United Kingdom	18.0	United States	7.1
France	9.0	Russia	3.8
Germany	7.3	Canada	3.7
United States	3.5	Argentina	3.0
Netherlands	2.0	Austria-Hungary	2.5
Belgium	1.5	Spain	2.5
Switzerland	1.5	Brazil	2.2
		Mexico	2.0
		India and Ceylon	2.0
		South Africa	1.7
		Australia	1.7
		China	1.6
Other	2.2	Other	11.2
TOTAL	45.0	TOTAL	45.0

Note: These are rough estimates of the international position, as of July 1, 1914. All the figures are "gross." No country is included in this table that had long-term "credits" or "debts" of less than $1.5 billion (we are using the terms "credits" and "debts" to include both equity and debt – bonds and loans). The home country is that of the "creditor"; it may not be the ultimate source of the capital. The "Other" in column 1 includes Japan and Russia (with investments especially in China), Portugal (especially in Brazil), Sweden (especially in Russia), and Canada (especially in the United States and the Caribbean), as examples. The figure for "Other" in column 4 includes the residual, *not* separately itemized: $4.7 billion for the rest of Europe, including the Ottoman Empire; $2.3 billion for the rest of Asia; $1.8 billion for the rest of Latin America, including the Caribbean; $2.3 billion for all of Africa except South Africa; and $.1 billion for the rest of Oceania.
Source: Mira Wilkins, *The History of Foreign Investment in the United States to 1914* (Cambridge, Mass: 1989), 145. She bases these estimates on compilations of data by the United Nations, Arthur Lewis, William Woodruff, Herbert Feis, Douglass North, Rondo Cameron, Raymond Goldsmith, F. Bartsche, Olga Crisp, and others, along with her own research.

nations to public and private sector activities abroad, in recipient countries.[2] The absence of foreign exchange restrictions and serious fluctuations in exchange rates for the major nations of the world opened the way for the vast enlargement of international trade and investments, resulting in the integration of the world economy. Information was transmitted more freely and more rapidly than ever in past history, as steamships and cables linked distant locales and as travel expanded. By 1913, it took less than a

2 There were some few exceptions to this overall pattern, as will be indicated later in this chapter.

Foreign Investments

Short-term	Long-term				

Portfolio				**Direct**	

Trade-finance,	**Government Debt**	**Private sector Debt**	**Equity**	**Multinational enterprises (MNEs)**	
Bank deposits, etc.	Bonds Other loans	Bonds Other loans	Shares	Free-standing companies	Classic MNEs

Figure 2.1. Capital abroad.

minute to communicate between the London and New York Stock Exchanges.[3] There was swift communication between London and Paris and Amsterdam, and St. Petersburg as well. D. K. Fieldhouse makes the remarkable statement that "the proportion of the world's land surface actually occupied by Europeans, whether still under direct European control as colonies or as one-time colonies [or as Europe itself]" was 84.4 percent in 1914.[4]

Indeed, in the years 1880–1914 probably there was greater worldwide integration through long-term international investment (with its network of ongoing obligations) than at any subsequent time between 1914 and the late 1980s, since the global integration of the 1880–1914 era was interrupted by the First World War and the Russian Revolution; the short-lived effort at restoration of worldwide investments in the 1920s was cut short by the 1930s depression and the Second World War; the post–World War II so-called "global economy" comprised only the West. Not until the late 1980s and particularly the 1990s, with the end of the Cold War, did we once more obtain a sustained worldwide integration in international investment that clearly surpassed that of the 1880–1914 period. The gold standard aided the movement of capital, sharply reducing exchange rate risks for investors in those countries whose currencies were backed by gold.

The international capital flows of the Gold Standard Era comprised two separate types of investments, which in today's terminology have been called foreign portfolio and foreign direct investments (see Figure 2.1). Foreign portfolio investments could be short- or long-term; they are in the realm

---

3 Ranald C. Michie, *The City of London: Continuity and Change, 1850–1990* (London, 1992), 134.
4 D. K. Fieldhouse, *Economics and Empire, 1830–1914* (Ithaca, N.Y., 1973), 3.

of finance, embracing banks, brokers, and stock markets. Foreign direct investments are all long-term and are what multinational enterprises do; they involve more than the transfer of capital, always including with that transfer the possibility of management. This chapter deals with long-term investments, both portfolio and direct investments. In the 1950s, in connection with balance of payments accounting, James Meade made the distinction between "accommodating" and "autonomous" investments; I do not follow Meade exactly (just in spirit).[5] The point I wish to stress is that certain investments were trade-related, were short-term in nature, and can be perceived as balancing items on the balance of payments. It is the long-term "autonomous" investments (in my sense and Meade's) that interest me and are tabulated on Table 2.1. Long-term, by my definition (and typically in the literature), is defined by the characteristics of the investment, not by how long it was held by the investor.[6] Thus, an investor in bonds or shares might hold the securities for a brief interlude. That is irrelevant; it is the nature of the instrument that defines it as "long-term." In this chapter, I do not want to repeat what is well known (owing to the huge literature on foreign investment in 1880–1914), but instead I want to focus specifically on the conduits through which the capital flowed – emphasizing the unique characteristics of portfolio and direct investments. I am going to look systematically at how the long-term international investment integration occurred and the different channels that created the basis for the figures presented in Table 2.1.

Before doing this, I want to note that the distinction I have made between short- and long-term is not absolute. Short-term investments could become transformed into long-term ones through roll-overs, defaults (and rescheduling), reinvestments, and changes in the strategy of the investor, and for other reasons. The large literature on foreign capital flows in the Gold Standard Era sometimes confuses short- and long-term, albeit it is principally concerned with long-term. My approach is consistent with that literature, although more straightforward in clarifying that I desire to include only the long-term investments.

In 1968, in keeping with the assumptions of the 1960s, Arthur Bloomfield wrote, "Portfolio investment was a far more important component of long-term capital movements before 1914 than direct investment; and it consisted much more of transactions in bonds and other debt instruments than

---

5 J. E. Meade, *The Balance of Payments* (London, 1952), 11–12.
6 See, e.g., Charles P. Kindleberger, *International Capital Movements* (Cambridge, 1987), 13.

in equities. In turn, the flotation of new issues on foreign capital markets appears with the possible exception of the United States, to have influenced the country totals of portfolio flows more than did net international transactions in outstanding securities."[7] Substantial research has taken place since 1968, which, as we will see, alters some of Bloomfield's conclusions, particularly on the ratio of portfolio and direct investments; there also seems to have been more transactions in outstanding securities in the Gold Standard Era than Bloomfield realized. As Charles Jones has written (in an article published in 1997), "Over the past 20 years [he could have made that thirty years] accepted views of the scale and character of British foreign direct investment (FDI) before 1914 have been upset. . . ."[8] The thrust of the "upset" has been the recognition, as we will see, that there was far more foreign direct investment in the pre-1914 period than had been previously acknowledged – and that this was true not only in the British case, but for all other nationalities as well.[9]

I have used the broad distinction between long-term portfolio and direct investments in exactly the same manner as Bloomfield and believe this distinction between the two forms of investment is fundamental to the study of conduits for foreign investments. It has long been evident – long before Bloomfield wrote and long before the last twenty or thirty years – that capital moved over borders through different channels. For tax purposes, the British Inland Revenue Department had in the early twentieth century divided income from British overseas investments into three categories:

Group I: "Dominion and Foreign Interest and Dividends" paid through paying agents or received by the cashing of coupons through bankers, coupon dealers, and so forth, in Great Britain.

Group II: (a) Income arising from business controlled within Great Britain, but mainly carried on abroad with assets located abroad and (b) interest and dividends payable abroad (not included in Group I) and income from other foreign possessions, arising abroad and payable abroad.

Group III: Income arising from trading operations carried on abroad by British concerns that operated principally at home but partly abroad.[10]

---

7 Bloomfield, *Patterns of Fluctuation*, 3–4.
8 Charles Jones, "Institutional Forms of British Foreign Direct Investment in South America," *Business History* 39 (Apr. 1997), 21–41.
9 For a summary of the recent reassessment, see Geoffrey Jones, *The Evolution of International Business: An Introduction* (London, 1996), 30.
10 See Gustav Cassel et al., *Foreign Investments* (Chicago, 1928), 126, 140, and G. D. N. Worswick and D. G. Tipping, *Profits in the British Economy, 1909–1938* (Oxford, 1967), 86.

These groupings, made in the British context, reveal a recognition of different conduits. Yet my use of the terms portfolio and direct investments are not those of the early twentieth century or even those commonly used in the British literature in the 1960s, but rather those of today superimposed on the past. My divisions are designed to assist me in asking and answering questions on how capital moved over borders, focusing on the channels, on the institutions, that facilitated and made possible the vast movement of long-term capital over borders during the Gold Standard Era. My data (and my approach) not only deal with capital movements, but with the emerging international obligations that formed the basis for integration. In addition to the variety of different conduits for foreign investments, the mix in the use of these conduits varied from one source-of-capital country to another; the mix also varied by recipient-of-capital country.

In my conclusion, I argue that looking at the different channels not only helps us understand the nature of capital movements, but also aids us in understanding the consequences (the impacts) of these capital flows. The mix of conduits is significant in that it enhances our knowledge of foreign investment and helps explain why in the Gold Standard Era the amounts were so great. Much of what I am including in this chapter has been implicit in prior studies; I am, however, asking of my material a unique set of questions.

In this chapter, I discuss the different conduits for long-term investments in the Gold Standard Era, with Figure 2.1 providing the guide. Unlike many other studies, I focus on 1880–1914, when there were the greatest capital movements, rather than on the entire pre-1914 period. To repeat, with very few exceptions, the sources of capital were nongovernmental, that is, from the private sector – individuals and firms. The capital went to foreign governments and to foreign economic activity (production of goods and services). And, if Table 2.1 is to be trusted, in 1914, over 95 percent of the international capital had come from seven countries (the United Kingdom, France, Germany, the United States, the Netherlands, Belgium, and Switzerland). The recipient countries were less concentrated.

PORTFOLIO INVESTMENTS: GOVERNMENT BONDS TRADED ON FOREIGN MARKETS

In much of the nineteenth century, prior to the advent of the Gold Standard Era, it seems likely that the largest share of the outflow of capital to foreign lands went into government securities. Yet as the nineteenth century progressed and into the twentieth century, government securities came to attract a far smaller proportion of capital flows.[11] What explains this trend? Two reasons stand out: (1) much of the early foreign government lending had proved risky and there had been sizable defaults,[12] and (2) as world markets became more integrated, alternative opportunities arose; new information was available and new conduits emerged to offer more options for international investment.

Lending to governments in this period took the form of portfolio investments and typically was through bond issues rather than commercial bank loans. Almost by definition, investors could not expect to control the government to which they provided funds.[13] In this period, foreign government borrowing took place principally in London and other European capital markets (the United States played a role as lender, but compared with London, it was not important); the loans, to repeat, took the form of bond issues. James Foreman-Peck found that the interest rates on government loans to every gold standard country (in 1889) were lower than to non–gold standard countries. Along the same lines, Michael D. Bordo and Hugh Rockoff point to the gold standard as a "good housekeeping seal of approval." It facilitated access to capital; they too concluded that a country's commitment to the gold standard meant that country could borrow at lower interest rates.[14]

To deal with the problems of risk in government lending (exchange rate risk where a country was not on gold, political risk, and economic risk), in Britain the Corporation of Foreign Bondholders (which had been organized in 1868) acted to assist investors who faced defaults.[15] Underwriters of bond issues developed their own in-house research on "sovereign risk." They

11 This is very evident in the data on the United States, Latin America, and Italy as recipient of capital areas: See Wilkins, *The History of Foreign Investment in the United States to 1914*, 188–9; Irving Stone, *The Composition and Distribution of British Investment in Latin America, 1865–1913* (New York, 1987), 60; Peter Hertner, "Free-Standing Companies in Italy, 1882–1912," in Wilkins and Schröter, *Free-Standing Company*, 151.

12 For a brief summary of the waves of defaults, see Peter H. Lindert and Peter J. Morton, "How Sovereign Debt Has Worked," in Jeffrey D. Sachs, ed., *Developing Country Debt and Economic Performance* (Chicago, 1989), 43.

13 Although the recipient government was not controlled in its domestic activities, it is true that the security for the loan might be controlled and this activity could impinge on the sovereign actions of governments. Thus, at the extreme, the foreign-controlled maritime customs administration in China collected revenues pledged to the service of foreign loans. See Feis, *Europe the World's Banker*, 459.

14 James Foreman-Peck, *A History of the World Economy, International Economic Relations Since 1850*, 2d ed. (New York, 1983), 172–3; Michael D. Bordo and Hugh Rockoff, "The Gold Standard as a 'Good Housekeeping Seal of Approval,'" *Journal of Economic History* 56 (June 1996): 386–428.

15 A group of investors had formed this organization in 1868; the Corporation of Foreign Bondholders of Great Britain was incorporated and took that name in 1873.

actively cooperated with governments to attempt to craft foreign government borrowings in a manner that would reduce the risk to lenders. Thus, when Spain wanted external funding of its post-1898 debt, the debt that would be held by foreigners had characteristics separate from the domestic debt: The exchange rate was fixed (Spain was not on the gold standard), and the Spanish law authorizing the debt stated no coupons were to be paid abroad "other than those detached from Bonds which have been sealed and inscribed, as being the property of foreigners." There had to be proof that these remained the property of foreigners. In short, Spain was trying to avoid Spaniards' investing in these fixed rate securities (through London, for example), while at the same time trying to encourage inflows of foreign finance.[16] Such arrangements notwithstanding, by 1914, because of the high risks of foreign government lending, a sizable portion of British overseas lending to governments had come to be within the Empire (over 70 percent by one estimate).[17] Empire set the rules of the game and lowered transaction costs.[18]

Merchant banks in London and "universal banks" on the Continent handled the placements of international loans to receiving governments; since the loans were typically in the form of new bond issues, the banks made arrangements for interest payments to investors. Some American bonds were issued that represented loans to governments abroad.[19] A single loan might be shared by a group of international bankers.[20] Unlike London, Paris, Amsterdam, and other European stock markets, the New York Stock Exchange in 1914 was basically a domestic market.[21]

---

16 On the Spanish loan, see Concepción García-Iglesias, "Fiscal Regime and Monetary Policy in Spain from 1880 to 1913," excerpt from Concepción García-Iglesias, "The Risks and Returns to Spain of Not Being on the Gold Standard, 1880–1913," unpublished Ph.D. dissertation, University of Illinois, 1998. My thanks go to Larry Neal for this reference.

17 According to Sir George Paish, "The Export of Capital and the Cost of Living," *The Statist, Supplement* (Feb. 14, 1914): vi.

18 See Ranald Michie, "The Canadian Securities Market, 1850–1914," *Business History Review* 62 (spring 1988): 38, on the ease by which Canadian Dominion bonds were issued in London.

19 E.g., see Lewis, *America's Stake in International Investments*, 334–41.

20 Thus, Morgan in the United States shared in the issues of its London house. The New York Morgan took, for example, a £50,000 interest in the Imperial Ottoman Bank's £7.8 million new Turkish conversion priority 4 percent loan in 1890; in 1892, it took a £100,000 participation in a Banque de Paris et des Pays Bas–managed £2 million loan to the Spanish government. See Vincent Carosso, *The Morgans* (Cambridge, Mass., 1987), 398, for a list of these shared loans. Note that Carosso gives them as denominated in pounds. On Russian banks' participation in shared loans, see B.V. Anan'ich and V. I. Bovykin, "Foreign Banks and Foreign Investment in Russia," in Cameron and Bovykin, eds., *International Banking*, 266–7.

21 There were some foreign securities traded, but not many; foreigners traded on the New York Stock Exchange – in *American* securities.

PORTFOLIO INVESTMENTS: RAILROAD BONDS TRADED
ON FOREIGN MARKETS

The age of the railroad started in Great Britain in 1825. By 1840, around the world there were 5,500 miles of railroad track; in 1870, 130,500; in 1910, 640,400.[22] A large share of this vast railroad growth was financed in international capital markets. The main developments took place during the Gold Standard Era. There was not always a clear line between government and railroad securities; governments borrowed to finance their nation's railroad expansion; in the early twentieth century, government securities (where the government held the obligation) provided a way of raising money to build railroads.[23] Some railroad bonds were issued with host government or colonial government guarantees.[24] Much of the international financing for railroads was done through the issuance of railroad bonds that would be traded in London, Amsterdam, Paris, and Berlin, and to a lesser extent on other European bourses. There were a wide variety of different kinds of railroad bonds, with different backings.

Foreign holdings of railroad bonds were not only based on new issues; when the Mexican government nationalized its railroad system, former direct investors obtained Mexican railroad bonds. Railroad bonds were traded, and investors bought traded securities. Bankers were active participants in new issues, introducing or listing new and also existing railroad bonds on source-of-capital stock exchanges, and in making arrangements for interest payments.[25] International groups of bankers would underwrite issues. If there were railroad defaults, bankers (and brokers) took part in protection committees. The Corporation of Foreign Bondholders paid substantial attention to railroad defaults, as did the English Association of American Bond and Shareholders, Ltd., formed in 1884 principally to deal with financial matters related to U.S. railroads.[26] By 1914, railroad bonds outstanding represented a sizable share of the level of European foreign investment. The interest on the bonds was typically paid to investors in London or Amsterdam

---

22 Kenwood and Lougheed, *Growth of the International Economy*, 13.
23 Sir George Paish estimated that in the seven years between 1906 and 1913, British investors had subscribed about £264,000,000 for foreign and colonial government loans, a large part of which (roughly £200,000,000 of this sum) had been spent on the construction of railroads. Paish, "The Export of Capital," iv. This was above and beyond the much larger sum, constituting securities publicly issued for railroads (without having the government as the borrower).
24 Bonds for Indian railways had British government guarantees.
25 The listing of a railroad security on a foreign stock market did not always take place at the time of the new issue. Outstanding securities were often listed after the new issue.
26 Wilkins, *History of Foreign Investment in the United States to 1914*, 209. See ibid., on similar organizations by the Dutch and Germans. Augustus J. Veenendaal, *Slow Train to Paradise* (Stanford, Calif., 1996), is splendid on the Dutch "protective committees."

or other major financial centers by the cashing of coupons through banking houses and brokers.

PORTFOLIO INVESTMENTS: OTHER SECURITIES TRADED ON FOREIGN MARKETS

Most of the portfolio investments in railroads were through bonds, but there were some portfolio investments in both preferred and common shares of railroads. Often bankers that arranged issues of railroad bonds also obtained shares, which were traded. Brokers handled both. A special section of the London stock exchange dealt in American rails, both stocks and bonds, albeit predominantly the latter. Although railroad securities were preeminent in the Gold Standard Era, the securities of other large foreign companies were also listed on and traded on European stock exchanges. For example, U.S. Steel Corporation's common stock, preferred stock, and bonds were traded in London and on certain continental European exchanges; American Telephone & Telegraph securities were traded in London, Amsterdam, and Paris. The shares of the big German mines were traded on the Paris stock exchange.[27]

GENERALIZATIONS ON THESE PORTFOLIO INVESTMENTS

The three categories so far discussed represented the bulk of (but not all of) foreign portfolio investment. They go under "Group I" of the British Inland Revenue Department description – although such investments were by no means confined to outward British investments. With these securities, bankers, brokers, and dealers within the financial center provided for the cashing of coupons and the transmission to the security holder of interest and dividends. Individual investors had no difficulties in obtaining returns in their own currencies (or a gold-backed currency, which was just as good). Bonds were often bearer bonds and easily traded. They moved across national frontiers with facility.[28] Indeed, this matter has generated substantial discussion over the level of British investments: Christopher Platt and others have maintained that although a security was issued (and traded) in Britain, it did not necessarily represent a British overseas investment; the stock or

27 Wilkins, *History of Foreign Investment in the United States to 1914*, 262–3, 523. Hobson, *Export of Capital*, 157.
28 This was true despite such restrictions as in the Spanish government loan described above; indeed, it may have been the reason such restrictions were attempted. The restrictions on capital movement imposed by the Spanish seem rare for the 1880–1914 period; overall, capital (and the securities that represented this capital) seems to have moved amazingly freely.

bond could be held (or acquired) by a French investor, for example, who bought the third-country security in London. The French investor might also buy the security from a Paris broker, who had contacts in London. So, too, securities issued in London for a particular host country (public or private sector obligation) could be shared by nationals of that country or, alternatively, "repatriated" over time by such individuals.[29] It should also be repeated that these securities were traded; thus, they represented a foreign investment (an obligation of the host country) when held abroad; since they were traded across countries, the "source-country" obligation of the host nation varied through time. Accordingly, in what nation a security was held at any particular date did not coincide with the amount of capital (the capital flow) that went from that country to the project abroad. This trade in securities was facilitated by the existence of the gold standard and minimal fluctuations in exchange rates.

Another reason for lack of coincidence between the capital flow and the obligation was that new issues of bonds were often priced below par; bankers were paid for their services; thus, even with the new issue, the face value of the bond rarely corresponded to the capital flow. What is important, however, is that the foreign investor (the purchaser of the securities) was in all these cases making financial decisions. Involved in these transactions were banks and brokers, and specialized dealers who cashed coupons. Although the actual size of the capital flow cannot be determined by the bond's face value, well-developed stock markets did facilitate the international flows of capital represented by these portfolio investments. The fact that the bonds could be sold on stock markets made them attractive. Investors in these securities could be individuals or firms. Wealthy individuals, but also firms (industrial enterprises, insurance companies, investment trusts, banks, and so forth) held "in their portfolios" out-of-country securities. This was particularly true of British investors. Surpluses not immediately needed for investment at home could be invested in these securities that brought higher returns than their domestic counterparts.

OTHER PORTFOLIO INVESTMENTS

Foreign portfolio investments did not necessarily involve securities traded on exchanges in the source-of-capital country. Investors could buy securities traded only on host country markets or, alternatively, provide long-term

---

29 D. C. M. Platt, *Britain's Investment Overseas on the Eve of the First World War: The Use and Abuse of Numbers* (New York, 1986), 34.

funds directly to businesses in a host country. Four examples will suffice: (1) Canadian brokers – because of close connections with the United States – could trade on their clients' behalf in American securities on U.S. stock exchanges; (2) some British and other investors bought securities of firms in foreign countries (especially the United States) using national (in the U.S. case, U.S.) financial advisers – brokers and bankers; (3) certain well-established multinational British trading houses (qua merchant bankers – Antony Gibbs & Son – for example) bought on foreign markets – through their houses abroad – (Gibbs traded on the Valparaiso bolsa for itself and others) and remitted securities to Europe; and (4) some foreign portfolio investment involved nonsecuritized bank lending to companies established outside the source country. In the British Inland Revenue Department categories, the returns on these investments seem to fall in Group II(b), that is, interest and dividends payable abroad (not included in Group I).

In these cases, the investor obtained an equity interest or a debt obligation of a locally established (foreign) company and generally would obtain returns in the host country currency. Stability in exchange rates tended to encourage such investments; at the same time, other uncertainties limited such investments. These uncertainties included the costs of finding out about companies abroad, the difficulties of obtaining adequate and reliable information on the prospects in foreign lands, and the general problems of unfamiliarity. Thus, often such international investments were confined to neighboring countries (U.S.–Canada, as an example), or were activities within Empires, or were conducted by well-established "houses" with close connections ("houses" or "branches") abroad. One important way that investors coped with such difficulties was by buying securities of home-domiciled companies, which, in turn, made direct investments abroad – and it is those companies we now must consider.

DIRECT INVESTMENTS: FREE-STANDING COMPANIES

Indeed, as it has long been known, investors in source-of-capital countries often participated in setting up companies in their home country and through these companies channeled investments abroad. The careful chronicler of British overseas investment, George Paish, identified many such British companies that did business overseas and included them in his surveys of "publicly traded companies" and "amounts subscribed."[30] The companies were engaged in many different economic activities; their overseas

---

30 See Paish papers reprinted in Wilkins, ed. *British Overseas Investments*.

investments tended to go to single countries (or colonies) or were confined to single regions. It seems that in the 1890s a sizable number and percentage of these companies were in railroad and transportation but that share declined over the years, so figures for the early twentieth century fail to capture the nineteenth-century involvement. The companies were engaged in transportation, canals and docks, banking, manufacturing, public utilities, mining, agriculture, and the like. They made their investments abroad both within and outside the Empire.

Discussing the British situation, Matthew Simon in the 1960s referred to such companies' investments abroad as "portfolio" ones.[31] Simon used the words "portfolio investments" to separate these companies from the Group III category of companies as defined by the British Inland Revenue Department. The latter invested abroad "directly," that is, they did not go through capital markets. The companies George Paish and Matthew Simon wrote about were typically publicly traded and listed in stock exchange manuals; they raised monies in British capital markets. This category coincided closely with those described in Group II(a) of the British Inland Revenue Department groupings.

With these companies, to be sure, many of the owners of their securities (equities and debentures) made purely financial investments and had no intention of controlling the business abroad. All the investors made *domestic* investments in the securities of the British company; the currency was the pound sterling. The balance sheet was in pounds sterling. The dividends were paid in pounds sterling, as was the interest on any debentures issued. It was, however, the company itself that in turn made the investments abroad. And, just as we see the modern company apart from the investors in that company, so too it is important to view these companies *as the investors abroad* (and not go up a tier to the stockholders and debtholders of these enterprises). Such companies, designed to do business abroad, were set up not only in Britain, but in all the other important source-of-capital countries as well. To repeat, they made the investments abroad. They provided a "familiar" conduit for the movement of capital abroad; they avoided the

---

31 See Harvey Segal and Matthew Simon, "British Foreign Capital Issues, 1865–94," *Journal of Economic History* 21 (Dec. 1961): 567–81; Matthew Simon, "The Pattern of New British Portfolio Foreign Investment, 1865–1914," in J. H. Adler, ed., *Capital Movements and Economic Development* (London, 1967) and republished in Hall, ed., *Export of Capital from Britain, 1870–1914*, 15–44; Matthew Simon, "The Enterprise and Industrial Composition of New British Portfolio Foreign Investment, 1865–1914," *Journal of Development Studies* 3 (1967): 280–92. This terminology had influence and thereafter, typically in the literature about British capital flows in the late nineteenth and early twentieth centuries, the term portfolio investments was used to cover those companies that raised money in Britain for capital export.

difficulties of the saver or the latter's agent (an investment trust, for example) investing abroad in unfamiliar foreign companies that had securities denominated in foreign currencies.

As students of portfolio and direct investments – who looked at financial (or passive) portfolio investments as against managed direct investments – reconsidered these companies as conduits for foreign investments, it became apparent that these companies were the investors abroad and should be seen as making foreign direct investments. In addition, during the 1960s and 1970s, new attention was paid to U.S. multinational enterprises and then, subsequently, to European and Japanese multinational enterprises. Their histories revealed formidable expansion of multinational enterprise in the Gold Standard Era.[32]

What characterized the modern multinational enterprise was the extension over borders not merely of investment, but of the firm itself, including the entire package of management, product, process, skills, and general know-how – what later came to be called firm-specific or proprietary assets. Students of contemporary, and past, multinational enterprises understood that they were not dealing with purely financial transactions. They were studying the growth of a firm that started at home, developed in the domestic market the firm-specific assets (or advantages, or core competencies), and employed their learned experience in their international expansion.[33] Such scholars used the phrase "foreign direct investment" as a measure of what multinational enterprises did.[34] Foreign direct investments as distinct from foreign portfolio investments carried with them from the start the control of the operations of the business abroad (or at least the potentials for control); the return to the investor was to come from

32 Wilkins, *Emergence of Multinational Enterprise*; John M. Stopford, "The Origins of British-Based Multinational Manufacturing Enterprise" and Lawrence Franko, "The Origins of Multinational Manufacturing by Continental European Firms," both in *Business History Review* 48 (autumn 1974): 303–35 and 277–302. Mira Wilkins, "Japanese Multinational Enterprise before 1914," *Business History Review* 60 (spring 1986): 199–231. The Japanese multinational enterprise activity before 1914 was, of course, far less substantial than that of American and European businesses.

33 For an influential rendition on the nature of multinational enterprise, see Charles P. Kindleberger, *American Business Abroad: Six Lectures on Direct Investment* (New Haven, Conn., 1969). Earlier, Kindleberger's student, Stephen Hymer, had written on the international operations of national firms. Raymond Vernon wrote of the expansion of American business based on home operations. All of the early theoretical work was done on American business abroad. Even John Dunning, the foremost British writer on multinational enterprise, did his initial work on American business abroad.

34 In doing this, they were following the pattern that had been adopted since the 1920s by the U.S. Department of Commerce, which as early as that decade recognized that "direct investments," investments by firms in affiliates abroad, were different from purely financial investments. In time, U.S. compilers defined foreign direct investment as a 25 percent equity interest in a firm abroad; later, the cutoff was reduced to 10 percent.

the controlled activity. The equation of multinational enterprise behavior and foreign direct investment has created endless difficulties. Students of multinational enterprise have often written about "theories of foreign direct investment" when they meant "theories of multinational enterprise." The measure overwhelmed and distorted the vocabulary. The correct formulation is that multinational enterprises make foreign direct investments (and do many other things as well).

As historians reexamined the history of capital flows in the Gold Standard Era, it seemed appropriate to analyze the thousands of companies set up in source-of-capital countries during that period to move capital over borders within the firm, using the theoretical framework that had emerged over the years on multinational enterprise. Like the familiar, what has been called the "classic," or "traditional," or "American-model" multinational enterprise, the many British companies (and also French, Dutch, Belgian, and other companies) did not merely dispatch capital over borders; a headquarters remained in the home country; it was the entire firm that stretched its business abroad.

I named such enterprises "free-standing companies," a label that has been challenged as inappropriate (and I will explain why), but I used the term to differentiate these firms so prevalent in the Gold Standard Era from the classic multinational enterprise. These many companies started afresh (hence free-standing), and they were set up with the purpose of initiating or acquiring a business abroad. Unlike the classic multinational enterprise, these companies did not evolve out of an existing source-of-capital-country business enterprise. Because they did not involve the expansion of a firm that had developed at home existing firm-specific assets, these new ventures had to acquire the assets (including the talents and experience) from elsewhere if the business was going to be a success. Initially, they had to rely on a cluster of services external to the firm.[35] They were structured to solve the problem posed earlier: Business abroad was risky; it was hard to obtain adequate and reliable information about firms in distant lands; returns were unpredictable. But there were clearly opportunities abroad; a company organized within the source-of-capital country, with a responsible board of directors, under source-of-capital country law, to mobilize capital (and other assets) and to conduct the business in foreign countries could take advantage of the opportunities while reducing transaction costs by providing a familiar conduit.

---

35 Mira Wilkins, "The Free-Standing Company, 1870–1914: An Important Type of British Foreign Direct Investment," *Economic History Review* 41 (1988), 259–82.

Since there were costs in setting up a business to carry on activities abroad, these firms tended to be quite sizable.[36] They typically were set up in capital-rich countries, with large international contacts (information about the rest of the world). Usually, the country in which they were headquartered had an active stock market. The headquarters of these companies, located in the source-of-capital country, were initially lean. By definition, there was a headquarters in the source-of-capital country and the extension of the firm abroad.

Part of the problem with these newly established companies (when seen in the context of the theory of multinational enterprise) was that by virtue of their being set up anew, they did not have the needed skills embodied within the firm. How could they then, how did they, effectively monitor, control, and manage the business abroad? A number of characteristics became evident about these firms. As in any collection of new companies, some failed (never getting off the ground or faltering in a few years), some had quasi-acceptable performance (and a modicum of longevity), and others were brilliant successes.

When I first studied these companies, I identified many scams and failures. I attributed some of the failures to the absence of internalized management control. Many individuals assumed that I saw these businesses as second-class, inferior, forms of direct investment. Scholars asked why, if there were so many "exits," did anyone invest in these companies? It became necessary to study in detail a number of these free-standing companies, particularly the ones that lasted.

It turned out that there were different experiences. Because these firms began afresh, they had to rely on outsiders. Often the outsiders were on the board of directors of the company. Outsiders provided assistance of various sorts. In my first article on free-standing firms, I identified various "clusters" of interested parties associated with the free-standing companies. The clusters revolved around promoters, solicitors, accountants, investment trust company representatives, trading companies, shipping companies, and mining finance houses. Clusters were often associated with expertise in a particular economic activity or a particular geographical location. Clusters could involve banking arrangements and the provision of short-term working capital to the venture abroad.

Sometimes the loose cluster itself constituted a firm and the use of the vocabulary "free-standing" was anomalous. Indeed, Charles Jones

---

36 On the costs of setting up these firms, see ibid. and Ben P. A. Gales and Keetie E. Sluyterman, "Dutch Free-Standing Companies, 1870–1940," in Wilkins and Schröter, eds., *Free-Standing Company*, 306.

argued that the term "free-standing" carried with it the "misleading implication that they lacked effective management."[37] As explained earlier, I did not use the phrase "free-standing" with that implication, although that could easily be read into my use of the term. Charles Jones has preference for the vocabulary: "MIGs" (members of mercantile investment groups) and "AOCs" (autonomous overseas companies).[38] Another criticism of the use of the term was that there was already a valid phrase to describe these companies – that is, "overseas companies."[39] The problem is that the terms autonomous overseas companies and overseas companies are fine for British business, but not for companies headquartered in countries where the foreign business was not overseas but rather overland. Thus, Belgian free-standing companies did business in Italy; French free-standing companies were in Spain; and U.S. free-standing companies operated in Mexico. Recognizing the validity of the criticisms, accepting that these firms often were closely linked with groups of various sorts, for want of a superior phrase (that does not have a British bias), I have stuck with the problematic label, free-standing company. The purpose of the nomenclature – to repeat – was to focus on the distinctions between the traditionally thought of multinational enterprise and this other form (or perhaps forms) of direct investment abroad.[40]

What is important is that these companies served as highly significant conduits for international investment. Free-standing companies, set up in capital-rich countries, were designed to control the business abroad and furnish returns to the investors that were higher than those available at home. They had the advantage over host-country incorporated companies in that the investors in the company, who lived in the source-of-capital country, typically did not have to bother with foreign exchange transactions (these investors were making purely domestic investments); they got their returns in the same currency in which they made the investment; they also had a readily available market for their securities. There were other advantages of having a headquarters in the source-of-capital country. Often, the headquarters of the free-standing company recruited skilled

37 Jones, "Institutional Forms of British Foreign Direct Investment," 21.
38 Ibid.
39 T. A. B. Corley, "The Free-Standing Company, in Theory and Practice," in Wilkins and Schröter, eds., *Free-Standing Company*; Corley does not make the distinction that Jones made between the MIGs and AOCs.
40 Mark Casson has argued that if the headquarters was weak then there was no direct investment. Casson, "An Economic Theory of the Free-Standing Company," in Wilkins and Schröter, eds., *Free-Standing Company*, chap. 3. I do not accept his argument. These free-standing companies were by definition direct investments; a headquarters was in the home country and it was the firm that extended abroad.

personnel, purchased machinery and certain intermediary inputs, provided information on markets, and so forth. The free-standing company form was frequently used for mining ventures and for plantation agriculture, where there was inadequate collateral for loans.[41] In certain countries, railroad investments took this form, but, as noted, the share devoted to this purpose seems to have decreased over time. The Suez Canal Company was a prominent free-standing company formed before the Gold Standard Era that functioned during (and after) it. Other infrastructure investments such as ports and docks were often developed using this particular form of doing business. In the case of public utilities, some in the pre-1914 period seem to fit comfortably into the free-standing company pattern(s), while others appear to lie more properly in the category of the classic multinational. There was, in fact, a wide range of additional uses of free-standing companies – from breweries to jute manufacture, from mortgage lenders to commercial banks. On a global basis, in and outside of empires, vast numbers of new businesses were established through free-standing companies. If foreign entrepreneurs wanted to set up businesses in their home lands or in a third country, it was easy to go to the capital-rich countries – to the United Kingdom or France – and arrange to have a company organized to undertake the business.

What is crucial about these free-standing companies is that they not only mobilized capital, but the successful ones came to mobilize business (including banking) expertise or, alternatively, they were in a cluster that in and of itself had the acquired, learned expertise. The free-standing companies that lasted took on several forms: (1) Some remained single product, single country entities; (2) others persisted in the corporate form, albeit they were closely networked into wider clusters; and (3) some became basically indistinguishable from the classic multinational enterprise, internalizing within the business firm the fundamental skills and needs appropriate to the type of enterprise. In the first category were companies such as the Antofagasta Railroad (a British company in Chile) and the Société de Sucreries Brésiliennes (a French sugar milling and growing company in Brazil). In the second category were a large number of jute manufacturers, tea plantations, coal mining and tin mining companies – in each case linked through different clusters. In the third category were well-known firms such as Rio Tinto, British Petroleum (its predecessor in the Gold Standard Era was Anglo-Persian Oil Co.), Royal Dutch Shell (the Royal

---

41 Jean-François Hennart, "Transaction-Cost Theory and the Free-Standing Firm," in Wilkins and Schröter, eds., *Free-Standing Company*, 65–6, 79–80. Hennart sees free-standing companies as nonintermediated, equity investments. See ibid., 75, 81.

Dutch part began as a free-standing company), and Standard Chartered Bank (its free-standing company predecessors took shape and form in the period 1880–1914).

The attention to management of the business abroad from the locale where the firm was headquartered varied substantially from one company to the next. Some firms kept small headquarters with limited control stemming from the source-of-capital country. Others maintained small headquarters, but created vast administrative structures abroad, while others would, in time, develop truly substantial headquarters in the source-of-capital country.

What seems evident is that research on free-standing companies has highlighted the fact that the capital going over borders through this channel was not sent to "strangers." There was a need for conduits to move capital: The free-standing companies became extremely important as channels in the Gold Standard Era. They transferred globally not only capital, but ways of doing things (from cultural attitudes to production processes). They provided a mechanism for combining the talents in capital-rich countries with the needs in capital-short countries. They offered rewards both to the investors and to the recipients of the capital. When they were part of a cluster, with a trading company or mining house at the center, they complemented the activities of that trading company or mining house.

Rather than being an inferior form of direct investments (as many critics thought that I implied), they were brilliant structures for mobilizing capital that provided information conduits and reduced risk for the investors. The gold standard lowered a different kind of risk. The gold standard world was a congenial one, in which these companies could multiply. They were not new to this era, but this was the time of their vast proliferation.

And, just as the typical traded security might not be held in the country of issue (see above), so too the free-standing company's stocks and bonds were not necessarily held in Great Britain, Holland, or Belgium, or wherever the free-standing company was domiciled.[42] The very mobilization of capital was international as well as its placement. Because there were the free-standing companies, companies such as Russian Tobacco could take advantage of the "conduit" form – not so much to bring capital into Russia, but

---

42 Mira Wilkins, "The Free-Standing Company Revisited," in Wilkins and Schröter, eds., *Free-Standing Company*, 36; Hobson, *Export of Capital*, 156, notes that a good many Belgian company shares were peddled in the northern provinces of France; Natalia Gurushina, "Free-Standing Companies in Tsarist Russia," in Wilkins and Schröter, eds., *Free-Standing Company*, 190, shows how the Russian Tobacco Company was set up in Britain, but was virtually entirely Russian owned. For more on international ownership, see Harm Schröter, "Continental European Free-Standing Companies; The Case of Belgium, Germany and Switzerland," in Wilkins and Schröter, eds., *Free-Standing Company*, 335.

to provide security to domestic investors (and thus aid in the mobilization of domestic capital); Russian Tobacco was registered in London yet controlled by Russian investors.

DIRECT INVESTMENTS: CLASSIC MULTINATIONAL ENTERPRISES

While the free-standing company, as described above, did not conform to the model of the classic multinational enterprise (although – as noted – the most successful of them, through time, came to internalize talents and to resemble the traditional multinational enterprise), many companies that operated internationally in 1880–1914 behaved exactly in the manner of the "classic" multinational enterprise. American business abroad was an outgrowth of the domestic expansion of U.S. companies in the late nineteenth and early twentieth centuries: Singer, National Cash Register, Standard Oil of New Jersey (the predecessor of EXXON), General Electric, American Radiator, Western Electric, American Tobacco, International Harvester, Ford Motor Company all set up or (less frequently) acquired businesses in foreign lands on the heels of domestic expansion – using the core competencies developed at home. And, this was not only true of manufacturing firms; American life insurance companies, for example, were multinational enterprises in the late nineteenth and early twentieth centuries. U.S. multinational enterprise emerged and flourished in these years. And, the expansion of business operations over borders was not confined to American companies: British-headquartered multinationals included, for example, J. & P. Coats (thread), Lever (soap), and Marconi (radio facilities).[43] And, then there were the German multinationals: Siemens, Bayer, Hoechst, Merck, for example, and the Swedish ones: from Ericsson to ASEA. An important French-headquartered multinational was Michelin, which by 1914 had plants in London, Turin, and Milltown (New Jersey) as well as in France. Dutch multinationals included Philips, Jurgens, and Royal Dutch-Shell (part Dutch and part British). Swiss multinational enterprises included Nestlé and Hoffmann–La Roche, both of which developed as international businesses with plants across Swiss national frontiers.[44] Once

43 On U.S. multinational enterprises see Wilkins, *Emergence of Mutinational Enterprise*; on British multinationals, see Geoffrey Jones, ed., *British Multinationals: Origins, Management and Performance* (Aldershot, U.K., 1986); on these British companies in the United States, see Wilkins, *History of Foreign Investment in the United States to 1914*.

44 There is now substantial material on the history of continental European multinationals, including some excellent company histories. For a start, see Lawrence G. Franko, *The European Multinationals* (Stamford, Conn., 1976); Geoffrey Jones and Harm G. Schröter, eds., *The Rise of Multinationals in Continental Europe* (Aldershot, U.K., 1993); Ragnhild Lundström, "Swedish Multinational Growth

most of the literature on multinational enterprise (on contemporary ones and on the history of multinationals) paid attention to "manufacturing" multinationals. Multinationals were, however, present in many other sectors, from United Fruit (which was integrated from plantation to retailing) to Metallgesellschaft (which traded but also had interests in companies that mined and refined metals), to the French Pathé (with its global film-making and distribution network).[45] Andrew Godley has been studying inward direct investments in the United Kingdom before 1914 in retailing.[46] Trading companies can also be viewed through the prism of multinational enterprise analysis.[47] And, most important, insurance companies were global in nature. American life insurance companies, which were multinational before 1914, were already by 1914 retreating from this involvement. British marine and fire insurance companies were formidable multinationals. There were also important French, Swiss, Russian, German, and even Bulgarian-headquartered companies in insurance (and reinsurance).[48] There were, in addition, in the Gold Standard Era many multinationals involved in banking.[49]

In the years prior to 1914, there was, accordingly, no absence of the "classic" multinational enterprise type of managed investment over borders. The idea that pre-1914 multinational activity was solely in infrastructure, agriculture, and mining is false. Multinational enterprises of a very modern variety were very much in evidence. They were conduits for capital, but also for technology (broadly defined to include not only machines but social technology – that is, ways of doing business), product, process, marketing methods, and, most of all, management. A word, however, needs to be said about the classic multinational enterprises as conduits of capital. It is more appropriate to see them as mobilizers of capital for use within the host country. Sometimes, they exported capital over borders from home to host; sometimes they raised capital locally and put it to productive purposes; and sometimes they brought capital from

---

Before 1930," in Peter Hertner and Geoffrey Jones, eds., *Multinationals: Theory and History* (Aldershot, U.K., 1986), 135–56. On Michelin's prewar plants, see Wilkins, *History of Foreign Investment in the United States to 1914*, 423.

45 On Pathé's international business, see Mira Wilkins, "Charles Pathé's American Business," *Entreprises et Histoire* 6 (Sept. 1994), 134–5.

46 He has identified a surprisingly large number of foreign-headquartered retailers that did business in Britain. Scott R. Fletcher and Andrew Godley, "Foreign Direct Investment in British Retailing," *Business History* 42 (2000), 43–62.

47 Geoffrey Jones, *Merchants to Multinationals: British Trading Companies in the Nineteenth and Twentieth Centuries* (Oxford, 2000).

48 The best sources on international insurance companies in the Gold Standard Era are *Best's Insurance Reports* that deal with both domestic and foreign insurance companies in the United States.

49 See Geoffrey Jones, ed., *Banks as Multinationals* (London, 1990).

third countries to be employed in particular projects. Often they reinvested their profits. With the classic multinational, there was no given bilateral capital flow, but rather multilateral flows (and sometimes no flows at
all). There is a true asymmetry between company and home/host country
relationships.

The major multinational enterprises were headquartered in countries
that adopted the gold standard, but many of the inward foreign investments
made by classic multinationals were in such countries as well; the firms were
attracted by the large market. Globally, the existence of the gold standard
reduced the inevitable uncertainties of doing business over borders.

DIRECT INVESTMENTS: THE MIX AND THE NUMBERS

If we transfer free-standing companies from the category of "portfolio" investments to that of "direct" investments and add the "classic multinational
enterprise" as well, it becomes evident that direct investments represented
a far greater share of total international investments in the Gold Standard
Era than earlier writers had realized. There have been attempts to measure
that share – and, even more specifically, to determine what portion of the
foreign direct investment took the form of free-standing companies. John
Dunning and T. A. B. Corley have done yeoman work in this regard.[50]
I am not going to reproduce their numbers in this text, for I have long
found myself uncomfortable with their calculations because of the prevailing ambiguities in defining what is a foreign direct investment and what
should be included as a free-standing company. There are also formidable,
still unresolved, problems with counting. For example, suppose we have a
French investment – portfolio or direct – in a British company that makes an
investment in Chile: Do we count it as one international investment, that of
a British company in Chile; or two investments, inward into Britain by the
French and outward by the British? And, what about the converse: Is this a
British investment in Chile or a British and French investment in Chile –
based on the size of the French investment in the British company; or if

50 John Dunning has published estimates over the years of foreign direct investment in 1913–14, most
recently in John H. Dunning, *Multinational Enterprises and the Global Economy* (Wokingham, U.K.,
1993), 117, where he gives global foreign direct investment in 1914 as $14.6 billion. T. A. B. Corley's
most recent estimate is in his "The Free-Standing Company, in Theory and Practice," in Wilkins
and Schröter, eds., *Free-Standing Company*, 136; in the latter essay, Corley revises upward Dunning's
total, finding the level of global foreign direct investment in 1914 was $18 billion, of which almost
45 percent was by free-standing companies. If the overall estimate of international investment in
1914 is $45 billion – see Table 2.1 herein – by Corley's estimate, this would make foreign direct
investment fully 40 percent of the total foreign investment.

the British company is controlled by the French investor, is this a French direct investment in Chile? The reader may say, the problem is not difficult; we deal with this with trade: exports and re-exports. It does, however, become difficult when one is seeking, as in the case of direct investment, to segregate the nature of the investment and separate out direct and portfolio investments. It is difficult to provide with confidence global numbers before criteria are accepted – and articulated.

There is, however, no question by those currently engaged in research on the history of international investment that free-standing companies and traditional multinational enterprise constituted crucial channels for capital flows in the Gold Standard Era. They were responsible for stimulating major economic change on a global scale. Aside from government finance and a certain amount of the railroad finance, it appears that managed direct investments were the most important conduits in the transmission of international capital in the pre-1914 years. Free-standing companies were very suitable for new mines and plantations; they did not engage in high-technology manufacturing. Whenever oil was found, the pattern was to internalize the expertise and link up with (or become integrated into) a classic multinational enterprise. High-technology projects as well as development, refining, and marketing of oil resources typically went through the "classic" multinational enterprise. The proportion of free-standing companies in the total foreign direct investment appears to have been highest in England, France, Holland, and Belgium, and substantially lower in the United States, Germany, and Switzerland, where the classic multinational enterprise predominated in the Gold Standard Era. There also seem to be systematic differences in the host countries that attracted these two different forms of multinational enterprise. While initially free-standing companies were in both developed and underdeveloped host countries, they lasted longer in the less developed than in the developed host countries; they were apparently more appropriate to the former than to the latter. The new literature changes our thinking about global integration in the Gold Standard Era in its attention to the different kinds of managed investments. It opens the way for an expansion of research on entrepreneurial behavior over borders and the relationships to capital flows.

CONCLUSION

In considering capital movements in the Gold Standard Era, too often the emphasis has been placed solely on "international finance"; as we have seen, much of the capital that moved internationally took the form of direct investment, managed investment. No matter what the conduit, there are problems in measuring the amounts of capital flows, their origins, and, most important, it is clear that the level at any time is not the sum of the flows; traded securities changed the nature of obligations. That said, clearly all the different conduits served to integrate the world economy. In each case, the ways of reducing uncertainties were very different. Whether we are talking about provisions in government bonds, or mortgages backing railroads, or the security of a home-country registration and headquarters, or the internalization within a classic multinational enterprise of the advantages that were sent abroad, each of the conduits served to reduce the risks of international transactions.

While it is not exactly clear how much of the capital movement went through free-standing companies or through classic multinational enterprise, it is obvious that far more was associated with firms that extended over borders than had been previously recognized. Also, multinational enterprise type investment (whether by free-standing companies or by the classic multinational enterprise) had the added benefit of moving not only capital but a bundle of other attributes, including management methods. The ways of the more advanced countries became diffused through the direct investments. With the free-standing companies, it was often the "culture" of the West, the ways of doing things, that was transferred along with the capital. With the classic multinational it was apt to be the new technologies, the branded goods (the trademarked products), and the new products that required careful managerial supervision. Foreign direct investors offered a large part of modern infrastructure, the spread of new technologies, and the introduction of a wide variety of new products into international trade. Foreign direct investors set up such infrastructure as ports and dock facilities, tramways, public utilities (electricity and telephones), and trading and shipping companies (crucial for an integrated world economy). We have no figures on intracompany trade before 1977, but available evidence suggests an extremely high level of intracompany trade in the Gold Standard Era. It was foreign direct investors that not only supplied capital, but through their continuing management over borders integrated the world economy. The conduits in these cases – far more than the conduits for international finance – became the basis for a deeper and longer lasting integration.

Even though stable exchange rates (or gold-backed bonds, or bonds that had guarantees of a fixed exchange rate, or bonds denominated in the currency of the source-of-capital country) helped accelerate the capital movement across borders, there remained the substantial uncertainties about investments in unfamiliar parts of the world; it was one thing for Europeans to invest money in American railroads, which were well known to British, Dutch, and most continental European investors; there was information on some other railroads. Beyond that, European investors desired the security of British, Dutch, Belgian, or French companies as they moved money internationally. These companies supplied familiar forms for investment purposes. They reduced risk. So, too, and with a quite different conduit structure, as American, British, German, Swiss, and other European companies grew in size in the late nineteenth and twentieth centuries and sought to expand their markets and to acquire the best sources of their inputs, their business operations extended over borders and they undertook international investment. Internalization of business within a multinational enterprise lowered transaction costs. Stable exchange rates facilitated the extension of corporate governance.

The discussion of the conduits for investments over borders has a purpose beyond mere description. First, it can be used to evaluate the success or failure for development purposes of different types of conduits (and the growth issues can be seen in terms of home as well as host countries). Second, it offers a more realistic understanding of the complex nature of capital flows, an understanding that can be applied to periods other than that of the gold standard; what changes occur as exchange rates fluctuate? Does the nature of the monetary system alter in a systematic fashion the conduits for international investment? Third, in that there appear to have been systematic differences in the mix of home and host countries' use of different conduits, we need to probe further into the significance of these differences and what they mean for the contemporary world. Fourth, it may matter substantially the way capital is embodied in institutional structures when we look at the nature of global technological change. There are sharp differences between the liquidity of securities markets and the aspirations of investors in financial markets and the lower liquidity of investment in business operations along with plant and equipment abroad. There is also a clear difference in the motives and thinking of the investors. Financial markets provide funding; direct investors furnish a package of other tangible and intangible benefits. Fifth, how much is internalized within a particular firm may affect the success or failure of the venture. Sixth, how much control the investor is able to exercise is likely to affect the performance of the venture. If control is an issue, if we are discussing direct investments, the performance of the recipient will be influenced by the competence of the international investors. The discussion of free-standing companies suggests that different types of multinational enterprises have different competencies and that the

3

The Gold-Exchange Standard

A Reinterpretation

STEPHEN A. SCHUKER

The gold-exchange standard of the 1920s, at least among economists, has suffered an infamous posterity. "There are few Englishmen who do not rejoice at the breaking of our gold fetters," Keynes declared when Britain elected to abandon the system in 1931.[1] In the current era, when monetary authorities have institutionalized flexible exchange rates with a modicum of success, most analysts looking backward tend to agree. The attempt to reconstitute the status quo ante by reestablishing the gold standard after World War I proved "a dreadful mistake," opines Peter Temin.[2] Barry Eichengreen insists that only when the monetary authorities repudiated the principles of "orthodox finance" could recovery from the Great Depression begin.[3] Allan Meltzer sees no compelling evidence that a gold-standard regime offers superior price stability to compensate for the easier transmission of shocks or the potential variability in output and employment.[4]

The classic older treatment by Charles Kindleberger does not fully echo those criticisms. Kindleberger concedes that monetary adjustment mechanisms did not work properly in the Depression, but he faults a cumulation of policy failures as much as insurmountable structural problems. Still, Kindleberger views the monetary regime of the 1920s as fatally impaired by the absence of a hegemon. Great Britain no longer possessed the financial clout to clear the market of distress goods, lend counter-cyclically, or

---

1 John Maynard Keynes, *Essays in Persuasion* (New York, 1932), 288.
2 Peter Temin, *Lessons from the Great Depression* (Cambridge, Mass., 1989), 37.
3 Barry Eichengreen, *Golden Fetters: The Gold Standard and the Great Depression* (New York, 1992), 21. See also Eichengreen's systematic comparison of the interwar gold-exchange standard with the pre-1914 gold standard and the postwar Bretton Woods arrangements in *Globalizing Capital: A History of the International Monetary System* (Princeton, N.J., 1996), esp. 45–92.
4 Allen H. Meltzer and Saranna Robinson, "Stability under the Gold Standard in Practice," in Michael D. Bordo, ed., *Money, History and International Finance: Essays in Honor of Anna J. Schwartz* (Chicago, 1989), 163–202.

discount in a crisis. The United States did not yet acknowledge a responsibility proportionate to its economic means to serve as the global stabilizer.[5] Although Kindleberger differs in emphasis from his Keynesian successors, he, too, regards the gold-exchange standard regime as inadequate in practice to the challenges of post–World War I reconstruction.

Every international monetary regime, however, reflects the political and cultural circumstances that attend its birth and sustain it. That proved true after both military cataclysms of our century. The familiar events of the more recent past illustrate the point. They provide a normative template by which we can measure the 1920s in retrospect. The shape of the Bretton Woods arrangements adopted after World War II did not turn mainly on the theoretical principles in contention, still less on the respective drafting skills of Harry Dexter White and Maynard Keynes. When the hostilities ended in 1945, the United States boasted half of global manufacturing capacity and two-thirds of world monetary gold. Those hard facts, as interpreted by policymakers with specific life experiences, bureaucratic loyalties, and economic preferences, inevitably determined the outcome.[6] The Bretton Woods system eroded in the 1960s when the disproportion between American resources and those of the rest of the world altered fundamentally.[7] The floating-rate system that developed after 1973 has also continued to evolve. The current regime retains the outward form but not the inner content of dispositions obtaining two decades ago. In the 1970s, central banks and treasuries could, and frequently did, manage rates in the service of domestic objectives. Today, outside regional groupings that have opted out of floating, exchange-rate movements largely register the

5 Charles P. Kindleberger, *The World in Depression, 1929–1939* [rev. ed.] (Berkeley, Calif., 1986), xv, 288–305.
6 Alfred E. Eckes, Jr., *A Search for Solvency: Bretton Woods and the International Monetary System, 1941–1971* (Austin, Tex., 1971); Robert Solomon, *The International Monetary System: An Insider's View* (New York, 1977); Harold James, *International Monetary Cooperation since Bretton Woods* (New York, 1996). The point emerges clearly from those who take a biographical approach, e.g., D. E. Moggridge, *Maynard Keynes: An Economist's Biography* (London, 1992), 721–55, and from those who approach the problems from the standpoint of political science, e.g., John S. Odell, *U.S. International Monetary Policy: Markets, Power, and Ideas as Sources of Change* (Princeton, N.J., 1982).
7 The most insightful overview remains David P. Calleo, *The Imperious Economy* (Cambridge, Mass., 1982). Among contemporary American economists, Robert Triffin was perhaps the first to draw attention to the paradigm shift; see *Europe and the Money Muddle* (New Haven, Conn., 1957); id., *Gold and the Dollar Crisis* (New Haven, Conn., 1960); idem., *The World Money Maze* (New Haven, Conn., 1966). Jacques Rueff, as financial adviser to President Charles de Gaulle of France, early advanced the theory that the United States had begun using its seignorage under the dollar-based Bretton Woods system to run a chronic balance-of-payments deficit. See Maurice Vaïsse, *La Grandeur: politique étrangère du général de Gaulle 1958–1969* (Paris, 1998), 396–412; note Rueff's polemic exposition of the theme in *L'Age de l'inflation* (Paris, 1963); and *Le Péché monétaire de l'occident* (Paris, 1971).

uncoordinated expectations of multinational corporate treasurers and bank arbitrageurs.[8]

To sum up, monetary arrangements and institutions represent an implicit bargaining framework for organizing international economic relations. Those arrangements and institutions may work more or less efficiently. When they fail, however, one should examine the political as well as the technical reasons for their breakdown. The gold-exchange standard ultimately collapsed because the leading nations of the Western world could not settle their intertwined domestic distributive controversies and international political conflicts after the most destructive of all wars up to that time.[9]

I

Among economists there currently exists a fair degree of consensus about the way monetary arrangements worked between the wars. One might describe that current orthodoxy with mild irreverence as the Gospel according to Saint Peter and Archangel Barry.[10] A gold-standard regime involves fixed currency values in terms of gold, the free flow of gold between countries, and the absence of a structured forum for international coordination. Adjustment is supposed to take place automatically. Deficit countries must contract their currencies and deflate until they balance external accounts. Surplus countries may expand their currencies, raise consumption, and import more. Significantly, however, they pay little penalty for not doing so and accumulating gold instead. The burden of adjustment thus falls asymmetrically on debtors. The latter must deflate rather than devalue. When labor-union power and a democratic ethos render wages inflexible downward, adjustment implies the fall of output and employment. Such a process transmogrified the severe but manageable downturn of 1929–30 – originally not qualitatively different from the recession of 1920–1 – into a catastrophic depression.[11]

---

8 Eichengreen, *Globalizing Capital*, 137–87; John H. Makin, *Capital Flows and Exchange-Rate Stability in the Post-Bretton Woods Era*, Essays in International Finance No. 103 (Princeton, N.J., 1974); Emmanuel Apel, *European Monetary Integration, 1958–2002* (London, 1998), 94–186.

9 This conclusion emerged implicitly even in the early analyses by William Adams Brown, Jr., *The International Gold Standard Reinterpreted, 1914–1934* (New York, 1940); and League of Nations [Ragnar Nurkse], *International Currency Experience: Lessons of the Interwar Period* (Princeton, N.J., 1944). Michael D. Bordo and Barry Eichengreen elaborate the notion that monetary regimes respond to historically specific factors in *The Rise and Fall of a Barbarous Relic: The Role of Gold in the International Monetary System*, National Bureau of Economic Research Working Paper 6434 (Cambridge, Mass., 1998).

10 Temin, *Lessons from the Great Depression*, 1–88; Eichengreen, *Golden Fetters*, 3–66.

11 Temin, *Lessons from the Great Depression*, 8–9.

When the guns fell silent in 1918, the United States remained the only major country with a currency still tied to gold, although severe price inflation had taken place even there. Yet the Cunliffe Committee in Great Britain expressed no doubt that that country should return to the gold standard as soon as feasible. Reputable authorities in London and New York differed only on the pace of the transition and the modalities of the return.[12] Russell C. Leffingwell of J. P. Morgan & Co. argued typically that, despite the temporary maladjustment of prices, "the way to resume is to resume." Maynard Keynes and his fellow publicist-economists seemed to think that price changes were "a disease rather than a symptom." In fact, the overriding issue, said Leffingwell, was to restore confidence. "When a bank's doors open again after a period of trouble, there are always heavy withdrawals at the outset by people who have been prevented from making withdrawals by the suspension. The trick is to pay everybody very promptly, and . . . to assure the world that the bank is open to stay."[13]

By early 1925, Governor Montagu Norman of the Bank of England and his Federal Reserve Bank of New York (FRBNY) counterpart, Benjamin Strong, had concluded that a failure to resume would lead to a long period of unsettled conditions, the recrudescence of paper-money expedients and uncontrolled inflation in Europe, the progressive deterioration of other currencies against the dollar, and a hemorrhage of gold to the United States.[14] Temin considers that view "tragically flawed." He contends that a sterling rate of $4.35 rather than $4.86 would not have improved British trade prospects decisively; the fixed-rate regime itself proved unacceptably rigid. He notes additionally that other countries returned to gold at misaligned parities: The Germans arguably overvalued the mark in 1924, and the French demonstrably undervalued the franc in 1926.[15]

Echoing the contemporary view of the British-dominated League of Nations Financial Committee, Temin claims that the United States and France, the two major nations with undervalued currencies, failed to expand

12 D. E. Moggridge, *British Monetary Policy, 1924–1931: The Norman Conquest of $4.86* (Cambridge, 1972), 21–8.

13 Russell C. Leffingwell to J. P. Morgan, 10 Sept. 1923, J. P. Morgan-Partners file, J. P. Morgan Papers, J. P. Morgan Library. Morgan stood in the middle of discussions about timing the return with his partner E. C. Grenfell and Governor Norman of the Bank of England.

14 Benjamin Strong Memorandum, 11 Jan. 1925, Benjamin Strong Papers, Federal Reserve Bank of New York; substantially reprinted in Lester V. Chandler, *Benjamin Strong, Central Banker* (Washington, D.C., 1958), 309–13. On the discussion between central bankers on the return to gold, see also Steven V. O. Clarke, *Central Bank Cooperation, 1924–31* (New York, 1967), 75–105.

15 Conclusive evidence now suggests that Finance Minister Raymond Poincaré deliberately undervalued the franc in 1926. See Kenneth Mouré, "Undervaluing the franc Poincaré," *Economic History Review* 49/1 (1996): 137–53; see also H. Clark Johnson, *Gold, France, and the Great Depression, 1919–1932* (New Haven, Conn., 1997), 44–62.

their economies sufficiently in the later 1920s. A maldistribution of gold resulted. Sterling suffered chronic weakness after the French began to convert their foreign currency holdings and to move toward a gold bullion standard after 1928. That fact assumed particular salience since the Bank of England had played the leading part in the financial reconstruction of other Continental countries; most central banks in Europe and the British Empire held sterling as a key reserve currency. Hence, the whole system rested on shaky foundations.[16]

The peculiar difficulties of German financial management added further complications. Germany financed reparations outpayments and its current-account deficit by long- and short-term borrowing abroad. Recalling the ravages of the 1923 hyperinflation on bondholders, domestic lenders insisted on a risk premium to hold government obligations. After a disastrous experiment in 1927, the Reichsbank found that it could attract foreign funds only by keeping the discount rate high, and that imparted a deflationary bias to the German economy. When in mid-1928 the United States allegedly curtailed capital exports and raised the discount rate to discourage stock market speculation, the weaknesses of the system stood dangerously exposed.[17] In other words, an unyielding policy regime constrained output and employment even before the downturn of 1929–30. Caught in the grip of economic orthodoxy, treasuries and central banks subsequently raised interest rates and balanced budgets in order to defend their currencies instead of expanding the money supply and embracing deficit finance to spur the real economy. When Britain abandoned the gold standard in September 1931, it nevertheless sought to accumulate reserves and thus transmitted deflation elsewhere. And when the United States finally depreciated its currency against gold in late 1933, it missed a chance to bolster the economy by expanding the money supply proportionately. Eichengreen, Temin, and their ideological bedfellows do not hesitate to embellish their ex post facto analysis with occasional heuristic grace notes. Eichengreen voices satisfaction that, after World War II, "the hegemony of the Keynesian model endowed policymakers in different countries with a common conceptual framework, facilitating efforts at international cooperation."[18] And Temin deplores the monetarist zeal displayed by "Fed" Chairman Paul Volcker in 1979 with the

16 See also Richard H. Meyer, *Banker's Diplomacy: Monetary Stabilization in the Twenties* (New York, 1970); and R. S. Sayers, *The Bank of England, 1891–1944* (Cambridge, 1976), esp. ch. 7–8, 15.
17 Eichengreen, *Golden Fetters*, 13–14, 392. For the details of German policy, see Harold James, *The Reichsbank and Public Finance in Germany, 1924–1933* (Frankfurt a.M., 1985); and Theo Balderston, *The Origins and Course of the German Economic Crisis, 1923–1932* (Berlin, 1993).
18 Eichengreen, *Golden Fetters*, 396.

aim of breaking the Jimmy Carter inflation. Volcker's "sharply deflationary" policies, he expostulates, almost led to an "economic meltdown."[19]

II

The financial history of the 1920s looks rather different to the archival historian who reads history forward rather than with Argus-eyed hindsight. The nineteenth-century version of the pure gold standard turns out not to work so differently from the gold-exchange variant as textbook models lead one to suppose. Bloomfield and Triffin show that countries violated the supposedly automatic rules for the adjustment of surpluses and deficits before World War I as well as after it. Export and import fluctuations, as well as relative prices, tended to move in parallel rather in contrast. Surplus countries sometimes neutralized gold inflows rather than expand; deficit countries rarely induced major downward wage adjustments. Nor did changes in discount rates play a uniform role in forcing cost discrepancies into line. Instead, huge international capital movements accommodated deficits or surpluses for decades at a time without compelling any correction on current account.[20]

While single-crop commodity producers on the periphery suffered periodically from capital shortages, the core industrial nations preserved exchange stability without restricting trade or frequently shipping gold. The system worked smoothly because of policy harmonization and substantial cooperation by central bankers, who shared a common outlook and a commitment to sound money, and because of the felicitous coordinating function played by the London City in extending credit and financing trade. By 1913, Triffin reminds us, paper currency and bank deposits accounted for nine-tenths of world monetary circulation, gold for only one-tenth. Moreover, central banks held sterling and other hard currencies as a substitute for gold reserves, although the prewar share of Devisen in total reserves amounted to only two-thirds the proportion reached in 1928.[21] Finally, the monetary authorities in advanced countries had already begun experiments in stabilizing silver currencies at the periphery through a gold-exchange standard. Britain introduced that arrangement in India in 1893; the United

19 Temin, *Lessons of the Great Depression*, 39–40.
20 Arthur I. Bloomfield, *Monetary Policy under the International Gold Standard, 1880–1914* (New York, 1959).
21 Robert Triffin, *The Evolution of the International Monetary System: Historical Appraisal and Future Perspectives*, Princeton Studies in International Finance no. 12 (Princeton, N.J., 1964), 15; Peter H. Lindert, *Key Currencies and Gold, 1900–1913*, Princeton Studies in International Finance no. 24 (Princeton, N.J., 1969), 12–15.

States did so in the Philippines in 1903 and studied its further use in the Caribbean.[22]

The floating exchange-rate regime that developed when pegging of key currencies ended in 1919 proved an unmitigated disaster. Unlimited fiat-money creation and hyperinflation brought the economies of the former Russian and Austrian empires to their knees. Speculative rings in Vienna and Amsterdam operating on forward exchange spurred the process on by turning their destructive ministrations successively to one gyrating currency after another. Heedless of the long-term social costs, Germany deliberately failed to arrest currency depreciation in 1921–3 in order to avoid the payment of reparations.[23] The ignominious collapse of European exchanges led the United States to protect its manufacturers from dumping through the emergency tariff of 1921 and through more permanent legislation a year later. Currency devaluation appeared not as a possible solution to under-utilization of capital and labor, as Keynesians would see it a decade later. Rather, economists and business leaders in the sounder-money countries regarded currency instability elsewhere as a generator of chaos and the chief obstacle to trade revival.

Yet a return to a gold-bullion standard did not seem immediately practicable. Having fallen steadily during the war, gold production reached its lowest point in 1920–2.[24] Although the gold price had not changed, the dollar had inflated by about 60 percent since 1913; thus, with the dollar as the standard unit of account, a given quantity of gold would buy proportionately fewer goods. Those conditions did not provide much incentive for additional gold exploration. Output at the mines rebounded relatively slowly; for the whole period 1914–28 monetary gold stocks increased on average only 2.5 percent annually, compared with 3.2 percent in the quarter-century before the war.[25]

A pure gold standard would therefore usher in a liquidity shortage. Nations recovering from war would perforce have to reestablish banking relationships on either dollars or sterling. Much international monetary debate

22 Elisabeth Glaser-Schmidt, '*Die Philippines den Filipinos!*': *Die amerikanische Debatte über die Wirtschafts- und Verwaltungspolitik auf den Philippines, 1898–1906* (Frankfurt a.M., 1986), 226–8; idem., "Amerikanische Währungsreform in Ostasien und im Karibischen Raum, 1900–1918," *Amerikastudien* 33 (1988): 359–75.

23 Stephen A. Schuker, "Finance and Foreign Policy in the Era of the German Inflation," in Otto Büsch and Gerald D. Feldman, eds., *Historische Prozesse der deutschen Inflation, 1914–1924* (Berlin, 1976), 343–61. Gerald D. Feldman, in *The Great Disorder: Politics, Economics, and Society in the German Inflation, 1914–1924* (New York, 1993), declines to concede the general point, yet brings one thousand pages of evidence to support it.

24 Eichengreen, *Golden Fetters*, 199.

25 See the figures in Triffin, *Evolution of the International Monetary System*, 79–80.

in the first postwar years turned on the rivalry between the two currencies. Governor Norman offered his "Genoa proposals" in 1922 with the hope that as many countries as possible would hold reserves in sterling and that London would resume pride of place as what Keynes later called (with characteristic national hubris) "the conductor of the international orchestra."[26] Although Strong wished to cooperate with Norman, he nurtured growing reservations about the key-currency idea. He worried about accepting responsibilities for stabilization abroad that might conflict with his primary responsibilities at home. He did not want to hand a "blank check to some of the impoverished nations of the world, or to their banks of issue, and especially to those whose government finances are in complete disorder and quite beyond control."[27]

Beneath the flowery language about central-bank cooperation, Norman pursued a tenacious rivalry with Strong over the basis for stabilizing European currencies in 1922–4. Norman talked the talk of cooperative endeavor with his FRBNY colleague, but revealed more nationalist inclinations to his European interlocutors. That is why he nurtured a cozy friendship with the arch-inflationist Rudolf Havenstein in Germany and why he labored indefatigably to line up the Dutch and Scandinavian central-bank governors on his side. Norman schemed relentlessly in the winter of 1923–4 to defeat the idea, implicit in the Dawes Plan, of stabilizing the new German currency on gold. Norman would have preferred to base the Reichsmark exclusively on sterling so that the Reichsbank would hold its external balances in London. Tempers ran high on the British and American sides; Hjalmar Schacht of the Reichsbank played the middle duplicitously against both ends. In the final analysis, Robert Kindersley and his fellow negotiators at the 1924 London Conference discreetly fudged the matter. But the fine print of the German banking law in essence linked the new Reichsmark to gold. That settlement magnified the pressure on London to resume its prewar parity as well.[28]

Sayers and Moggridge have detailed the extensive policy discussions that Chancellor of the Exchequer Winston Churchill orchestrated in early 1925

---

26 Clarke, *Central Bank Cooperation*, 73; quotation in Eichengreen, *Golden Fetters*, 8. There is much evidence for Norman's political motives at Genoa in files G8/55 (Committee of Treasury), and G30/8–9 (Governor's Misc. Correspondence), Bank of England.

27 Benjamin Strong to Montagu Norman, 14 July 1922, File 1116.3, FRBNY.

28 Clarke, *Central Bank Cooperation*, 45–67, provides a sanitized version of these events. The biographer Andrew Boyle, *Montagu Norman* (London, 1967), 157–78, also smooths the rough edges. The Bank of England files on German monetary reconstruction, OV34/117–120, and also the correspondence files with the Reichsbankdirektorium, OV34/71–72, provide evidence of a far less cooperative environment. See also Hans Otto Schötz, *Die Kampf um die Mark, 1923/24* (Berlin, 1987).

before agreeing to resume gold payments at $4.86 to the pound. The high-level expert debate that preceded resumption, carried on within the bureaucracy as well as the public prints, has few models or parallels in diligence.[29] No doubt policymakers lacked the statistical knowledge that might have led to better forecasting. Yet it is far from obvious, even today, whether as a political matter the decision to go back on gold was right or wrong.

A. W. Phillips later claimed that, by examining experience over the half-century before the war, one could fairly accurately have predicted the level of unemployment that would persist given the average decline of wage rates in 1925–9. But Samuelson and Solow offer a generally persuasive response.[30] One cannot easily separate the effects of cost changes and demand shifts on the price level. Hence, Governor Norman and his colleagues in the Treasury could not have predicted the high unemployment and sluggish growth rate of the later 1920s without supplementary data on the mobility of labor markets and without knowing how international trade would develop once other trading countries had returned to stable currency values. Perhaps the British should have realized that German coal mines, idled during the Ruhr occupation, had modernized sufficiently to drive British coal from international markets. But such details seemed to hold at most peripheral significance.[31]

Compelling political reasons mandated an early return to gold. The key Dominions, as well as several European nations, had already determined to resume gold payments. In effect, Britain could merely choose to lead the movement or to bring up the rear. If Britain lagged behind, the gold bill would ineluctably replace the sterling bill as the chief medium of exchange. The country would lose on revenue from invisibles what it potentially gained on export trade.[32] Josiah Stamp, one of the Dawes Plan architects in 1924, articulated the fear of the average manufacturer lest overseas political pressure price British goods out of world markets. "New York cracks the whip," he complained, "and London obeys the signal." His fellow expert Owen Young, a director of the New York "Fed," articulated the broader vision that

---

29 Moggridge, *British Monetary Policy*, 37–112; details in his earlier study, *The Return to Gold 1925: The Formulation of Economic Policy and Its Critics* (Cambridge, 1969). Sayers, Bank of England, chap. 7.

30 See A. W. Phillips, "The Relation Between Unemployment and the Rate of Change of Money Wages in the United Kingdom, 1861–1957," *Economica* 25 (Nov. 1958): 283–99; and the reply by Paul Samuelson and Robert Solow in *American Economic Review* (1960): 177–94; also Robert M. Solow, "Recent Controversy in the Theory of Inflation," in Stephen W. Rousseas, ed., *Inflation: Its Causes, Consequences, and Control* (Wilton, Conn., 1968).

31 See, however, the continued debate in John Redmond, "The Sterling Overvaluation," *Economic History Review* (1984): 528ff. Barry Supple, *The History of the British Coal Industry*, vol. 4, *1913–1946: The Political Economy of Decline* (Oxford, 1987), 214–67, provides useful sectoral analysis.

32 See Sir Otto Niemeyer memorandum, 2 Feb. 1925, cited in Moggridge, *British Monetary Policy*, 264.

actuated the transatlantic proponents of a return to gold from the Dawes
Plan deliberations onward. Both countries, Young replied, would have to
take discernible risks to foster stability of the international structure:

> Quite apart from the question of whether the gold standard is the best, I am
> satisfied ... that it is unwise to introduce ... the speculative elements of any new
> experiment.... We should use, so far as we can, well-known and well-understood
> machinery in order that we may the more quickly, and with a greater certainty, get
> back to stable exchanges, and thereby take the first step toward freer international
> markets.[33]

III

The historical record reveals that sterling remained a weak link in the key-
currency chain throughout the later 1920s. We can plausibly classify that
development, however, as a contingent political outcome rather than a systemic flaw in the monetary regime. After all, the London City had smoothly
coordinated discount markets before World War I with relatively slender
reserves. And Montagu Norman deliberately misstated gold holdings and
secretly sterilized the inflows in order to make the situation seem more
precarious than it was.[34] Precisely as predicted, moreover, Britain's return
to gold in 1925 paved the way for an ambitious program of central-bank
cooperation to stabilize currencies and revive trade on the European continent over the next three years. The respective central banks of France and
England cultivated an unseemly rivalry over the details of financial reconstruction that burst into the open in the Rumanian case.[35] The struggle had
political overtones, for beneath a diaphanous banking figleaf Norman allied
himself with Schacht and covertly sought to undermine French political
influence in Eastern Europe. Nevertheless, after numerous excursions and
alarms, most nations in Europe (as well as Latin America) heeded the prescriptions of the "money doctors" and returned to stable rates.[36]

   Poincaré admittedly undervalued the franc when France stabilized de
facto in 1926 at one-fifth of the 1914 par. One can argue, however, that
a middle-sized country faced with containing Germany and upholding
the Versailles treaty virtually alone might bolster international security,

---

33 Owen D. Young to Josiah Stamp, 3 March 1925, Owen D. Young Papers, St. Lawrence University.
34 See J. R. Garrett, "Market Control Techniques and the Bank of England," *Journal of Economic History*
    (Sept. 1995): 612–36.
35 Sayers, *Bank of England*, 195–9.
36 For the readoption of gold in Latin America, see Paul Drake, *The Money Doctor in the Andes: The
    Kemmerer Missions, 1923–1933* (Durham, N.C., 1989); also Paul W. Drake, ed., *Money Doctors, Foreign
    Debts, and Economic Reforms in Latin America from the 1890s to the Present* (Wilmington, Del., 1994).

broadly conceived, by modestly underpricing its tradeables to spur domestic economic growth. True, the consequent gold inflow into France outpaced most expectations. Yet that need not have resulted in gold maldistribution if Paris had developed more sophisticated money-market institutions allowing it to recycle resources outward, or if the political menace that Germany posed to the status quo had not made it imprudent to do so.[37]

The evolution of the British domestic economy reflected policy choices as well. Prime Minister Stanley Baldwin aimed to dish the Diehards and re-fashion the Conservative Party as a center party attractive to the skilled working class.[38] He therefore preferred an indecisive end to the 1926 General Strike that would promote class unity to an open defeat for organized labor that would keep the lid on wages. For similar reasons, the Baldwin government did not dare tackle an overgenerous welfare system that fostered labor immobility by allowing the long-term unemployed to remain in their familiar social settings within the Depressed Areas. In light of later experience, it seems implausible that any untargeted macroeconomic policies could have overcome the specific regional problems of declining industries in the Midlands, Scotland, and Wales.[39] Nor did world trade generally expand as fast as optimists had hoped. The World Economic Conference of 1927 deadlocked between British advocates of open markets and French proponents of cartel restrictions and failed to produce a practical result.[40] What seer could have foreseen all that?

By 1927, both Strong and Norman acknowledged that they were presiding over a managed-currency system and not one that could adjust to shocks automatically.[41] For various reasons, however, the notable Central Bankers meeting of July 1927 did not consolidate the movement toward closer monetary cooperation. Instead, each country pursued national objectives with renewed zeal. This did not demonstrate a regime failing so

37 On the problems created by the influx of foreign money into France, see particularly the 1927–8 exchanges between Norman and Siepmann of the Bank of England with Moreau and Quesnay of the Banque de France in file G1/34, Bank of England. For a more critical account of Banque de France monetary policy than the one advanced here, cf. Kenneth Mouré, *Managing the Franc Poincaré: Economic Understanding and Political Constraint in French Monetary Policy, 1928–1936* (New York, 1991), ch. 1–4.

38 On Baldwin's strategy, see Philip Williamson, *National Crisis and National Government: British Politics, the Economy, and the Empire, 1926–1932* (Cambridge, 1992); also Stuart Ball, *Baldwin and the Conservative Party: The Crisis of 1929–1931* (London, 1988).

39 Bentley B. Gilbert, *British Social Policy, 1914–1939* (Ithaca, N.Y., 1970); Sean Glynn and Alan Booth, "Unemployment in Interwar Britain: A Case for Relearning the Lessons of the 1930s?" *Economic History Review* 36 (Aug. 1983): 329–48.

40 Robert Boyce, *British Capitalism at the Crossroads: A Study in Politics, Economics, and International Relations* (Cambridge, 1987), 119–22.

41 See Benjamin Strong to Montagu Norman, 19 Oct. 1927, in Benjamin Strong Papers 1116.7, FRBNY.

much as a failure to practice the regime. Contrary to received opinion, the United States did not substantially drain net gold from the rest of the world in 1925–8.[42] However, when selective credit controls failed (as they almost always do), the "Fed" saw no alternative to raising interest rates in 1929 in order to curb the New York stock market boom. That inevitably put pressure on sterling. The French and Germans also added to Britain's secular problems by reducing their sterling balances toward the end of the period.[43]

From their own point of view, given popular preferences, French monetary authorities had sound reasons for moving toward a gold-bullion standard after 1928. With open-market operations restricted by the stabilization law, the Bank of France believed that it could control domestic finance better by reducing holdings of Devisen.[44] In addition, given Anglo-French divergencies over German affairs, politicians in Paris saw no compelling reason to finance John Bull's alleged financial imperialism on their own centime. While expert opinion differed whether a true gold shortage had developed by 1929, international cooperation could have solved the putative problems within the four corners of the existing monetary regime. During the Young Plan negotiations of 1929, W. Randolph Burgess of the New York "Fed" adumbrated plans for a type of special drawing rights as a feature of the prospective Bank for International Settlements. Ideally, the BIS could serve as an intermediary in the payment of reparations, and reparations deposits could serve as the basis for an expansion of international liquidity.[45] The BIS did not wholly fulfill its promise. Plans for paper gold never came to fruition. But the obstacles were political, and not technical.

A political explanation for the breakdown of the gold-exchange standard must focus primarily on Germany. It must track that nation's resolve, at virtually any cost, to repudiate the strictures of Versailles. The Reich fulfilled the Dawes Plan for reparations only so long as the partial moratorium continued. By a very large margin, it imported more foreign capital than it delivered in reparations. It utilized that capital not in productive plant and equipment, but largely on the amenities of public infrastructure and in financing a higher living standard than domestic productivity could justify. Owing to political pressures and Socialist domination of the arbitration process run by the Labor Ministry, hourly wage rates rose to the point where German industry became internationally uncompetitive. In 1928, Germany demanded another investigation of its capacity to pay reparations, although

---

42 Brown, *International Gold Standard Reinterpreted*, 1: 542–3.
43 Clarke, *Central Bank Cooperation*, 123–41.   44 Mouré, *Managing the Franc Poincaré*, 46–79.
45 See the several Burgess memoranda to Owen D. Young in the "International Bank" files for Feb.–June 1929, Owen D. Young Papers.

the real variable remained as always German will to pay. The Young Plan negotiations of 1929, envisioned as a final liquidation of the war, led instead to bitter acrimony. Right-wing nationalists mounted a demagogic campaign against the Young Plan, even though that plan reduced Berlin's annual obligations by one-quarter.[46]

In fact, the German economy turned down in 1929 before that of the United States.[47] Yet the world recession that began in that year need not have proven substantially worse than the 1920–1 downturn except for one factor: It happened to coincide with a last-ditch German attempt to repudiate its obligations under the Versailles treaty. Contrary to the general impression, President Herbert Hoover slightly cut U.S. taxes in 1930. The full-employment budget proved mildly stimulative in that year; it grew even more expansive in 1931 (when it reached 2 percent of GNP).[48] The Labour government in Britain similarly declined to take more than a modest dose of the prescribed deflationary medicine.[49]

As Temin has pointed out, most of the traditional explanations for the depth of the American downturn in 1930 do not fully work. The stock market plunge of October 1929 did not initially go further proportionately than the crash of 1987. Many qualified observers considered the first jolt downward a salutary correction, and the limited decrease in private wealth it engendered cannot fully account for the autonomous fall in consumption.[50] The collapse of commodity prices hurt commercial farmers, but benefited city dwellers. The Smoot-Hawley tariff had at most marginal consequences.[51] The first round of bank failures in late 1930 really featured the insolvency of the pushcart peddlers' bank in New York and did not produce a significant shock to the quantity of money.[52]

---

46 Stephen A. Schuker, *American 'Reparations' to Germany, 1919–33*, Princeton Studies in International Finance no. 61 (Princeton, N.J., 1988), 14–46; see also Philip Heyde, *Das Ende der Reparationen. Deutschland, Frankreich und der Youngplan, 1929–1932* (Paderborn, 1998), 35–98.

47 Peter Temin, "The Beginning of the Depression in Germany," *Economic History Review* 24 (May 1971): 240–8.

48 Figures in E. Cary Brown, "Fiscal Policy in the Thirties: A Reappraisal," *American Economic Review* 46 (Dec. 1956): 857–79.

49 Robert Skidelsky, *Politicians and the Slump: The Labour Government of 1929–31* (London, 1967); Williamson, *National Crisis and National Government*, 255–424.

50 Contemporary observers, who did not suffer from exposure to the sirenic prose of John Kenneth Galbraith, realized this perfectly well at the time. See Joseph S. Davis, *The World between the Wars, 1919–39: An Economist's View* (Baltimore, 1975), 189–223; cf. Galbraith, *The Great Crash, 1929* (Boston, 1955).

51 Alfred E. Eckes, *Opening America's Market: U.S. Foreign Trade Policy since 1776* (Chapel Hill, N.C., 1995), 100–139; Barry Eichengreen, "The Political Economy of the Smoot Hawley Tariff," *Research in Economic History* 11 (1989): 1–44.

52 Excellent analysis in Temin, *Did Monetary Forces Cause the Great Depression?* (New York, 1976); also in idem., *Lessons from the Great Depression*, 45–63.

By contrast, contemporaries abandoned hope of a normal recovery in the spring and summer of 1931. Deflationary expectations – the so-called Mundell effect – then began to feed on themselves. This second leg of the Depression had its primary roots in international politics. Trying to draw right-wing opinion away from the Nazis by outflanking them in nationalist fervor, Chancellor Heinrich Brüning launched a customs union with Austria as a prelude to political union and the extension of German economic dominance in the East.[53] The Versailles treaty had strictly forbidden such an *Anschluss.* The French reacted with predictable dismay. The ensuing crisis exposed the fact, already known to insiders, that Austria's largest bank had made improvident agricultural loans and become insolvent. The Austrian banking crisis led to a banking crisis in the Reich, in which the dependence of the universal D-banks on short-term foreign loans to finance long-term equity investments became patent.

At this point, it was far more important for the Reich to maintain the confidence of short-term private lenders than to obtain relief from its modest reparations obligations. State Secretary Fritz Schäffer of the German Finance Ministry forcibly reminded Brüning of the relative magnitudes involved. Yet the chancellor felt that to satisfy public opinion he had to manipulate the crisis to obtain reparations relief as his highest goal.[54] Largely owing to German rigidity and incredibly poor management by Reichsbank President Luther, the French dragged their feet in accepting the Hoover moratorium for reparations and war debts. By the time that international bankers had put together a rescue package for Germany, the forces of deflation elsewhere had spun out of control. No smoking gun has yet emerged from the Threadneedle Street archives to prove that the Bank of England voluntarily abandoned gold in September 1931. But Labour leaders crudely observed that their constituencies would decline further sacrifices for the sake of sterling's world role. And the Bank of England handled its market intervention in defense of the pound with unwonted inexpertise. Governor Norman remained on holiday while the crisis mounted. Younger Bank officials like Kershaw, Siepmann, and Clay expressed no great sorrow to see Downing Street throw in the towel.[55]

---

53 Andreas Rodder, *Stresemanns Erbe. Julius Curtius und die deutsche Aussenpolitik, 1929–1931* (Paderborn, 1995); Edward W. Bennett, *Germany and the Diplomacy of the Financial Crisis, 1931* (Cambridge, Mass., 1961); Aurel Schubert, *The Credit-Anstalt Crisis of 1931* (New York, 1991). For Brüning's emphasis on the primacy of foreign policy, see the ingenious defense in William L. Patch, Jr., *Heinrich Brüning and the Dissolution of the Weimar Republic* (New York, 1998), 172–219.

54 Balderston, *Origins and Course of the German Economic Crisis*, 296–326.

55 Diane B. Kunz, *The Battle for Britain's Gold Standard in 1931* (London, 1987). The present writer attempted without success to find a "smoking gun" in the Bank of England archives. It seems clear, however, that Whitehall faced a virtual "workers' ramp" in the summer of 1931 and concluded that

Once Britain had abandoned the gold parity, retrospective wisdom suggests that other countries should have followed to obviate the propagation of deflationary forces. Still, the possibilities for rescuing the gold-standard regime were not wholly exhausted. After an initial panic, sterling did not depreciate radically owing to gold dishoarding in India. The Treasury therefore set up an Exchange Equalisation Account to "keep down the pound," although it would not trumpet that rationale so bluntly in Parliament.[56] Manipulation of sterling – leaning against the wind harder than the wind was blowing, as Howson delicately puts it – figured as only one of several interlocking British schemes to beggar their neighbors.[57] In 1932, Whitehall created the Ottawa system and constructed a tariff wall around the British Empire. Those challenges fairly invited a nationalist response elsewhere.

In Germany, however, Brüning quickly realized that he could not possibly follow Britain with a competitive devaluation. A trained and able economist, Brüning surveyed the possibilities more keenly than later critics suggest. Brüning knew that uncompetitive wage rates in Germany would have to come down, one way or another. But, unlike Britain, Germany had no empire. Other countries could and would retaliate if he openly devalued. Moreover, not only did the Young Plan legally require Germany to retain gold parity; a weaker mark would also increase the real weight of the foreign debt that the country had run up with open eyes. Above all, Brüning realized that, after Germany's experience with the 1922–3 hyperinflation, there could be no such thing as a controlled devaluation in the Reich.[58] Indeed, all European nations that had suffered from high inflation in the early 1920s hesitated to repeat the experiment. As the Italian finance minister explained colloquially in 1933: "A man who has drunk too much must be a teetotaler, while the ordinary man can take his wine without danger."[59]

it could not ask the nation to make further domestic sacrifices to save the nation's international position; archival citations in Schuker, *American 'Reparations' to Germany*, 55n.

56 Howson, *Sterling's Managed Float: The Operations of the Exchange Equalisation Account, 1932–39*, Princeton Studies in International Finance No. 46 (Princeton, N.J., 1980), 6.

57 Ibid., 56. Howson observes, however, that even "clean" floating requires targets, and she maintains that Britain managed the float more vigorously in support of domestic policy goals from 1935 onward than earlier.

58 The classic treatment is by Knut Borchardt, "Zwangslagen und Handlungsspielräume in der grossen Wirtschaftskrise der frühen dreissiger Jahre: Zur Revision des überlieferten Geschichtsbildes," in Bayerische Akademie der Wissenschaften, *Jahrbuch 1979* (Munich, 1979), 87–112; also id., "Zur Frage der währungspolitischen Optionen Deutschlands in der Weltwirtschaftkrise," in Knut Borchart and Franz Holzheu, eds., *Theorie und Politik der internationalen Wirtschaftsbeziehungen. H. Müller zum 65. Geburtstag* (Stuttgart, 1980), 165–82. Carl-Ludwig Holtfrerich attempts – without notable success – to poke holes in the argument in "Zu hohe Löhne in der Weimarer Republik? Bemerkungen zur Borchardt-These," *Geschichte und Gesellschaft* 10 (1984/1): 122–41.

59 Per Jacobsson Diary, 5 July 1933, London School of Economics Library.

Undoubtedly the Federal Reserve deepened the American Depression by raising rates in the fall of 1931 to prevent speculators from attacking the dollar after they had finished with sterling. The Fed had little other choice, other than an abrupt devaluation, when the Bank of France peremptorily withdrew all its earmarked gold from New York. Courageously, however, the Fed carried out vast open-market operations in the spring of 1932 despite the lack of clear technical data on their effects. That open-market intervention essentially brought the worst of the American deflation to an end.[60]

The prospect of international cooperation for recovery had still not wholly disappeared. As Robert Mundell has recently reminded us, fixed exchange rates have obvious advantages – at least when they prove feasible.[61] Transparency of pricing, stability of expectations, and lower transaction costs foster trade. When countries accustom themselves to fixed currency relationships, wages, prices, and interest rates tend to harmonize across borders. The integration of commodity, factor, and capital markets strengthens the ability of all trade partners to promote comparative advantage. Per Jacobsson and his colleagues in the Monetary Division of the Bank for International Settlements had those benefits firmly in mind when they advocated the restoration of fixed rates with a coordinated joint devaluation against gold to overcome the existing shocks in 1932–3.[62] At the World Monetary Conference of June/July 1933, neither the British nor the Americans expressed genuine interest in stabilizing at a rate that the other would find acceptable.[63] But it would be erroneous to blame what Franklin Roosevelt called "the old fetishes of so-called international bankers" for the result. Although Keynes lauded Roosevelt's bombshell message torpedoing the conference as "magnificently right," the president expressed more concern to his newspaper friends to appear ideologically left.[64] One cannot examine the tiny scraps

---

60 Milton Friedman and Anna Jacobson Schwartz, *A Monetary History of the United States, 1867–1960* (Princeton, N.J., 1963), 362–419. The Fed also took the lead in setting up Banking and Industrial Committees that could spur housing construction, offer mortgage relief, fund self-liquidating public works, and stabilize the bond and commodities markets. It is nevertheless broadly true that monetary rather than national fiscal policies turned the tide. For a nuanced appreciation of the B&I Committees, see Josephine Young Case and Everett Needham Case, *Owen D. Young and American Enterprise* (Boston, 1982), 575–96.

61 Editorial page, *Wall Street Journal*, March 24–5, 1998.

62 The successive memoranda by Jacobsson and his staff received wide circulation among Central Bankers. See especially G1/51–33 (Governor's files on League of Nations Monetary and Economic Conference, Nov. 1932–July 1933); also OV4/28, 73–74 (BIS files), Bank of England.

63 Herbert Feis, *1933: Characters in Crisis* (Boston, 1966).

64 For Keynes's comment in context, see D. E. Moggridge, *Maynard Keynes: An Economist's Biography* (London, 1992), 577; for Roosevelt's candid remarks to journalists, consult Charles Hurd, *When the New Deal Was Young and Gay* (New York, 1965), 146–71.

of paper on which Roosevelt instructed his fellow "chicken farmer" George Warren about monetary-policy preferences in the fall of 1933 without concluding that he had no theoretical grasp of the economic issues involved.[65] The World Economic Conference demonstrated, as a practical matter, that international monetary cooperation was dead. Yet the outcome tells us less about the principles of the gold-exchange-standard regime than about the politicians who ran it into the ground.

65 George W. Warren Papers, Cornell University Archives; also Frank Freidel, *Franklin D. Roosevelt: Launching the New Deal* (Boston, 1973), 454–89; bombshell message quoted in ibid., 483.

4

The Bank of France and the Gold Standard, 1914–1928

KENNETH MOURÉ

The gold standard is back, as the great villain of interwar economic history responsible for the origins, the rapid spread, the depth, and the duration of the Great Depression in the 1930s. The Bank of France advocated restoration of the prewar gold standard, opposed its dilution as a gold-exchange standard, and by its gold policy contributed significantly to the onset and the severity of the Depression.[1] In 1928–31, the Bank of France drew more than 30 billion francs in gold from central banks abroad, aggravating the monetary contraction and the price deflation that set off the Depression. After sterling went off gold in September 1931, the Bank withdrew 24 billion francs in gold from the international monetary system, increasing the contractionary force of the gold standard. From 1931 to 1936, France remained committed to the gold standard, organizing a handful of countries in a Gold Bloc to preserve convertibility while the international gold standard disintegrated around them. France was the most consistent and adamant proponent of the gold standard, yet the most disruptive in its actions.

Recent work on the interwar gold standard has paid little attention to gold standard belief: to what policy makers believed and how their beliefs shaped policy. This chapter reviews French experience *off* gold from August 1914 to June 1928, examining how the Bank of France conceived of the gold standard and the return to convertibility, its role in the depreciation of the franc from 1920 to 1926, and its views on returning to gold in 1928.[2] The

---

1 See Peter Temin, *Lessons from the Great Depression* (Cambridge, Mass., 1989) and Barry Eichengreen, *Golden Fetters: The Gold Standard and the Great Depression, 1919–1939* (Oxford, 1992). The gold standard and French policy decisions in particular are central in H. Clark Johnson's account of the origins of the Depression in *Gold, France, and the Great Depression, 1919–1932* (New Haven, Conn., 1997).

2 On French monetary policy on gold from 1928 to 1936, see Kenneth Mouré, *Managing the Franc Poincaré: Economic Understanding and Political Constraint in French Monetary Policy, 1928–1936* (Cambridge, 1991), and the revised and augmented French edition, *La politique du franc Poincaré:*

first section covers the Bank's views and actions from August 1914 to June 1924, stressing the commitment to restoring the franc's prewar parity and the dismay caused by postwar inflation and currency depreciation. The second section examines the Bank's part in the increasing crisis from June 1924 through July 1926 until Raymond Poincaré, "savior" of the franc, returned to office as premier. It seeks to clarify the nature of the regime change effected by Poincaré. The third section follows Bank policy during the period of de facto stabilization from 1926 to 1928, crucial to understanding French opposition to the gold-exchange standard.

THE PROMISE TO RETURN TO GOLD, AUGUST 1914–JUNE 1924

The suspension of gold convertibility by most European belligerents in August 1914 ended the era of the "classical gold standard." The duration of the war, the extent of currency inflation, and the difficulties of reconstructing an international system that had evolved without conscious design were unforeseeable. French rhetoric off gold from 1914 to 1919 reflected an absolute commitment to restoring the gold convertibility of the franc at prewar parity as soon as possible after the war; this proved impossible as postwar financial decisions took their toll on French finances. France suspended convertibility of the franc on August 5, 1914, one of a series of measures to finance mobilization for war. French plans were based on experience in the Franco-Prussian War of 1870–1. The Bank of France had increased its gold reserves by more than 500 million francs since December 1913 to serve as "a larger base for the issue of currency needed in the event of war."[3] In suspending convertibility, Governor Georges Pallain affirmed that the Bank's "strict duty" to which all other concerns must yield was "to maintain intact the credit of its bank note."[4]

Unlike in England, where gold convertibility was maintained and gold reserves were intended to be *used*,[5] French policy sought to conserve gold

---

Perception de l'économie et contraintes politiques dans la stratégie monétaire de la France, 1926–1936 (Paris, 1998).

3 Banque de France, *Compte rendu des opérations de la Banque de France pendant l'année 1914* (Paris, 1915), 4.

4 Délibérations du Conseil Général (DCG), Archives de la Banque de France, Aug. 12, 1914.

5 On the purpose of gold reserves in wartime, see R. G. Hawtrey, *Currency and Credit*, 4th ed. (1922; reprint, London, 1950), 359–61; for wartime contrast of Continental and British policy on gold use, see John Maynard Keynes, "Memorandum Against the Suspension of Gold," and "Russia," in Elizabeth Johnson, ed., *The Collected Writings of John Maynard Keynes*, vol. 16, *Activities, 1914–1919: The Treasury and Versailles* (London, 1971), 7–15, 72. Also "The Function of Gold Reserves," *The Times* (London), Apr. 1, 1916.

reserves. Jules Décamps (of the Direction des Études économiques at the Bank of France) explained that French authorities concentrated gold disbursements where they would have the maximum effect in order to maintain a strong gold reserve as the basis for confidence in the franc.[6] Prior to the war, the gold was intended to be a *trésor de guerre* (war chest), the purpose of which was not clearly stated. During the war, the gold became a *trésor de la paix*, preserved as the basis for postwar restoration of the franc. The economist Charles Gide rationalized this transformation in claiming that even "hidden" in the Bank of France, the gold served as a trésor de guerre by its potential for use, just as the British fleet, "sheltering who knows where," maintained the liberty of the seas and the security of French shores.[7] The difference in French and British views proved a frequent source of friction during and after the war.[8]

When France prohibited the export of gold by private citizens in July 1915, the government launched a campaign to encourage the exchange of gold coin for bank notes. Remittances from the public brought in 2.4 billion francs in gold. As initial enthusiasm for voluntary contributions ebbed, gold committees were organized throughout France, on the Bank's initiative and with its financial support. Lectures, posters, postcards, and moral fables were employed to encourage gold remittances. One pamphlet told of an elderly peasant woman turning in 150 gold francs at a post office, her son having written asking her to do so, telling her that "it may be your gold, you see, that will save me."[9] The campaign to "harvest gold" collected roughly half the specie coins held by the public before the war. It promised that French citizens could exchange their gold for bank notes at the Bank of France, "without losing any part of their savings, without running any risk, without having to pay more for anything they wish to buy."[10] "Verser de l'or, c'est gagner sans rien perdre" ("To give gold is to gain without losing a thing") was one slogan used to encourage gold remittances and subscription to interest-bearing Bons de la Défense Nationale.[11] In a lecture titled "The

---

6 Jules Déscamps, "L'or et les règlements internationaux pendant la guerre," *Journal des économistes* (Apr. 1918).

7 Charles Gide, "L'or et le change," *Revue d'économie politique* 30 (1916): 94. Gide nonetheless thought the Bank could and should ship more gold in support of the franc exchange rate.

8 Martin Horn covers diplomatic aspects of this conflict to April 1917 in "External Finance in Anglo-French Relations in the First World War, 1914–1917," *International History Review* 17, no. 1 (1995): 51–77.

9 Pamphlet in Comité National de l'Or files, Archives de la Banque de France (BdF), 1060193601/11.

10 Notice of the Comité National de l'Or to French mayors, encouraging them in their *duty* to encourage exchange of gold and purchase of Bons de la Défense Nationale, 1916; in BdF, 1060193601/11; Comité National de l'Or, 1915–18.

11 Pamphlet from BdF, 1060193601/11.

duties of those holding gold" (Le devoir des détenteurs d'or), the president
of the gold committee in Calvados promised:

You can exchange your gold for bank notes, *which have exactly the same value. May
those who have any fear in this regard consider seriously that the State will never harm the
interests of those who have given their gold for the defense of the nation, as is only just.* The
notes of the Bank of France will have the same purchasing power and the same
liberating force, *equal to that of gold.*[12]

The Catholic Church was mobilized, using sermons, pamphlets, and articles in local issues of *La Semaine religieuse,* to encourage gold remittances;
the clergy collected gold from congregation members in parishes. Catholics
were told, "Become apostles of gold payments for your country"; handing
in gold was a duty of their "Christian conscience."[13] Thus, the gold value
of the franc was *sacrosanct.* The "harvest of gold" campaign broadcast an absolute conviction that wartime inflation would be reversed and the *normalcy*
of the prewar gold standard restored. The postwar situation proved profoundly disquieting. The state continued to spend far in excess of revenue,
requiring further advances from the Bank. For the Bank, the fundamental
problem was the increased note circulation backed by wartime advances to
the state. In 1914, 92 percent of its note issue had been backed by gold
and commercial paper; in December 1918, 70 percent of a note issue that
had increased fivefold was backed by advances to the state.[14] Pallain emphasized the harmful effects of the notes put in circulation by this means:
"We must...reduce our note circulation. Reimbursing the state's debt to
the Bank is the necessary condition for its reduction, and the unique means
of restoring a normal regime."[15] The Bank desired an explicitly *deflationary*
policy, to reduce the quantity of notes in circulation.[16] The most efficacious
means of doing so was to repay the Bank advances to the state, which the
state had promised to make its absolute priority after the war.[17]

12 M. Villey, "Le Devoir des détenteurs d'or" (Paris: Comité National de l'Or, s.d.); copy in BdF,
   1060193601/11. Emphasis in original.
13 Copy of lecture by Canon Gaudeau, undated; BdF, 1060193601/5.
14 See the analysis in Marcel Netter, *Histoire de la Banque de France entre les deux guerres, 1918–1939*
   (Pomponne, n.d.), 30–8; also Jean Bouvier, "The French Banks, Inflation and the Economic Crisis,
   1919–1939," *Journal of European Economic History* 13, no. 2 (1984), 43.
15 Banque de France, *Compte rendu des opérations pendant l'année 1918* (Paris, 1919), 9.
16 For the various definitions of deflation at the time, see Charles Rist, *La déflation en pratique* (1923;
   reprint, Paris, 1927), 1–7.
17 Bank advances to the state had been agreed upon as necessary to finance mobilization in secret conventions signed in November 1911; at the first increase beyond this mobilization measure, Minister of
   Finance Alexandre Ribot solemnly promised that repayment of the advances would be accomplished
   "in the shortest time possible" (dans le plus court délai possible). The Bank repeatedly invoked this
   engagement in pressing the state to repay the advances after the war. Ribot to Pallain, Sept. 18, 1914;
   Lois et statuts qui régissent la Banque de France (Paris, 1926), 208.

The Bank agreed, reluctantly, to raise the ceiling on advances by 3 billion francs in February 1919; and to a temporary increase of 3 billion francs in April (to 27 billion francs). The limit on note issue was similarly increased (to 41 billion).[18] When the Treasury could not repay the "temporary" advance one year later and refused to issue a loan to reduce Bank advances, Pallain insisted upon a formal state commitment to amortize the Bank's advances each year by the "extremely moderate figure of 2 billion francs." This *minimum* would leave open the possibility of more rapid reimbursement, and "certainly does not exceed the effort the Treasury must impose upon itself."[19] The resulting François-Marsal Convention was an unhappy compromise. The repayment of the "temporary" advance at the end of 1920 was abandoned, with annual 2-billion-franc reimbursements to begin in December 1921. The Bank saw repayment delayed and prolonged; the Treasury had no idea how it would meet its reimbursement requirements. Governor Georges Robineau (who replaced Pallain in August 1920) saluted the convention's anticipated effects with the claim that "No single act . . . could be more useful for the economic restoration of France and the preservation of its credit abroad." The reimbursements were necessary "not in order to provoke a deflation more rapid than circumstances would allow but, on the contrary, to apply deflation in the degree necessary to the needs of industry and commerce."[20] The first repayment was made without difficulty thanks to the recession in 1920–1, which had increased idle funds on deposit in Treasury accounts.[21] As Treasury difficulties increased thereafter, state repayments declined; full payment was not made again until December 1926. The François-Marsal Convention was transformed from the *least* the state could do in 1920 to the *most* the Bank could expect and, by default, the sole plan to restore the franc to its prewar parity.

The Bank did not officially define its beliefs in the gold standard and deflation. The most articulate analysis of the gold standard came from Jules Déscamps, director of economic studies, 1920–6. In his view, the gold standard provided the "central axis" for regulating prices and exchange rates in the international economy. Both were controlled automatically. An increase in note circulation in excess of new production of goods and services would

---

18 Reconstruction and recovery pushed the budget deficit to nearly 27 billion francs in 1919 in a budget of 40 billion francs. Alfred Sauvy with Anita Hirsch, *Histoire économique de la France entre les deux guerres*, rev. ed. (Paris, 1984), iii: 379.

19 Pallain to François-Marsal, Apr. 8, 1920; DCG of same date.

20 Banque de France, *Compte rendu des opérations de la Banque de France pendant l'année 1920* (Paris, 1921), 16–17.

21 Rist, *La déflation en pratique*, 67–8; Georges Lachapelle, *Les finances de la IIIième République* (Paris, 1937), 103.

raise prices, discourage exports, encourage imports, and produce a loss of gold to cover the trade deficit. Order was restored by the central bank raising its discount rate. "Monetary policy was reduced . . . to surveying and maintaining the sound functioning of the gold standard; in this way, the relative stability of prices and the exchange rate is assured."[22]

Déscamps's views were those of an individual, not an institution. The Bank's collective view was undoubtedly less moderate and less coherent. For journalists and economists close to the Bank, currency notes issued against gold represented existing metallic reserves, and notes issued against discounted bills represented existing goods and services. Notes issued against Bank advances to the state, however, were claims on future production, and as such not true bank notes at all, but "*a paper money that takes on the appearance of a bank note in order to live as a parasite on the sound circulation.*"[23] Arch-deflationists Arthur Raffalovich and Yves Guyot referred to this as "borrowing from the circulation" and "the worst of loans." Their arguments, propounded in the *Journal des économistes* and in their disorderly collection of articles, *Inflation et déflation* (which, as Charles Rist noted, was a prolonged attack on inflation without at any point considering the problems of deflation), were probably closer to most regents' views.[24] Guyot's arguments for deflation at the Bank-sponsored *Semaine de la Monnaie* in June 1922 are representative. He criticized Keynes's program for currency stabilization at the Genoa conference (as "a widespread bankruptcy") and fully endorsed the François-Marsal Convention as the moderate path to the restoration of sound money. He concluded: "Everyone must be solidly convinced that the steps to restore French credit will be those of deflation, and that French credit will only be restored on the day that the currency is completely liberated from the worst of loans."[25] With the suspension of allied assistance to peg the franc in March 1919, the franc fell. There were rare interventions to support the franc, the most notable being the counterattack on speculation in March 1924.[26] (See Figure 4.1.) Persistent

22 Jules Décamps, "La question monétaire," 414; also Décamps, "La stabilisation du change," *Journal des économistes* (Dec. 1921): 460–1.

23 Jules Décamps, "La question monétaire," *Revue de Paris* (Mar. 15, 1922): 423; Décamps's emphasis. He makes the same point in "La Semaine de la Monnaie et les expédients inflationnistes," *Revue de Paris* (May 1, 1922): 196–7, and in "La Crise du franc," *Revue de Paris* (Mar. 1, 1924): 216–18.

24 Arthur Raffalovich and Yves-Guyot, *Inflation et déflation* (Paris, 1921); Charles Rist, review in *Revue d'économie politique* 36 (1922): 94.

25 Yves Guyot, "La déflation," in Semaine de la Monnaie, *La politique financière et monétaire de la France* (Paris, 1922), 151.

26 See Stephen A. Schuker, *The End of French Predominance in Europe: The Financial Crisis of 1924 and the Adoption of the Dawes Plan* (Chapel Hill, N.C., 1976), chap. 4; Jean-Noël Jeanneney, *François de Wendel en République: L'argent et le pouvoir, 1914–1940* (Paris, 1976), 185–93; Raymond Philippe, *Le drame financier de 1924–1928* (Paris, 1931), 25–56.

budget deficits, with heavy reconstruction expenditure classed as "recoverable expenses" (*dépenses recouvrables*) and financed by short-term domestic borrowing (hoping German reparation payments would permit "recovery" of these expenditures) created a huge overhang of floating debt. This debt, mostly Bons de la Défense Nationale, could be quickly monetized by nonrenewal. Although a large part of it was held by financial institutions, the legal ceiling for the note issue meant that a comparatively small volume of reimbursements would "break" this ceiling, a matter presented to the public as of colossal significance, with utterly incalculable adverse consequences.

French governments were thus prone to a combination of fiscal impasse and capital flight should their actions provoke nonrenewal of the floating debt, fears of increased taxation, or simply an adverse shift in trade and payments. The exchange rate of the franc, the strained financial situation of the Treasury, and the vulnerability of fragile coalition governments were interlinked and highly sensitive, creating a regime in which maintaining "confidence" became critical to sustain an unsound edifice of public finance and government. As the franc depreciated and the goal of restoring it to prewar parity receded, the Bank ceased to speak of doing so. But the disappearance of claims to restore the franc did not mean that the Bank had ceased to believe it could be done, even if it had retreated beyond the immediate policy horizon.

For the Bank, advances to the state had been a departure from sound practice, admissible in order to mobilize resources for national defense. Policy since 1919 had met political demands for reconstruction rather than restore the sound finances necessary to repay Bank advances, undo wartime inflation, and reestablish the gold standard as the ultimate return to "normalcy." The Bank limited its own responsibility to providing technical advice and guarding against any resumption of inflationary policies. The extent and quality of Bank assistance depended upon its willingness to help successive governments. Given that postwar policy relied heavily on short-term borrowing, the Bank found much to protest and little to condone as sound monetary reconstruction. Even with the ideologically sympathetic Bloc National in power, led for two years by Robineau's childhood friend Raymond Poincaré, Bank assistance was reluctant.

The Morgan loan negotiated in March 1924 is a case in point. The franc had been falling since the previous November. The government blamed international speculators, but according to Maurice Bokanowski, *rapporteur général* on the Finance Committee in the Chamber of Deputies, the fundamental cause was the budget deficit. The ordinary budget had been balanced in 1923. The problem was the special budget of recoverable expenses.[27] Poincaré and his minister of finance, Charles de Lasteyrie, introduced a rigorous financial program on January 17, its key element being a 20 percent increase in most existing taxes (the *double décime*). The program took five weeks to clear the Chamber of Deputies, stalled by long debates of which "the most striking characteristic . . . was the extent of their irrelevance."[28] The Senate Finance Committee did not report on the legislation until March 13. In the meantime, speculation increased, the exchange rate fell, and the government sought means to defend the franc.

Most bankers advocated intervention by the Bank of France.[29] The Bank had opposed the negotiation of any loan that would engage its gold reserves, but agreed to intervention on March 9 after a meeting in the office of the president of the Republic. The step was exceptional, given the Bank's determination to maintain its gold reserves intact and to leave *assainissement* to the government. The regents argued that market intervention could be effective only "if immediate measures are taken to remedy the situation of the Treasury." On March 7, Robineau had been unwilling to set out a financial program for the government. On March 9, he made specific suggestions. The Bank would negotiate a loan guaranteed by French gold reserves if the government would take the measures necessary to reduce expenditure, to cease borrowing, and to restore public confidence and hasten consolidation of short-term debt.[30] Robineau arranged the loan from J. P. Morgan and Co. Despite the private character of the loan, Morgan's attached particular importance to announcing it in New York, stressing the French government's commitment to balance its budget and avoid all new expenditure not covered by tax revenue.[31]

The loan provided the means to defend the franc and rout speculators. The franc had fallen to nearly 130 francs to the pound on Saturday, March 8. Hastily negotiated credits brought it back to 116 frs./£ on March 10 and 11. The Morgan loan was announced on March 13 and the franc recovered rapidly, to 78 francs to the pound on March 24. The success of the intervention depended upon a convincing demonstration of the government's will to prevent further inflation and on close cooperation between the Bank and the government. Although technical personnel recommended against

27 Bokanowski report, *JO Chambre documents*, no. 6980.
28 Schuker, *End of French Predominance*, 61.
29 Schuker, *End of French Predominance*, 104–8; Philippe, *Le drame financier*, 31–6.
30 Annexe to DCG, Mar. 9, 1924.
31 J. P. Morgan to secretary of state, Mar. 21, 1924; U.S. Record Group 59, 851.51/444; Georges Lachapelle stresses the importance of the announcement for the New York market in *Les batailles du franc: La Trésorerie, le change et la monnaie depuis 1914* (Paris, 1928), 128–9.

letting the franc rise above 80 francs to the pound, the Bank, demonstrating "an absolute lack of understanding" allowed it to rise to 63.50, and spent $30 million to maintain the franc at 68 through the first round of parliamentary elections on May 6.[32] The victory of the Cartel des Gauches in the second round thus coincided with a falling franc, and cooperation between Bank and state was rendered more tenuous. The Bank would find little to its liking in Cartel policy and practice.

THE CARTEL DES GAUCHES AND THE CRISIS, 1924–1926

The Bloc National defeat in May 1924 was narrow, owed in part to public dislike of Poincaré's fiscal measures.[33] Ironically, the new majority produced a succession of crises, fundamentally political in nature, that returned Poincaré to the premier's office in order to lead the June 1924 Chamber back from the brink of monetary disaster. The victorious Cartel des Gauches, a strictly electoral alliance of Radicals, Left Radicals, and Socialists, was profoundly divided on the financial issues requiring immediate attention. The Radicals were fragmented on financial questions; the Socialists refused to participate in government; the Communists were "less a parliamentary party than a permanent scandal."[34] It was not an auspicious combination. The financial situation inherited by the Cartel was precarious, and after an initial period of grace it deteriorated steadily.

The first Cartel government received conflicting advice from the Bank of France and the Treasury. Treasury director Pierre de Moüy advised raising the legal limits on the note circulation and advances from the Bank. The Treasury was perpetually under threat that the nonrenewal of floating debt would require increased advances and currency.[35] The Bank could conceive of no policy more catastrophic; such inflation must be avoided at all cost.[36] Premier Edouard Herriot and his minister of finance, Etienne Clémentel, chose to work with the Bank to restore French finances and currency

---

32 Philippe, *Le drame financier*, 51.
33 See Charles S. Maier, *Recasting Bourgeois Europe: Stabilization in France, Germany and Italy in the Decade after World War I* (Princeton, N. J., 1975), 475–6; Jean-Noël Jeanneney, *Leçon d'histoire pour une gauche au pouvoir: La faillite du Cartel, 1924–1926* (Paris, 1977), 13–19; and Jean-Jacques Becker and Serge Berstein, *Nouvelle histoire de la France contemporaine*, vol. 12, *Victoire et frustrations, 1914–1929* (Paris, 1990), 245–50.
34 D. B. Goldey, "The Disintegration of the *Cartel des Gauches* and the Politics of French Government Finance, 1924–1928," Ph.D. diss., Oxford University, 1961, 92. As Goldey put it, the Cartel were united on everything except financial policy; the National Union that replaced it was united on nothing else. Ibid., ix.
35 Schuker, *End of French Predominance*, 135–6; Jeanneney, *François de Wendel*, 203.
36 Robineau in DCG, July 17, 1924.

without "inflation." The best course, they argued, was "to defend the first trench, to hold out there until the end, and not to begin with a retreat, even strategic."[37] It was a fateful choice. Since March 1924, the Bank had been falsifying its weekly balances to publish a note circulation below its true level.[38] It also made indirect advances to the state which, while not technically illegal, disguised the extent of state reliance on advances from the central bank. The margins within which the Treasury struggled were thus significantly narrower than published figures revealed. In October, the note circulation exceeded the legal ceiling, a fact concealed in the Bank's published weekly balance. The Cartel chose to rely on the forbearance of the Bank in continuing this deception, hoping vainly that the "inflation" could be undone. The Cartel thus assumed responsibility for the deception, which the Bank had initiated on its own authority before the Cartel took power.

Clémentel and Herriot had repeatedly declared their willingness to work with the Bank and had accepted Robineau's counsel on fiscal policy in an effort to rebuild confidence; the high levels of taxation introduced by the Bloc National were continued. Cartel financial policy must have seemed anodyne and inept, rather than threatening. But the rise of the note circulation beyond its legal ceiling required effective action to resolve the Treasury's difficulties. The spread of knowledge of the falsified Bank balances was inevitable, and when it became public, it would reflect badly on the Bank if it was revealed as a Bank initiative taken without governmental knowledge or approval.

Deputy Governor James Leclerc discovered the deception in October and insisted on informing Clémentel; he alerted Moüy in November. In December, Clémentel offered Leclerc the post of director of the Caisse des Dépôts et Consignations. Leclerc refused to leave the Bank under the circumstances. Clémentel met the next day with Robineau and Albert Aupetit (the secretary general of the Bank who initiated the falsification) at Herriot's bedside. Clémentel declared that he would resign rather than increase the legal limit on note circulation. Herriot proclaimed he would do likewise; Robineau joined the chorus. This stirring collective suicide pledge ignored the fact that the inflation they renounced had already taken place. They

---

37 Clémentel, cited in Édouard Herriot, *Jadis*, vol. ii, *D'une guerre à l'autre, 1914–1936* (Paris, 1952), 205.
38 The most careful examination of the falsified balances is the reports by an *inspecteur des finances*, Drouineau; his reports of May 9 and 25, 1925, are in Service des Archives Économiques et Financières (SAEF), B 18675. Bertrand Blancheton provides a detailed account of Drouineau's reports in "Les mécanismes des faux bilans de la Banque de France entre le 13 mars 1924 et le 2 avril 1925," *Etudes et documents IX* (1997), 455–70.

hoped it could be undone before anyone else noticed.[39] In February, the knowledge spread to the finance committees of the Chamber and the Senate, and began to provoke capital flight in the Paris market.

Clémentel and Herriot's desire to cooperate with the Bank trapped them into continuing the falsification rather than introducing legislation to legalize the increase that had already taken place. Robineau's care not to inform them that the falsification had begun the previous March distorted the problem. But even had they known, their choice to work with the Bank had set them in opposition to the Treasury case for increasing the legal limits on advances and note circulation. According to the Bank, "no measure could be more disastrous than an increase in the legal maximum of the note circulation. It would ruin French credit abroad and open the way to a progressive inflation that neither the government nor the Bank would be able to control." Reducing the note circulation depended exclusively on the actions of the government and parliament.[40] The hapless Cartel accepted responsibility for correcting a measure initiated by the Bank, without government approval, prior to their taking office.

The measures proposed to reduce the note circulation never came close to offering a credible solution: The government had no program for effective deflation.[41] In late February, as news of the *faux bilans* spread, the regents decided that palliatives would no longer suffice and sent an ultimatum. The Bank would publish a true balance on March 5. On appeal from Herriot, they granted a stay of execution. On March 30, Clémentel admitted the circulation could not be brought below the legal ceiling and promised to introduce legislation to raise the ceiling.[42] Herriot then decided to "fall to the Left," introducing a capital levy proposed by the Socialists (and opposed by Clémentel), and going down to defeat in the Senate on April 11, two days after the Bank published an accurate balance showing the note ceiling exceeded by 2 billion francs. Herriot snapped to those on the Right as he left the Palais de Luxembourg, "Gentlemen, the battle begins!"[43] In fact, having taken his stand in the "first trench," the battle had been lost, and the Cartel's retreat would turn to a rout.

---

39 See the account in Jeanneney, *François de Wendel*, 207–14.
40 Robineau to Clémentel, Dec. 27, 1924; DCG of same date. The letter was addressed to Clémentel personally, and was not seen by directors of the Treasury until after Clémentel's resignation.
41 The measures included subtracting the notes circulating in the Sarre and in Madagascar from the Bank's official count, and calculating and subtracting the notes destroyed or lost during the war. Robineau believed this would amount to more than 1 billion francs. See Georges Lachapelle, *Le crédit public* (Paris, 1932), vol. ii: 234–5.
42 DCG, March 30, 1925.   43 Jeanneney, *François de Wendel*, 235.

Financial policy in the next fifteen months concentrated on eliminating the budget deficit, judged to be the fundamental cause of exchange depreciation, inflation, and the declining confidence both domestically and abroad. The Bloc National had already accomplished a great deal; the 1926 budget was balanced on paper in April 1926, and was balanced in fact by Poincaré's tax increases in the summer of 1926.[44] But focus on the budget balance destroyed the Cartel, promoting the idea of a capital levy, the Socialist cure for the deficit. The idea resurfaced as a potential solution to Cartel difficulties in February 1925; Léon Blum proposed it formally in late March, and Herriot chose to fall on this issue in April.[45] Clémentel's successor at the rue de Rivoli, Joseph Caillaux, renounced the idea and passed the 1925 budget in mid-July with the support of the Right. Division within the Radical party and Herriot's opposition provoked a disavowal of Caillaux at the Radical party congress in October.

The budget deficit was but one element in the recurrent Treasury difficulties in renewing short-term debt. When subscriptions to Bons de la Défense Nationale declined, advances from the Bank and the note circulation increased. Caillaux raised the legal ceilings by 4 billion francs in April 1925 and by 6 billion francs in June; a further rise of 7,500 million was needed in November–December. There was no massive nonrenewal of bonds (a good part of the decline of the short-term debt by nearly 15 billion francs from August 1924 to July 1926 was through consolidation),[46] but

---

44 Corrected budget figures shown in a memorandum prepared for Poincaré for debate on 1927 budget in SAEF, B 33985, show a much more substantial contribution by the Bloc National; in the following table they are compared with figures from Sauvy, *Histoire économique*, iii: 379. Figures are millions francs:

Year	Sauvy	B 33985
1918		−49,858
1919	−26,688	−42,601
1920	−17,139	−25,171
1921	−9,275	−16,726
1922	−9,761	−13,715
1923	−11,806	−10,233
1924	−7,121	−3,455
1925	−1,507	−1,195
1926	1,088	362

45 Becker and Berstein, *Victoire et frustrations*, 267; Berstein, *Edouard Herriot*, 133–8.
46 Jacques Néré argues the floating debt was a faux problème in *Le problème du mur d'argent: les crises du franc (1924–1926)* (Paris, 1985), 55–9. There was a significant reduction in the term of obligations held, increasing the problem of renewal.

it required only incremental nonrenewals to provoke fears of inflation, for repayment required funds unavailable without increasing the advances from the Bank of France.

Caillaux's fall revived proposals for a capital levy to balance the budget and reduce the level of public debt. The cabinets that followed from November 1925 to March 1926 tried various tacks to impose new taxes and balance the budget. Resistance from the Finance Committee in the Chamber and the Senate rendered the various projects ineffective. Caillaux's successors at the rue de Rivoli were unable to rally parliamentary support for increased taxation, regardless of the measure proposed.[47] "Impotence!" declared *Le Matin* in mid-February; "The proof is in: there is no majority to vote any tax increase, whether direct or indirect."[48] In the process of cabinet reshuffling, Cartel cohesion crumbled. An increasing number of Radicals looked to solutions from the Right, and the capital levy preferred by the Socialists became less and less acceptable.[49]

Minister of Finance Raoul Péret managed to impose new taxes on April 4 and to pass a nominally balanced budget on April 28. His fiscal program adapted measures introduced previously; its passage reflected despair rather than innovation. The franc declined through April 1926 and fell more steeply in May. (See Figure 4.2.) The budget balance depended on maintaining the value of the franc; high tax rates discouraged capital imports and caused some capital flight.[50] Contemporaries stressed that the problem was political. In mid-April, Herman Harjes, head of the J. P. Morgan affiliate Morgan, Harjes & Cie., took Thomas Lamont to meet with the minister of finance and governor of the Bank of France. Everyone at the meeting,

---

47 See summaries in Robert Murray Haig, *The Public Finances of Post-War France* (New York, 1929), 124–37, and in Lachapelle, *Le Crédit public*, ii: 261–7. In January 1926, Keynes wrote in his well-known "Open Letter to the French Minister of Finance (whoever he is or may be)" [*Essays in Persuasion* (London, 1931)] that de facto stabilization of the franc and allowing domestic prices to rise to reach parity with prices abroad, which would increase tax revenues and diminish the burden of servicing domestic debt, would suffice to solve French budget difficulties. Criticized by Néré, *Mur d'argent*, 89.

48 *Le Matin*, Feb. 16, 1926, cited in Philippe, *Le drame financier*, 89.

49 For the drift of Radical deputies from support for the Cartel to support for a government of republican concentration (relying on the center-right), Gregory C. Schmid, "The Politics of Currency Stabilization: the French Franc, 1926," *Journal of European Economic History* 3, no. 2 (1974): 360–9.

50 A decline of the franc would increase domestic prices and the cost of exchange needed for foreign payments; Maurice Bokanowski's criticism of the budget was particularly important; cited in Myron T. Herrick to Sec. of State, Apr. 30, 1926, no. 6283; in U.S. Department of State Record Group 59 [R.G. 59], 851.51/814.

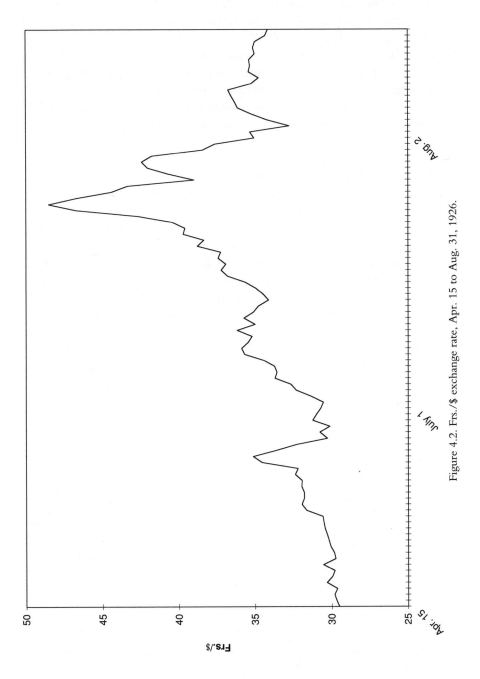

Figure 4.2. Frs./\$ exchange rate, Apr. 15 to Aug. 31, 1926.

and Paris commercial bankers consulted later that day, agreed that "the uncertainty of the political outlook" was the main difficulty in an otherwise improving financial situation.[51]

The Bank remained on the sidelines during the budget altercations; it would play an important role in the subsequent crisis and stabilization. With the budget balanced on paper, Péret hoped for a "natural stabilization" of the franc. He consulted the Bank about intervention to support the franc and was told that it could provide only temporary improvement in the exchange rate.[52] Morgan bankers confirmed this view; they had their own prescription to avert the developing crisis. With significant progress on the budget and war debts, prompt action was needed to deal with the floating debt and the fall of the franc. Their solution for the floating debt was to pay the market price for money. The interest rate on Bons de la Défense Nationale had been fixed as if immutable while the Bank's discount rate and money market rates increased: "Until the French Treasury is dynamited out of this fantastic disregard for the elementary principles of finance and political economy and becomes aware of the fact that like every other borrower it must pay the market price for money, there can be no hope for the franc."[53] This should be coupled with a comprehensive stabilization plan to restore gold convertibility.[54]

In the meantime, Péret asked the Bank to consider use of the Morgan loan and to find additional credits to defend the franc. Robineau stated that intervention could provide only temporary relief "without gaining any real

---

51 Morgan, Harjes & Cie. [MH&C] to J. P. Morgan & Co. [JPM&C], no. 84.171, Apr. 14, 1926; J. P. Morgan papers [JPM], The Pierpont Morgan Library, New York, 532C; similar comment on political uncertainty in Harjes report on subsequent meeting with Robineau and Picard, MH&C to JPM&C, no. 84.183, Apr. 21, 1926; JPM 532C.
52 DCG, Apr. 20, 1926.
53 JPM&C to HM&C for Harjes, no. 63.470, Dec. 18, 1925; JPM 532C; probably written by Leffingwell. He observed that the two previous major government loans, the 5 percent Clémentel in 1924 and the 4 percent Caillaux exchange–guarantee loan, were both offered on terms "calculated to exaggerate apprehension as to the future" without paying current market rates. A second problem was the persistent discussion of forced consolidation, a moratorium, and a reduction in interest rates; "Nothing could be more destructive of credit...." This explanation was invoked several times in April and May 1926. Harjes cabled back the same day his "Hearty congratulations on masterpiece." MH&C to JPM&C, no. 84.043, Dec. 19, 1925; JPM 532C.
54 The Morgan suggestions that France plan to stabilize the franc were consistently ignored by French bankers and politicians alike. The most significant proposal was Russell Leffingwell's plan for a revival of the Latin Monetary Union, taking advantage of prospective war debt settlements to make a cooperative effort at stabilization of the French and Belgian francs and the Italian lira at a ratio of $5^1/_2$ or 6 francs to one prewar franc. Leffingwell's suggestion was relayed in JPM&C to MH&C for T. W. Lamont, no. 63.641, Apr. 22, 1926. For the fate of this proposal, see MH&C (Lamont) to JPM&C for J. P. Morgan, no. 84.194, Apr. 28, 1926; MH&C (Lamont and Harjes) to JPM&C, no. 84.202, Apr. 30, 1926; and MH&C (Lamont and Harjes) to JPM&C, no. 84.203, Apr. 30, 1926; JPM 532C.

advantage."[55] He refused when Péret asked that the Bank negotiate a $100 million credit with the FRBNY using French gold as a guarantee. Such a measure would damage the credit of the franc, which it was the Bank's "essential mission" to safeguard.[56] Péret shopped abroad for credits with no greater success. Benjamin Strong refused to discuss the matter except with the Bank of France and encouraged Robineau to resist.[57] Strong and Montagu Norman opposed granting any such credit – in the absence of a "thoroughgoing program of financial and monetary reform" with the cooperation of the Bank of France and the commercial banks.[58] Péret's approaches to private banks were rejected, straining relations with J. P. Morgan & Co. when word got back to them.[59]

Péret believed the situation was analogous to that in March 1924; private bankers and the Treasury favored intervention. The Bank, however, stressed the differences between the two situations, attributing the 1924 crisis to foreign speculation. The current problem was the flight of French capital, which could only be remedied by government action. "The day it is clear that, no matter what the pretext, the government and the parliament will not give in to the deadly facilities of inflation, the *redressement* of our currency will take place of its own accord, and confidence will be reborn."[60] The Bank absolved itself of responsibility for dealing with the crisis. The fall of the franc was not its problem; it would preserve its gold reserves for use when the franc returned to gold.

On May 19, in imitation of March 9, 1924, Péret convoked the regents, Treasury directors, and several private bankers to meet in the Elysée Palace. Péret, Premier Briand, and President Doumergue appealed for intervention to arrest the fall of the franc. Robineau invoked the views of Benjamin Strong (who had met with Robineau and Péret earlier that day)[61] to buttress

---

55 DCG, May 6, 1926.   56 DCG, May 11, 1926.

57 See Parmentier's report on his trip to London, cited at length in Lachapelle, *Le crédit public*, ii: 269–70, and R. B. Warren, "Conversation with Monsieur Péret," May 19, 1926; in Central Records Office of the Federal Reserve Bank of New York [FRBNY], Strong Papers, 1000.7.

58 Strong to Pierre Jay, May 9, 1926; Norman to Strong, May 19, 1926; Warren, "Conversation with Monsieur Péret," May 19, 1926.

59 See Lamont to Harjes, May 1, 1926; JPM, 532C; MH&C (Lamont and Harjes) to JPM&C, no. 84.214, May 10, 1926, and Lamont to Clarence Dillon, May 13, 1926; JPM 532D.

60 From a meeting of directors of the Treasury, regents of the Bank of France, and private bankers on May 15; DCG, May 17, 1926.

61 Strong stressed his complete accord with the Bank of France that a gold-backed credit was inadvisable, owing to fears that *without a comprehensive stabilization plan supported by Paris bankers*, the credit would have to be repaid in gold. When Péret asked directly whether the FRBNY would extend a gold credit to the Bank of France if the government came up with an acceptable stabilization program, Strong replied that although a gold pledge was undesirable, "the really important thing was to get a thoroughgoing program of financial restoration," which commercial bankers would support, and then "the way would be open for the two central banks to cooperate." Warren, "Conversations

his argument that under current circumstances, intervention could produce no more than temporary relief. The fundamental problem was not foreign speculation but the flight of French capital fearing inflation. Although he declared that it was not the Bank's place to specify details of a fiscal program, he provided a list of what not to do: no more inflation, no *plafond unique*, no "arbitrary and artificial stabilization." François de Wendel called for "a clearly deflationary policy." It would entail a decline in domestic consumption, a loss of foreign markets, a certain slump in production, and increased unemployment, but these were necessary to end inflation.[62]

Yet the regents agreed to intervention, admitting that there were now signs of speculative activity. Péret emerged from subsequent negotiations convinced that he had obtained the full cooperation of the Bank. He had not, and from May 21 to June 2, $56 million in Morgan funds were spent to bring the franc back from 178 to 150 francs to the pound, only to have it fall back and keep falling when support using the Morgan loan ended. The Bank refused to negotiate an international credit to sustain intervention. An embittered Péret resigned on June 15, alluding to a lack of support from the Bank on which the government had a right to depend.[63] French and American bankers were angered by Robineau's refusal to support the government. Two things had gone wrong.

First, successful intervention required solidarity and cooperation between the Bank and the government. When the question of using Bank gold to guarantee a loan was rumored, the Bank mobilized the press amenable to its influence in order to oppose any commitment of French gold.[64] This rendered public a fundamental discord between the Bank and the government, and revealed that resources to support the franc were limited.

Second, the Bank misrepresented the views it conveyed between the French government and American bankers. The government had taken a major step in forswearing fiscal innovation and announcing the appointment of a committee of experts to develop a comprehensive program for financial and monetary stabilization on May 26. Such a committee could inspire confidence only if it was weighted with bankers and proffered solutions

---

with Monsieur Péret," May 19, 1926; copies in FRBNY, "French Situation" files, and in George L. Harrison Papers [GLH], Butler Library, Columbia University, box 15. Strong sent a careful account of the meeting to the FRBNY via Morgan's, cable 84.257, May 20, 1926; FRBNY, Strong Papers, "European Trips."

62 DCG, annex to the procès-verbal of May 20, 1926.

63 Péret's letter of resignation is reproduced in Lachapelle, *Le crédit public*, vol. ii: 272.

64 See Harjes to Lamont, June 9, 1926; JPM 532E; Jeanneney, *François de Wendel*, 290–3; Philippe, *Le drame financier*, 102–3.

acceptable to the Right. Its appointment marked a clear break with Cartel policy. Robineau hoped the committee would decisively alienate the Socialists.[65] Many observers saw this as a major opportunity to regain control of French finances and stabilize the franc. Morgan's was suddenly willing to offer a loan secured by French Treasury bills rather than gold.[66] Robineau, however, opposed any such credit, misled the Briand government as to the views of the Morgan bank, and insisted that the restoration of confidence was a *precondition* for intervention to defend the franc.[67]

Condemnation of the Bank was widespread. The committee of experts, with the exception of the Bank's Deputy-Governor Ernest-Picard and the economist Gaston Jèze, urged continued intervention to support the franc. (Harjes and others feared that Ernest-Picard's presence on the committee of experts would frustrate its worthwhile efforts.)[68] Jean Parmentier, a former director of the Treasury, stated that the Bank had "left the Government in the lurch, stabbing it in the back."[69] R. B. Warren reported that the Bank "has no plan of its own, except to hoard its gold," and lamented, "I cannot disguise my conviction that financial reform in France should begin with the Bank of France."[70] Harjes saw no prospects for improvement without changing the current directors of the Bank. "I am as convinced as can be that they have no sound reason and simply don't want to do *anything* or take the slightest responsibility towards any programme."[71]

Péret's resignation was followed by that of the Briand government, and nine days elapsed before a new Briand government with Caillaux as minister of finance and vice-premier took office. Caillaux immediately removed Robineau, appointing Emile Moreau in his place, and sent Ernest-Picard to Moreau's post as governor of the Banque d'Algérie. Leclerc was promoted to first deputy-governor, and Charles Rist took his place as second deputy-governor. Moreau and Rist reoriented the Bank's direction in favor of monetary stabilization; both served on the committee of experts, and Rist drafted their report's section on monetary stabilization. The report called

---

65 Harjes to JPM&C, no. 84.274, May 26, 1926; JPM 532D; Herrick to Sec. of State, no. 6357, May 28, 1926, R.G. 59, 851.51/827.

66 Harjes to JPM&C, no. 84.290, May 31, 1926; JPM&C to MH&C, no. 63.730, June 2, 1926; Harjes to JPM&C, no. 84.293, June 2, 1926; in JPM 532E.

67 DCG, June 3 and 4, 1926.

68 Warren reported: "Picard has made a most unfortunate impression on the Experts' Committee. He has had absolutely nothing constructive to offer, and has generally appeared in opposition to other proposals." "Memorandum," June 24, 1926; FRBNY, Strong papers, 1000.7.

69 Harjes to Lamont, June 22, 1926; Thomas W. Lamont papers, Baker Library, Harvard University [TWL], 113–15.

70 Warren, "Memorandum," June 24, 1926.

71 The quotes are from Harjes to Lamont, June 9, 1926, JPM 532E, and Harjes to Lamont, June 22, 1926, TWL, 113–15.

for stabilization of the franc on gold, a budget balanced through sharply increased indirect taxes, reduced direct taxes to encourage the return of capital, and a sinking fund to retire volatile short-term Bons de la Défense Nationale. In Rist's view, "The entire text of the report was above all a condemnation of the policy of immobility of the Bank of France, which claimed it could not change the legal purchasing price of gold, and believed that the government alone, by balancing its budget, could restore the franc to its former parity."[72] Caillaux requested decree powers to implement the experts' program; he was refused them by the Chamber of Deputies. The Radical Party split. Herriot stepped down from his chair as president of the Chamber to speak against the government. Forty-eight Radicals voted against the government (defeated by a 45-vote margin). The vote was not a matter of principle or program (the same Chamber would support Poincaré two weeks later), but a vote of antipathy to Caillaux.[73] Herriot was called to form a new government which stood no chance of survival; Doumergue was determined to finish off the Cartel.[74] The prospect of a Herriot government pushed the crisis to its zenith. On July 20, the franc touched 243 francs to the pound. When Herriot presented his government on July 21, a crowd of several thousands gathered outside the Palais Bourbon shouting "Down with Herriot! Dissolution!" When word spread that the government had been defeated, the demonstrators fell silent, then began to sing the "Marseillaise."[75] The franc's recovery was already under way.

Poincaré stopped France on the brink of hyperinflation and accomplished a clear change from an inflationary regime to one of relative price stability. Just *what* he changed, however, has been subject to debate. Thomas Sargent, examining the ends of inflationary regimes in the light of rational expectations, argued that the problem was essentially budgetary. Poincaré's return to power settled a long-standing dispute over whose taxes would be raised "in a fashion acceptable to the country's monied interests." His success was based on essential preconditions: a general political truce, a "high degree of political and intellectual consensus" with regard to the policies necessary, a strong reputation as a fiscal conservative, and the imposition of a

---

72 Rist, "Notice biographique," *Revue d'économie poltiique* 65 (1955): 998. As Caillaux put it, insistence on the chimera of revalorization was "the great error that marvelously reconciled patriotism and inaction." Cited in Edouard Bonnefous, *Histoire politique de la Troisième République*, vol. 4, *Cartel des gauches et Union nationale (1924–1929)* (Paris, 1960), 151.

73 For hostility to Caillaux see the draft petition by Chamber deputies in reaction to Caillaux's demand in the Wendel Papers, AN 190 AQ 20; see also Berstein, *Édouard Herriot*, 146–7; Allain, *Joseph Caillaux*, 359–61; Bredin, *Joseph Caillaux*, 259–62; and Jeanneney, *François de Wendel*, 312.

74 Georges Bonnet, *Vingt ans de vie politique, 1918–1938* (Paris, 1969), 120–1; Goldey, "Cartel des Gauches," 312.

75 *Le Figaro*, July 22, 1926.

fiscal regime restoring confidence in the government's ability to convert its debt.[76] But satisfying these preconditions was really the greater part of the problem. In subsequent "Second Thoughts," Sargent revised his analysis, giving a greater role to the Committee of Experts and Moreau.[77]

Makinen and Woodward, noting that the budget problem had been nearly resolved in 1926, found the origins of French inflation in the monetization of government debt. Poincaré changed the monetary regime, raising interest rates on government debt and creating a sinking fund. The latter alone, they claimed, would have sufficed for stabilization.[78] Their argument ignores essential factors in the 1926 crisis: The threat of a capital levy and the high direct taxes, both encouraging capital flight, are dismissed as insignificant. Political instability becomes a factor that should have inspired confidence, demonstrating the Cartel's inability to impose a capital levy.[79] This seriously underestimates the political element in the crisis. The cumulative impact of political instability on public confidence was substantial, provoking fears of governmental *inaction* or *misdirected action* as the crisis developed.[80] *Le Temps* commented in May 1926 that the franc could not be maintained without recognizing "the imperious necessity for a policy of order, of security, of confidence. No more lethal experiments, no more miraculous promises. That is to say: no more Cartel."[81]

Other reinterpretations of the crisis have accorded greater weight to politics. Prati explained the capital flight as fear of confiscatory taxation and the repeated threats of a capital levy. He concluded that consolidation of the short-term debt was the key to ending the crisis.[82] Sicsic and Dornbusch have both argued that monetary and fiscal explanations are insufficient to explain the crisis or the steep decline of the franc;[83] Eichengreen gave politics

---

76 Thomas J. Sargent, "Stopping Moderate Inflations: The Methods of Poincaré and Thatcher," in Rudiger Dornbusch and Mario Henrique Simonsen, eds., *Inflation, Debt and Indexation* (Cambridge, Mass., 1983), 58–64.

77 Thomas J. Sargent, "Stopping Moderate Inflations: The Methods of Poincaré and Thatcher," in Thomas J. Sargent, *Rational Expectations and Inflation*, 2d ed. (New York, 1993), 153–4.

78 Gail E. Makinen and G. Thomas Woodward, "A Monetary Interpretation of the Poincaré Stabilization of 1926," *Southern Economic Journal* 56 (1989): 205–8.

79 Ibid., 203.

80 As contemporary observers noted, the severity of the crisis in July "led almost inevitably to the recovery which followed so quickly," when the political conditions promoting panic were ended by Poincaré taking power. Eleanor Lansing Dulles, *The French Franc, 1914–1928: The Facts and Their Interpretation* (New York, 1929), 414. French economists produced a psychological theory of money and exchange rates to account for the crisis and recovery in 1926.

81 *Le Temps*, May 20, 1926.

82 Allesandro Prati, "Poincaré's Stabilization: Stopping a Run on Government Debt," *Journal of Monetary Economics* 27 (1991): 213–39.

83 Pierre Sicsic, "Was the Poincaré Franc Deliberately Undervalued?" *Explorations in Economic History* 29 (1992): 71–4; Rudiger Dornbusch, "Credibility, Debt and Unemployment: Ireland's Failed Stabilization," *Economic Policy* 8 (1989): 178–80.

an essential role in his account of the crisis and stabilization.[84] Even Makinen
and Woodward admitted, in their monetarist interpretation, that the crisis
occurred just when confidence should have been restored, and that "No
good reason exists for the flight from the franc to have occurred at the time
when it did."[85]

Monetary policy, the budget, the exchange rate, the situation of the
Treasury, and the political instability of the Cartel Chamber were closely
interwoven. No single altered factor could effect the change from an inflationary policy regime to one of stable prices. The nominally balanced
budget in April 1926, dubious in itself, depended on exchange rate stability.
The tough fiscal program introduced by Poincaré borrowed heavily from
the committee of experts, differed little from that proposed by Caillaux, and
disappointed many financial critics. The recovery of the franc began before
Poincaré had been called to form a new government, and was threatened by
his attempt to ratify the war debt accords. In this volatile mix of influences,
three factors were critical in the change of policy regime.

First, Poincaré's return as premier (and minister of finance) created the
political truce sought in vain by Briand and Herriot. The new government
excluded Socialists and their confiscatory tax policies; it included Herriot
and moderate Radicals now willing to support a government of the center
in order to resolve the monetary crisis.[86] Poincaré had twice refused the
ministry of finance – in June because his tax program was unacceptable to
the Radicals, in mid-July because the crisis required that the premier take
the finance portfolio.[87] He understood the crisis as primarily psychological,
requiring measures to impress public opinion.[88] His political position was
not secure; his actions were constrained by the need to maintain a majority
in the Cartel Chamber of 1924. The July crisis had temporarily realigned
support within the Chamber. His coalition posed persistent problems of
political management, which influenced his monetary policy, most notably
in delaying legal stabilization.[89] Poincaré's mastery of the hostile Chamber

84 Eichengreen, *Golden Fetters*, 172–83.
85 Makinen and Woodward, "A Monetary Interpretation," 204.
86 Schmid's analysis of the Radicals' defection to the center remains fundamental; "Politics of Currency
   Stabilization."
87 Bonnet, *Vingt ans*, 118.
88 "The French malaise is more imagined than real, more moral and sentimental than physical or
   monetary. . . . A prudent and reasonable policy would promptly expose this strain of passing neuras-
   thenia, which has carried off a part of the population, making it fear catastrophe." Interview with
   Poincaré in the Spanish newspaper *Vanguardia*, cited in "Dans la presse," June 28, 1926; AN F7/12594.
89 As Goldey commented many years ago, by relying on "confidence" rather than foreign credits,
   Poincaré made himself indispensable to the stabilization process. I treat this matter in more detail in
   the first chapter of *La politique du franc Poincaré*.

was vital to the survival of the Union nationale, and thus to public confidence that the era of inflation had ended. Second, the Committee of Experts provided the comprehensive plan for stabilization that financial advisors outside France had long insisted was necessary. Even though not followed in all its details, it provided the framework for bringing the budget, the floating debt, and the exchange rate under control. It rallied the support of Paris bankers, the Treasury, the new directors of the Bank of France, and foreign bankers. The *Economist* likened the report to that of the Cunliffe Committee in England. It was more important, in that it synthesized the various policy recommendations to provide a coherent plan for action in the midst of a major crisis.

Third, the change in direction at the Bank was essential. Robineau, Ernest-Picard, and key regents adamantly opposed stabilization. A hostile governor could frustrate government plans, particularly those that depended upon close state-bank cooperation. Moreau was committed to a prompt stabilization of the franc, and his actions as governor limited and eventually frustrated Poincaré's desires for a substantial revalorization. Robineau would not have resisted Poincaré's initial demand to monetize short-term debt (when Poincaré himself pointed this out on July 26, Moreau coolly replied, "Recall Robineau"),[90] would not have resisted Poincaré's demands for Bank intervention to regulate exchange rate fluctuations in the autumn of 1926, and would have sympathized with regents desiring revalorization in 1927. The planning for stabilization, the timing and the choice of rate, and thus the return to the gold standard were the work of the Bank of France under Moreau's direction. Poincaré provided the political calm and consensus essential to make this possible.[91]

RETURNING TO GOLD, 1926–1928

The Committee of Experts called for a balanced budget and monetary stabilization on gold as complementary and inseparable measures: "Without stabilization, neither a balanced budget, nor a solvent Treasury can be reestablished, nor can equilibrium in the balance of payments be restored."[92] Their plan relied on foreign credits, from the United States in particular, after

90 Emile Moreau, *Souvenirs d'un Gouverneur de la Banque de France: Histoire de la Stabilisation du Franc (1926–1928)* (Paris, 1954), 45.
91 "Our task is . . . laid out clearly" Moreau had recorded in his journal with regard to the experts' report; "but will the politicians know how to accomplish theirs? Will they let us work in peace?" Moreau, *Souvenirs*, 17.
92 *Rapport du Comité des experts (Décret du 31 Mai 1926)* (Paris, 1926), 41.

ratification of the Mellon-Béranger debt accord. Poincaré had criticized the accord and opposed ratification; at the end of July he decided to attempt ratification in order to obtain foreign credits.[93] Opposition within his coalition dissuaded him from following through, and ratification was delayed, eventually to July 1929. The immediate crisis having passed and the Treasury crisis resolved by his fiscal reforms, Poincaré was content to let events develop and allow the franc to rise. Moreau and Rist, partisans of the experts' report, began planning for stabilization. Poincaré's refusal to ratify the debt accords and adopt a definite stabilization program frustrated their plans.

Throughout the autumn of 1926, Poincaré sought Bank intervention in the exchange market to reduce fluctuations in the exchange rate of the franc, and thus to moderate (but not to prevent) its rise. On August 7, he passed a law authorizing the purchase of foreign exchange and gold with this object in view. But Moreau refused to act without a definite stabilization program, foreign credits to counter pressure on the franc, and a guarantee of continuity in the direction of the Bank.[94] It was only the prospect of an uncontrollable rise of the franc and a sharp economic crisis in December 1926 that forced Moreau to abandon his demands. The nascent crisis was of sufficiently forbidding aspect to compel compromise. The Bank would stabilize the franc until January 15, and Poincaré would allow the Bank to control a temporary stabilization, despite his desire for revalorization.

Three factors prolonged the de facto stabilization. First, strong demand for francs allowed the Bank of France to accumulate foreign exchange reserves that replaced the foreign credits believed essential to successful stabilization. Second, the slump that began in November 1926 was relatively mild, but sufficient to increase reluctance to allow the franc to rise higher until the economy had adjusted. In fact, key economists at the Bank of France advocated lowering its value.[95] Third, Poincaré realized the political utility of de facto stabilization. It kept alive the threat of capital flight should the Radicals choose to challenge his policies, while offering determined *revalorisateurs* on the Right the prospect of further revalorization.

Moreau accepted the political impossibility of stabilization prior to the 1928 elections and devoted his energies to preparing the Bank for stabilization. He accelerated repayment of the Bank's advances to the state, and

---

93 Moreau, *Souvenirs*, 55.

94 This argument developed in Mouré, *La politique du franc Poincaré*, 63–70.

95 Mouré, "Undervaluing the franc Poincaré," 145. On the French slump, see James Bradford De Long, "Returning to the Gold Standard: A Macroeconomic History of Britain and France in the 1920s," Ph.D. diss., Harvard University, 1987.

determined the technical aspects of the return to gold.[96] French experience with foreign exchange holdings during the de facto stabilization increased their distrust of the gold exchange standard. In the spring of 1927, the rapid growth of foreign exchange reserves posed a problem. A reduction in Bank rate in London, coinciding with pressure in France to let the franc appreciate, increased an already strong flow of capital to France and threatened the stability of the exchange rate and domestic prices. Moreau feared that the franc unpegged could rise to 60 francs to the pound, causing a severe economic crisis.[97] His director of economic studies, Pierre Quesnay, blamed the change in the London rediscount rate, reasoning that easy money in London facilitated Continental speculation. Their "gold standard" solution was to convert sterling to gold in London in order to tighten credit there, which would in turn curb speculation in Amsterdam and Berlin.[98]

On May 16, Moreau requested the purchase of gold in London and New York with French sterling and dollar balances. This caused little difficulty in New York, where Moreau converted $100 million to gold, as the FRBNY purchased Treasury bills to return the money to the market. In London, however, his conversion of £20 million caused alarm. The demand was met over several weeks by Bank of England purchases of gold in the London market. Norman termed the French demand "capricious" and feared that France would threaten sterling's convertibility. The problem, in his view, could only be solved in Paris, where a long-term interest rate "higher than anywhere else in the world," low security prices, confidence in French fiscal policy, and the possible revalorization of the franc made an irresistible combination. He recommended raising prices, reducing the discount rate, and a firm commitment to maintain the present value of the franc.[99] Although the two banks disagreed on the nature of the problem, a collaborative solution was found by increasing market rates in London and concentrating French gold purchases in New York.[100]

---

96 From December 1926 to the end of May 1928, advances were reduced from 35.4 billion to 17.9 billion francs; on the eve of the monetary reform they had been further reduced to 13.6 billion. These advances were repaid from the revaluation of French gold and foreign exchange held by the Bank.

97 Moreau, *Souvenirs*, 293–6, 305–6.

98 Moreau, *Souvenirs*, 324–6; H. A. Siepmann to Norman (writing from Paris), May 20, 1927, Archives of the Bank of England [BoE], G 1/34, and Frederick Leith-Ross, "Conversation with Monsieur Quesnay (the Secretary of the Banque de France) on French monetary policy," June 9, 1927; Public Record Office [PRO], T 176/29.

99 Moreau, *Souvenirs*, 324–6; "Collaboration des marchés de Paris et de Londres," s.d., AN 374 AP 6. Also Sir Henry Clay, *Lord Norman* (London, 1957), 228–32; Siepmann, "Note of a conversation in Paris on Friday, May 27, 1927," BoE, G 1/34.

100 Siepmann, "Note of conversations with Monsieur Quesnay in London on the 1st, 2nd and 3rd June, 1927," BoE, G 1/34; Siepmann to Quesnay, June 4, 1927, AN 374 AP 6; Moreau, *Souvenirs*, 357–8, 371, 373, 389, 394.

Discussion of the working of the gold standard continued when central bankers met on Long Island in early July. Rist represented the Bank of France. He characterized recent French gold policy as "a *politique de circonstance* owing entirely to our need to slow as much as possible the influx of foreign exchange now taking place." Once convertibility was restored, the Bank would let the favorable balance of payments produce its "natural effect" – a continued gold flow to France. Rist disagreed with Strong's view that French policy disrupted the international monetary system. The current (mal)distribution of gold was a result of the war; the flow of capital and gold to France would help right the imbalance. France would naturally draw gold from the market where it could be acquired at lowest cost – London. Strong suggested that lower interest rates would facilitate recovery in Europe, "obviously an indirect criticism of the policy we have followed in recent weeks." Rist replied that the gold standard required large gold reserves if one wished to maintain a low discount rate; otherwise a high rate was essential.[101] High interest rates were necessary in Europe in order to draw back European gold reserves from the United States. Rist was deaf to American and British concerns that a rapid deflation induced by the reconstitution of European gold reserves would depress world prices and produce prolonged depression.[102] If the weak situation of London were to be relieved, it was New York's responsibility to do so, for America should have been facilitating the return of gold to Europe by running a balance of payments deficit paid off in gold.

In September, Quesnay discussed the theory and practice of the gold exchange standard with H. A. Siepmann of the Bank of England, stating: "At last I have understood its exact significance; the experience of having these formidable reserves was necessary to enable us to grasp the rights and wrongs of this theory."[103] Quesnay asked who paid the interest earned by central banks holding foreign exchange as reserves. In his analysis, because gold reserves in the United States had been sterilized to prevent domestic

---

101 Rist, "Aide mémoire des conversations du 29 et 30 juin entre M. Rist, M. Strong et M. Harrison," July 1, 1927; AN 374 AP 6 and BdF, 1397199403/181.

102 This was discussed at a dinner on June 29, with Leffingwell in particular. Leffingwell noted Rist's opposition to managed currency without realizing that "the French franc today is a managed currency, and that it was the Banque's management of the franc that caused the recent difficulty in the money markets. . . . But he doesn't see any alternative to the classically operated gold standard even as a transitional measure. Heaven send he may!" Leffingwell to Lamont, July 12, 1927; Russell C. Leffingwell papers [RCL], Sterling Library, Yale University, box 4, folder #83. Leffingwell had earlier expressed his concerns about French gold policy in Leffingwell to Lamont, June 13, 1927; RCL, box 4, folder #93.

103 Siepmann quotes a Quesnay letter of September 12, 1927 in his summary of Quesnay's gold standard views, "Monsieur Quesnay on the Gold Exchange Standard," Sept. 22, 1927; BoE, OV 48/1.

inflation, the Federal Reserve System paid interest to foreign central banks, interest foregone by "its present inability to build up American credit on its metal surplus." In London, because Bank of England gold reserves were needed to back the domestic currency, there was no guaranteed convertibility of the sterling balances held by foreign central banks as reserves. Their sterling holdings were a credit granted to the London market; foreign banks holding reserves in sterling were not on the gold standard at all.[104] Quesnay was not reassured by the reply. The gold exchange standard, Siepmann explained, was intended to economize gold, and this goal would be frustrated if foreign currency claims had to be backed 100 percent by gold. A country reverting to the gold standard could claim "more gold than there is any reason to expect the gold center to have held in reserve against legitimate Gold Exchange Standard demands," and would threaten the gold standard itself.[105] The system was less secure than the gold standard and depended on the sufferance of countries holding foreign exchange as currency reserves.

The Bank of France had no desire to compromise its gold standard to benefit London. Quesnay would have been more concerned had Siepmann revealed his own reservations. In a letter to Henry Strakosch, to whom Siepmann circulated Quesnay's questions and his own response, Siepmann expressed his own dissatisfaction with his reply to Quesnay. "The real trouble" with the gold exchange standard was that it failed to deal with "catastrophe risks": Europeans countries would prefer "continuous credit contraction" to the risk of leaving foreign balances on deposit in London.

If they were rich enough, I am sure they would like to hoard gold and be self-sufficient in this as much as in any other way. It seems to me to be quite useless to try to get over this difficulty by appealing to their virtues. Our best hope is, I think, to exploit their misfortune and their vices. Some of them are poor, and they are all greedy. That is to say, some of them cannot afford to accumulate large gold stocks and all of them enjoy earning interest on the equivalent of gold.[106]

French policy after returning to gold attempted to draw the best of both worlds, rich enough to hoard gold, but unwilling to forego the interest earnings on their foreign exchange reserves. The Bank categorically rejected

104 Siepmann, "Monsieur Quesnay on the Gold Exchange Standard," and Quesnay's margin comments; Quesnay found Siepmann's summary of his views accurate and added margin comments "to complete and fortify" the summary. Quesnay to Siepmann, Sept. 23, 1927; BoE, OV 48/1. Margin comment on the copy of Siepmann's summary in Quesnay's papers notes that his questions were not fully answered by Siepmann; AN 374 AP 9.
105 Siepmann, "Reply to some observations by M. Quesnay on the Gold Exchange Standard," Nov. 8, 1927; copies in BoE, OV 48/1 and AN 374 AP 9.
106 Siepmann to Strakosch, Nov. 9, 1927; BoE, OV 48/1.

the gold exchange standard: "There is no question of adopting a monetary system condemned by the experience of recent years, the Bank of France policy of de facto stability being nothing other than the integral application of the gold exchange standard."[107]

The parliamentary elections in May 1928 returned Poincaré with an increased majority, and the Bank imposed de jure stabilization. A surge in demand for francs threatened to overwhelm the Bank's capacity to maintain the franc without substantial inflation. Both Moreau and Poincaré employed threats of resignation to demonstrate their determination; on June 25, the monetary reform passed by impressive majorities in both the Chamber and the Senate.[108] The new law defined the franc for the first time solely in terms of gold; it restored convertibility and promised the eventual issue of gold coins. The value of the franc was set to maintain French prices below the level of world prices in order to preserve domestic economic stability.[109] The franc's return to gold was supposed to be the final step in the reconstruction of the gold standard: According to the *Economist*, it would "mark the close of the epoch of Europe's post-war currency chaos."[110] But the respite from currency chaos was short-lived, and the new gold standard proved vulnerable to the "catastrophe risk" Siepmann feared in 1927.

French policy on gold from 1928 to 1936 was conditioned by experience off gold from 1914 to 1928 in several important ways. First, the strength of commitment to the prewar parity of the franc, evident in the claims made during the wartime campaign to "harvest gold," made acceptance of devaluation more difficult. The "four-sous franc" may have been a victory snatched from the jaws of hyperinflation, but it was nonetheless a default on the promises made in good faith throughout the war, and resented long after 1928. Preserving the franc Poincaré and the gold standard would harden French resistance to devaluation and domestic measures to stimulate economic recovery in the 1930s. Second, the failure of wartime allies to support French economic and monetary recovery and to compel Germany to pay reparations, and the accomplishment of stabilization by French efforts with little foreign assistance and no foreign credits, increased skepticism with regard to international cooperation. It had done little to help

---

107 Original: "Il ne saurait être question d'adopter un système monétaire condamné par l'expérience des dernières années, la politique de stabilité de fait de la Banque de France n'étant pas autre chose que l'application intégrale du gold exchange standard" ("Méthodes propres à assurer le maintien de la stabilité du franc," June 1928; AN 374 AP 8).
108 The reform passed in the Chamber by 448 to 18, with 133 abstentions, mainly socialists; in the Senate the vote was 256 to 3.
109 Mouré, "Undervaluing the franc Poincaré," 146–9.
110 *Economist*, June 23, 1928, 1278.

France after the war, and French cooperation in response to the depression reflected this skepticism. Third, French experience of budget deficits, inflation, and currency depreciation established a model for the evils against which the gold standard would stand as safeguard, and hardened resolve against rethinking that model when budget deficits recurred in the context of international deflation in the 1930s. Fourth and last, French experience with foreign exchange holdings increased their hostility to the very idea of the gold exchange standard, which seemed clearly intended to benefit London and to constitute a perversion, rather than an improvement, of the prewar gold standard.

5

Keynes's Road to Bretton Woods

An Essay in Interpretation

ROBERT SKIDELSKY

The delegates did not reach an "agreement." They merely signed a paper which looked like an agreement.[1]

INTRODUCTION

As the well-known story of Bretton Woods has it, there were two plans, the White Plan and the Keynes Plan. The White Plan, from the U.S. Treasury, championed liberal internationalism; the Keynes Plan, from the British Treasury, tried to secure for Britain sufficient freedom from international pressures to be able to pursue full employment and other desirable social policies. The British saw internationalism as a constraint, the Americans as an opportunity. The Bretton Woods Agreement was a successful attempt to reconcile these two views; each country accommodated the requirements of the other, without sacrificing its own aims. The result was the "golden age" of the 1950s and 1960s, so different from the interwar years. In 1946, President Truman called the Agreement "a cornerstone upon the foundation of which a sound economic world can – and must – be erected." And a leading historian of the Agreement wrote in 1978 that "during a quarter of a century" it had stood as the "foundation upon which world trade, production, employment and investment were gradually built."[2]

The trouble with this canonical text is that it does not square with the facts. For the first fourteen years after the war, the Bretton Woods System was in virtual cold storage. Its cornerstone, currency convertibility at fixed, though adjustable, exchange rates, was not restored in the main European

I am indebted to Professor Paul Davidson for his comments on an earlier draft of this chapter.

1 *Commercial and Financial Chronicle*, Sept. 14, 1944, on the Bretton Woods Agreement, Armand van Dormael, *Bretton Woods: Birth of a Monetary System* (New York, 1978), 240.

2 Dormael, *Bretton Woods*, 289; the author's view is on 307.

countries till the end of the 1950s, by which time "the golden age" was in full flower. It was not adherence to the Bretton Woods rules which rebalanced the economies of the United States and Europe, but a combination of large sterling, deutschmark, and franc devaluations against the dollar and the huge outflow of American dollars on government account, particularly for military spending abroad. These events were reflected in the rundown in U.S. and the buildup of European (and Japanese) reserves. But this trend in the reserve positions of its leading members also meant that the System was in crisis from the moment of its "completion" till it broke down in 1971.

I am not arguing that the "rules of the game" agreed by forty-four nations in 1944 had no influence on the course of history. Like any international treaty, the Bretton Woods Agreement bound its signatories to follow certain rules and procedures. To the extent that the rules concerning fixed exchange rates, convertible currencies, etc., were accepted and followed, they made for more stable and predictable monetary conditions. The fact that the System was not *explicitly* hegemonic – though it soon became a dollar standard – also made it more generally acceptable. But would the Agreement have "stuck" without the special incentives provided by the United States and the general atmosphere of the Cold War? It was U.S. overseas disbursements, which far exceeded the obligations that the United States had undertaken under the Bretton Woods Agreement, which made it relatively easy for the leading countries to follow, for a time, the "rules of the game." I agree with Stanley Hoffman that the postwar economic order was shaped by a "more or less explicit deal between the United States and its allies in Western Europe and Japan. The latter accepted Washington's favourite rules of the game in exchange for military protection, but Washington accepted certain exceptions to these rules to safeguard important allied interests."[3] That is to say, the course of events was dominated by the logic of the Cold War, the fact of U.S. power, the initial strength and the gradual weakening of the mighty dollar.

So much I think would be widely accepted by historians of the postwar period.[4] The System set up in 1944 could not have produced, far less sustained, the "golden age." The argument of this chapter is more radical. Its central contention, which cannot be fully established here, is that there was never enough agreement between Britain and the United States on the

---

3 Stanley Hoffman, *Primacy or World Order: American Foreign Policy Since the Cold War* (New York, 1978), 13.
4 For an account of the early irrelevance of the IMF, see Harold James, *International Monetary Cooperation Since Bretton Woods* (New York, 1996), chaps. 3, 4.

"rules of the game" to make the Bretton Woods Agreement any more than a form of words to paper over the cracks. There were far too many contractual escape clauses and "voluntary misunderstandings." My contention is that the Agreement was kicked into touch in the act of setting it up, because both the British and U.S. governments regarded it as marginal, or even antithetical, to their policy objectives. The economists' attempt to make it the centerpiece and showcase of a new world order failed to get off the ground.

There are exemplary accounts of the technical issues at stake in the Bretton Woods negotiations. One of them is by D. E. Moggridge.[5] The key issue was creditor versus debtor adjustment. The fact that, under the gold standard, adjustment, as Keynes noted in 1941, was *"compulsory* for the debtor and *voluntary* for the creditor" was the main reason for his hostility to it.[6] Under the gold standard, the duty of adjustment fell on those countries losing gold; those countries gaining it were free to sterilize it. All Keynes's plans for a reformed gold standard were designed to make a degree of creditor adjustment compulsory or automatic. The Americans accepted that creditors had responsibilities. They were willing, during and after World War II, to exercise them with unparalleled generosity. But they consistently upheld the doctrine of voluntarism. The Bretton Woods Agreement failed to bridge this divide. The United States retained discretion concerning the degree of creditor adjustment it would undertake. As a result, Britain secured for itself discretion to retain its "discriminatory" prewar system.

These technical debates are only *fully* understandable in light of the fact that Britain, the world's leading creditor before 1914, had become its leading debtor over the space of thirty years, and the United States had become the world's leading creditor. When Keynes talked about the duty of creditor adjustment he was generalizing about Britain's particular problem, which was also the point of reference for his own economic theorizing. Keynes's proposition could also be stated theologically. The doctrine of debtor adjustment had strong Old Testament overtones: Justice demanded that the profligate should be punished for their extravagance. The doctrine of creditor adjustment was New Testament: Debts, like sins, might be "forgiven."

Keynes and the British fought to institutionalize New Testament doctrine in international economic relations. The Americans upheld Old Testament doctrine. What I aim to do in a preliminary way is to try to understand how the two countries, particularly Britain, came to view the postwar problem

---

5 D. E. Moggridge, "Keynes and the International Monetary System 1909–1946."
6 John Maynard Keynes, *The Collected Writings of John Maynard Keynes* [hereafter JMK CW], 30 vols. (London and New York, 1971–89), XXV: 28.

in this way. This focuses the discussion on Keynes, who dominated the British approach, both intellectually and as de facto or actual leader of the two British missions to the United States that hammered out the Bretton Woods compromise in 1943 and 1944.

Before embarking on the story, I should set out my own methodological credo in telling it. I accept Schumpeter's verdict that Keynes's advice "was in the first instance always English advice, born of English problems."[7] This does not mean that he argued his case in crudely nationalistic terms, or that the technical debates between Keynes and White were simply a cover for conflicting national interests. Economics often enables intractable political conflicts to be resolved by assuming (or the cynic would say, pretending) that political issues are technical at heart and imposing a language of debate consistent with this assumption. The fact that technicians handled all the stages leading to the Bretton Woods Agreement meant that, by the time political opposition surfaced in both countries, it was too late to scupper the actual Agreement. But there is no reason for the historian to follow this convention. His job is to explain why people acted in the way they did. To accept the convention that positions were adopted for technical reasons is to omit a large part of the explanation. It fails to explain, for example, why British and American economists were usually to be found on different sides of the technical argument. All this is well understood by most economists; but the fact that they are constrained to write, even about historical episodes, in the language of economics, does not make them very good historians. The ideal is to use technical language where that is necessary and historical language where that is appropriate. But few people can do this well; and the danger is that one does both badly. But this is a risk I shall have to take, as indeed I have in writing about Keynes at all.

Emphasizing the *Britishness* of Keynes's international thinking helps explain two things about his Clearing Union plan: first, why it was so readily accepted by the British Treasury; second, why it was so unpersuasive to the Americans. That part of Keynes's economics, which insisted on the overriding importance of national monetary sovereignty, was not at issue between Keynes and the Treasury after the collapse of the gold standard in 1931. Even today the notion unites many (perhaps most) British monetarists and Keynesians against Britain's membership in the EMU. As for the Americans, it seemed to them that Keynes was setting up the United States as Britain's milk cow. The Americans were willing to be milked, but on their own terms.

7 Joseph A. Schumpeter, *Ten Great Economists, from Marx to Keynes* (London, 1952), 274.

THE POLITICAL ECONOMY OF THE 1930S

To state the conflict between Britain and the United States in this way is to be alerted to a paradox. Historically, Britain was internationalist, the United States protectionist and isolationist. In the 1930s, these historical attitudes started to shift. Britain became more "nationalist," the United States more "internationalist." Generalized reference to the background of the Great Depression cannot itself explain this shift. The interwar years were differently experienced by the two countries, and the Great Depression itself figured differently in their respective mythologies.

The shift in values should not be exaggerated. In the 1930s, Britain still retained a sense of responsibility for the health of the international economy: The only "world economic conference" of the 1930s took place in London, in 1933. By contrast, the United States practiced a policy of monetary nationalism and political isolationism. These attitudes reflected vastly different historical experience. Britain had virtually created the "world economy" in the nineteenth century; it was its lynchpin as well as its main beneficiary. The United States, by contrast, was a largely self-sufficient periphery, with a founding myth of freedom from foreign entanglements. By the 1930s, these historical perspectives were no longer viable. Because of its great size, the U.S. economy could affect economic conditions in the rest of the world, without itself being much affected by them; Britain, by contrast, was still highly vulnerable to external shocks, but could no longer "conduct the international orchestra." The 1930s was thus a decade of transition – but transition to what was unclear. The ostensible trend was toward the economics of blocs and regions. This reflected the breakdown of international cooperation during and after the Great Depression. But the hope of a revived internationalism was never quite extinguished in Britain and was stirring in the United States. This was to make the Bretton Woods Agreement possible; it did not guarantee that the Agreement would be put to work.

The interwar years presented themselves very differently to the Americans and the British. The 1920s were a "good" decade for the United States; its troubles started only with the catastrophic collapse of 1929–33. Although Herbert Hoover claimed – naturally enough – that "the hurricane that swept our shores" was of European origin,[8] this was not the majority view of the New Dealers, who attributed the Depression to structural weaknesses in the U.S. economy and banking system. The New Deal was essentially a domestic reform program, with a neo-Keynesian "recovery" element tagged on.

---

8 Herbert Hoover, *The Great Depression, Memoirs*, vol. 3 (New York, 1952), 79–80.

Unlike in Britain, there was no lasting reaction against the gold standard. For most of the interwar years, the United States held the largest share of the world's monetary gold, and the gold standard was viewed as a constraint on recovery – probably wrongly – only in the eighteen months following the downward float of sterling and its allied currencies against the dollar in September 1931. Roosevelt's aggressive gold-buying policy of 1933 deliberately drove down the international value of the dollar, restoring the dollar-sterling rate in January 1934 to what it had been before September 1931 and wiping out Britain's temporary competitive advantage. Though the gold-dollar rate was fixed at $35 to an ounce of gold in January 1934, Roosevelt kept open the threat of currency retaliation to prevent sterling from depreciating again.[9]

The monetary events of 1931–3 highlighted the fact that the gold system lacked an agreed set of adjustment rules. Deliberate exchange rate depreciation was ruled out. Suspending convertibility into gold was allowed only in grave emergencies. Britain argued that the 1931 sterling crisis was such an emergency: As Keynes quipped, sterling did not leave gold, gold left sterling. The Americans did not agree. Britain should have deflated, they argued, and raised fresh loans. Because the United States refused to accept sterling's devaluation as involuntary, it forced down the value of the dollar to restore the previous rate of $4.86 to the pound. The lack of an agreed set of adjustment rules opened the way to competitive devaluations and "dirty floating."

Why did the United States refuse to accept a sterling devaluation? The answer lies in a combination of interest, suspicion, and ignorance. Although America still ran a current account surplus between 1931 and 1933, it had one large and influential class of debtors – food and raw material producers, whose incomes had been catastrophically hit by the collapse of world food and raw material prices. Farmers and miners welcomed currency inflation as the route to higher prices at home and increased exports abroad. Politically, Roosevelt's tirade against the "fetishes of international bankers" pandered to a rural paranoia dating back to William Jennings Bryan and even earlier. A related paranoia gripped parts of his administration. U.S. Treasury policy under Henry Morgenthau was dominated by a grotesque overestimation of Britain's financial strength and a corresponding suspicion of Britain's motives. Vigilance against British Machiavellianism rather than the production of constructive ideas was the watchword of U.S. Treasury's policy in the 1930s, a tendency reinforced by British secretiveness. These

---

9 Ian M. Drummond, *The Floating Pound and the Sterling Area, 1931–1939* (Cambridge, 1981), 257.

attitudes did not disappear with the war; they were overshadowed by more urgent imperatives.

Roosevelt's monetary policy was regarded as bizarre by many at the time – even Keynes described his gold-buying policy as "the gold standard on the booze" – and a longer perspective has not altered this verdict. It did nothing for U.S. recovery, and strengthened the trend to currency and trading blocs abroad by failing to address the problem of America's unbalanced creditor position. Carried to its logical conclusion, it would have prevented three out of four continents from trading with the United States, leaving its huge gold stock largely redundant.

This realization was starting to break through in the later 1930s. A Tripartite Monetary Agreement was signed on September 25, 1936, by which the United States and Britain accepted the need for a devaluation of the franc, and agreed to promote stable exchange rates between themselves. On October 13, the United States agreed, subject to revocation at twenty-four hours' notice, to sell gold for immediate export at $35 an ounce or earmark it for exchange equalization funds willing to reciprocate. These monetary arrangements soon embraced the core Western democracies. The United States also negotiated a series of stabilization arrangements with Latin American countries; while the Bank for International Settlements in Geneva offered central banks facilities for granting one another reciprocal credits in their own currencies or in gold. All this marked the end of the era of competitive exchange depreciation, though it fell far short of a full-blooded return to the gold standard. Harry Dexter White's Plan for a fund that would stabilize currencies and avoid devaluations and payments' restrictions directed at the United States harks back to these tentative steps.[10]

The economic problem posed by America's overwhelming creditor position was better appreciated by the State Department. Secretary of State Cordell Hull understood that the United States must be prepared to import if it wanted to export. Although his particular animus was directed at Britain's Ottawa Preference system, which he called "the greatest injury, in a commercial way" to the United States in a long career,[11] he recognized that it was Britain's response to the Hawley-Smoot tariff put up by America in 1930. The Hull program required reciprocal tariff reductions and the ending of discrimination against American goods. Hull

---

10 For a summary, see J. Keith Horsefield, *The International Monetary Fund, 1945–1965*, 3 vols. (Washington, D.C., 1969), 1: 6–7.

11 Arthur M. Schlesinger, Jr., *The Coming of the New Deal* (Boston, 1959), 253.

regarded currency stabilization as the essential condition for trade liberalization and embraced it accordingly, colliding thereby with the monetary nationalism of Roosevelt and Morgenthau.[12] His successes were the Trade Agreements Act of 1934 and the Anglo-American Trade Agreement of 1938, the latter bringing "a marked benefit to American agriculture."[13] However, Hull's free trade outlook was vitiated by an economic determinism which even Cobden would have blanched at: namely, that political conflicts were the result of trade barriers, and that their removal was therefore a necessary and sufficient condition for a harmonious world. The attraction of this doctrine for American opinion in general, and for exporting and banking interests in particular, was obvious: It extended America's economic reach, while preserving political isolationism. This combination made it unattractive to the British, especially in the run up to the second European war.

The lessons the British drew from the interwar years were very different. Despite the huge changes in the relative positions of Britain and the United States wrought by the First World War, Britain still attempted to play its traditional role in the 1920s, repegging the pound to gold in 1925 at its prewar parity with the dollar, allowing unlimited capital exports, and maintaining a virtually unmodified free trade system. Although sterling was forced off gold in 1931, official British policy at the London World Economic Conference of 1933 was to re-establish an international gold standard purged of its previous defects.[14] Britain would not join the gold bloc led by France, but "MacDonald and Chamberlain were eager for a temporary de facto stabilization of the pound, dollar, and franc vis-à-vis one another."[15] Roosevelt, however, refused any commitment to limit dollar depreciation, and the Conference collapsed. After 1933, British policy was "to manage sterling so as to suit our own economy."[16]

This retreat from internationalism reflects, above all, the British experience of the 1920s, when Britain slumped while the United States boomed. The Great Depression was not the defining event for Britain as it was for the United States, but was viewed as superimposed on the difficulties of the British economy dating from World War I. It therefore gave rise to no New Deal, but was rather seen as an opportunity to liberate monetary policy from a long-standing external constraint. Britain's

---

12 Benjamin Rowland, ed., *Balance of Power or Hegemony: The Interwar Monetary System* (New York, 1976), chap. 5, 203.
13 Cordell Hull, *The Memoirs of Cordell Hull*, 2 vols. (New York, 1948), 1: 530.
14 Drummond, *Floating Pound and the Sterling Area*, 163.
15 Ibid., 173.   16 S. G. Waley, 1936; ibid., 205.

abnormally high unemployment in the 1920s was largely concentrated in the export sector, and was attributed both at the time, and subsequently, to the malfunctioning of the gold standard, particularly to the failure of the United States and France to play by the "rules of the game." France was believed to have deliberately undervalued the franc in 1926; the United States had discouraged imports with its high tariff, while insisting on payment of its war debts. Britain's departure from the gold standard in 1931 was seen not just as having directly helped British exports, but as having made possible the "cheap money" policy of the 1930s, which laid the basis of home market recovery. Thus, a British return to the gold standard was premised on the removal of these structural imbalances. Roosevelt's hostility to a realignment of the two currencies strengthened Britain's resolve to manage the exchange rate in its own interest.

The Sterling Area was anathema to Morgenthau, but its role in British thinking, or recovery, before 1939 is uncertain. It took shape in 1931 when twenty or so countries followed sterling in a downward float against the dollar. It consisted of countries, mainly in the British Empire, but including a varying number of others with strong trade links with Britain, which held their reserves in London and kept their currencies freely exchangeable and virtually stable in terms of sterling, either because they were compelled to, or from convenience. It protected most of Britain's external trade against exchange risk, and, with freedom to export capital within the area, preserved the role of the City of London as banker and lender, though on a much reduced scale. The accumulation of sterling balances in London, which reached £780 million early in 1938, also offset Britain's deteriorating current account balance. But few Englishmen before 1940 regarded the sterling area as a permanent system. It compromised British monetary independence without securing the much larger advantages of a stabilized international monetary system.

Nor, except for a minority of Imperialists, was the Ottawa Preference System, set up in 1932, regarded as a permanent replacement for free trade. The inspiration behind it, which went back to Joseph Chamberlain's tariff reform campaign of 1903, was to convert an empire of sentiment into a commercial and political union on the basis of reciprocal tariff preferences for each other's products granted by the mother country and its colonial offshoots. Neville Chamberlain, the British Chancellor of the Exchequer, to whom it fell to implement his father's grand design, found little warmth in the imperial bargaining at Ottawa. The theory was that Britain would use its quasi-monopsonist buying power in foodstuffs and raw materials to secure preferential tariffs for its manufactured exports in Empire countries heavily dependent on exporting to Britain. The basic flaw in this strategy, which Ottawa exposed, lay in the notion of a "natural" division between British manufactures and Dominion primary products. In practice, Canada, Australia, South Africa, and India were all interested in developing their manufactures, while Britain, for many different reasons, wanted to protect its agriculture. An additional problem was how to reconcile the imperial vision with Britain's trade relations with third countries, many of which were members of the sterling area. The Ottawa Preference System turned out to be a device for tariff increases all round – the preferences taking the form of lower tariff increases for empire products – coupled with a complicated duty and quota system to protect British agriculture and preserve third party entry into the British market. Judging by results, the British were comprehensively outnegotiated at Ottawa: a classic case of the weak exploiting the strong. Britain achieved only a tiny increase of exports to the Dominions; its exports to third countries were restricted, as it was deprived of bargaining flexibility and suffered increased competition in non-empire markets; and empire and foreign countries benefited largely from Britain's home-market-based recovery. As a result, Britain's trade deficit soared, while income from "invisibles" shrank. What is important to note, in this context, was that the Ottawa System did not solve Britain's balance of payments problem; it almost certainly worsened it. Although Hull might rail against "discrimination," differential tariffs were a very inefficient form of discrimination. They antagonized everyone else, without in fact doing the job.

By the end of the 1930s, the monetary and commercial relations between Britain and the United States had reached something of an impasse. In Kindlebergian terms, the United States would not, and Britain could not, take the lead in reconstructing a functioning world economy – this despite the growing realization that the state of their economic relations put a limit on the ability of both countries to recover from the Depression. It took another world war to break the deadlock, and then only partially.

KEYNES AND THE INTERNATIONAL MONETARY ORDER

Writing in 1943, Keynes said that there were two main objections to the old gold standard. The first was that it "does not provide the appropriate quantity of money." The second – and more modern – complaint was that it failed to deal with the problem of differential wage movements except by "creating unemployment." A new international currency scheme should aim therefore to prevent those evils resulting from "a chronic shortage of international money due to the draining of gold into the creditor countries" and to provide an orderly exchange-rate adjustment mechanism to reconcile national differences in wage movements.[17] This was economic-speak for saying that Britain must have freedom to "choose" its own rate of wage inflation. Thus, Keynes and the British Treasury at Bretton Woods sought an agreement that would "combine an international system with the maximum of national monetary independence."[18]

The fact that Keynes had been saying much the same things in the 1920s alerts us to the dominant source of the policy problem which preoccupied him over his professional lifetime: how to deal with the effect on the British economy of the unbalanced creditor position of the United States. In most of his writing on international monetary arrangements, Britain and the United States can be substituted for debtors and creditors. Only at the end of his life did he foresee that dollar scarcity would eventually give way to dollar glut.

Bearing this perspective in mind, the highlights on Keynes's road to the Clearing Union can be summarily listed as follows:

1. His *Grand Scheme for the Rehabilitation of Europe* (1919). This was the first of Keynes's ingenious plans for channeling American savings to Europe through a quasi-automatic mechanism. It provided for the issue by Germany and its defeated allies of bonds to a present value of £1,445 million. Of the sum raised, £1 billion would go to the European Allies on account of reparations, to finance reconstruction of their devastated areas and to discharge inter-ally war debts, and £445 million would be retained by the Central Powers to buy food and raw materials and pay off debt to neutrals. The plan was accepted by the British Treasury and the prime minister, Lloyd George, on the understanding that American investors would take up about 90 percent of the issue. It foundered on the refusal of the U.S. Treasury to underwrite an unconditional transfer of American funds abroad. As Thomas Lamont observed, American credits should be extended through "normal commercial and banking channels."[19]

2. *The Tract on Monetary Reform* (1923). This was Keynes's first assertion of the doctrine of national monetary sovereignty, as against the consensus view that Britain should return to the gold standard as quickly as possible. Keynes claimed that a restored gold standard was bound to be a managed standard,

---

17 JMK, *Economic Journal*, July–Sept. 1943, reprinted in CW, XXVI: 30–3.
18 Moggridge, "Keynes and the International Monetary System," 80.
19 Robert Skidelsky, *John Maynard Keynes: Hopes Betrayed* (London, 1983), 370; see also D. E. Moggridge, *Maynard Keynes: An Economist's Biography* (London, 1992), 309.

and managed by Washington, not London. "With the existing distribution of the world's gold, the reinstatement of the gold standard means, inevitably, that we surrender the regulation of our price level and the handling of the credit cycle to the Federal Reserve Board of the United States." The American monetary authorities would determine their monetary policy by reference to domestic conditions, not to the requirements of countries like Britain.[20] In the short run, the Federal Reserve Board's policy of sterilizing gold gains to prevent inflation would impose deflation on the rest of the world if it returned to the gold standard. In the longer run, Keynes feared that the eventual dishoarding of America's gold stock would lead to worldwide inflation – as it did, but not till the 1960s! The best solution was to divide the world into "managed" sterling and dollar currency blocs. "So long as the Federal Reserve Board was successful in keeping dollar prices steady the objective of keeping sterling prices steady would be identical with the objective of keeping the dollar-sterling exchange steady." Keynes's unwillingness to entrust Washington with de facto responsibility for managing a restored gold standard reflects in part his disappointment at the way the United States had shuffled off its responsibility, as he saw it, for restoring Europe after the First World War. After the experience of the restored gold standard between 1925 and 1931, Keynes's view became Treasury orthodoxy.

3. *Does Unemployment Need a Drastic Remedy?* (1924). This was one of a sheaf of articles and lectures that year arguing for the "diversion of national savings from relatively barren foreign investment into state-encouraged constructive enterprises at home." Keynes's argument was that, with an inflexible domestic labor market, increased foreign lending would not automatically create a corresponding flow of exports. Its main effect would be to raise the rate of interest on domestic borrowing, thus curtailing employment. The Treasury should use its powers under the Trustee Acts "strictly to ration overseas borrowers."[21] From this point onward, rejection of unlimited capital mobility became a constant in his thinking.

4. *The Economic Consequences of Mr. Churchill* (1925). This was the first clear statement of Keynes's view that the price of debtor adjustment was mass unemployment. Keynes's insistence in the *Tract* that price stability, rather than exchange stability, should be the aim of (what would now be

---

called) macroeconomic policy rested on the assumption of sticky money wages. "Deflation does not reduce wages 'automatically.' It reduces them by causing unemployment."[22] By 1928, this had become Keynes's standard explanation for the "abnormal" British unemployment of the 1920s: "We have deflated prices by raising the exchange value of sterling and by controlling the volume of credit, *but we have not deflated costs.* The fundamental blunder of the Treasury and Bank of England has been due, from the beginning, to their belief that if they looked after the deflation of prices the deflation of costs would look after itself."[23] The idea that a country's wage system was an exogenously given variable dominates his thinking from this point onward.

5. *A Treatise on Money* (1930) was the first clear statement of Keynes's doctrine of the need for interest rate autonomy. The central object of national monetary policy, as here defined, was not to maintain stable prices, but to maintain a rate of interest consistent with full employment at a price level governed, in the long run, by the behavior of "efficiency wages." Interest rate autonomy, Keynes argued, was incompatible with the gold standard and its corollary of a "laissez-faire attitude to foreign lending." Hence he doubted whether "it is wise to have a currency system with a much wider ambit than our banking system, our tariff system, and our wage system."[24] This was a pretty extreme statement of monetary nationalism, yet Keynes toyed with the idea of a reformed gold standard that would combine the advantages of fixed exchange rates with monetary autonomy. The essential condition was to ensure that countries never had to deflate because of a shortage of gold. As a "minimum" step toward coordinated management of the gold standard, Keynes proposed that all central banks be allowed to hold at least half of their legal reserve requirements in foreign currencies. But the "ideal arrangement would surely be to set up a supernational bank to which the central banks of the world would stand in much the same relation as their own member banks stand to them." The bank would have power to create a fiduciary reserve asset (supernational bank money or SBM) that would count equally with gold as legal reserves of the member banks. It would be able to lend SBM to the central banks of countries in temporary balance of payments difficulties in proportion to their deposits of gold and securities. It would vary the total quantity of SBM (by bank rate and open-market policy) so as to stabilize its value in terms of a tabular standard of the major

22 JMK, CW, IX: 219.
24 JMK, CW, VI: 299.

23 JMK, CW, XIX: 762.

traded commodities and to stabilize the world business cycle.[25] This was the first of Keynes's plans to secure a *compulsory* redistribution of reserves from surplus to deficit countries and to provide *automatic* overdrafts (at a price) for countries in temporary difficulties.

The plan for this ideal standard was sketched out before the gold standard system itself broke up in September 1931. In foreign editions of the *Treatise*, written in late 1931 and early 1932, Keynes reverted to the ideas of the *Tract*, envisaging two blocs, one adhering to a gold standard and the other to a sterling-based currency union. This latter would embrace the British Empire, Japan, South America, Central Europe, and Scandinavia, with a common currency unit (sterling), the value of which would be kept stable within 5 percent of a composite commodity made up of the principal articles of international trade, in a fixed, but not invariable, relationship to gold. The United States, still on the gold standard, would be outside this union. "If, on the other hand, *all* the leading countries were to show themselves disposed . . . to abandon a rigid gold standard and to join in an international scheme of management, drawn up scientifically and without reference to obsolete prejudices, that would be another matter, and I would warmly welcome and explore the possibilities which it would offer."[26]

6. *The Means to Prosperity* (1933) Here Keynes propounded a reflationary variant of the *Treatise of Money*'s "ideal" scheme, aimed explicitly at raising, and thereafter stabilizing, the world price level. An international authority would create additional international reserves by issuing gold certificates to the amount of $5 billion, which all countries would accept as a means of international payment. Each country would receive a quota equal to its gold reserves in 1928, up to a maximum of $450 million. These *caches* of gold certificates would enable their recipients to return to a modified gold standard, with wider bands (Keynes suggested 5 percent) and at adjustable parities; they would renounce exchange restrictions, reduce tariffs, eliminate quotas and embargoes on foreign lending, and write down their debts. In the long run, there should be "an elasticity in the quantity of additional reserves outstanding, so that they would operate not as a net addition to the world's monetary supply, but as a balancing factor to be released when prices were abnormally low as at present, and to be withdrawn again if prices were rising too much."[27] Limiting national quotas to $450 million would secure a redistribution of total reserves, since Britain and four other

25 Ibid., 354–61.   26 JMK, CW, V: xxi–xxii.
27 JMK, CW, IX: 355–64.

countries would receive the same share of additional gold certificates as the United States and France on the basis of much smaller gold stocks. The distribution of additional reserves, Keynes wrote, should "not be of an eleemosynary [i.e., discretionary] character, but should be available, not only to the exceptionally needy, but to all participating countries in accordance with a general formula."[28] That redistribution from creditor to debtor should be compulsory, not discretionary, was the cardinal principle of his Clearing Union plan of 1941. He did not feel the need to emphasize the fact that the formula was set in such a way that Britain just qualified for the maximum of additional reserves.

7. *National Self-Sufficiency* (1933). The general theme of this chapter is that the economic advantage of the international division of labor had been greatly reduced, since "most modern mass production processes can be performed in most countries and climates with almost equal efficiency." But Keynes adduced, as an additional reason for "national self-sufficiency," the desire of nations to be free to experiment with different political and social systems. "We each have our own fancy. Not believing we are saved already, we each would like to have a try at working out our own salvation. We do not wish, therefore, to be at the mercy of world forces working out . . . some uniform equilibrium according to the ideal principles of *laissez-faire* capitalism. . . . We wish . . . to be our own masters, and to be as free as we can make ourselves from the interferences of the outside world."[29] Keynes's insistence, embodied in Article IV, Section 5(f) of the Articles of Agreement of the IMF, that "domestic social or political policies" which create "fundamental disequilibrium" should be immune from Fund criticism, harks back to this line of thought.

8. *The General Theory* (1936). A crucial (some would say *the* crucial) theoretical innovation in this book was Keynes's liquidity preference theory of the rate of interest, which Keynes used to explain why the rate of interest did not "automatically" equilibrate the economy at full employment. It followed that any undue propensity to hoard international reserves (gold) would inflict deflation and unemployment on the world economy as a whole, irrespective of the location of the hoarding, by keeping the world interest rate higher than it should be. This liquidity preference analysis underpinned the conclusion that the accumulation of creditor balances (international liquidity) was to the ultimate detriment of both creditor and

28 Ibid., 358.   29 JMK, CW, XXI: 239–40.

debtor by depressing economic activity in the "closed" economy; and that it is the simultaneous pursuit by all countries together of "the policy of the autonomous rate of interest, unimpeded by international preoccupations, and of a national investment program directed to an optimum level of domestic employment" which is most likely to restore "economic health and strength internationally."[30] This was the theoretical basis of Keynes's Clearing Union plan for automatic creditor adjustment. There is one (congested) passage which gives an indirect explanation, in terms of Keynes's liquidity preference theory of the rate of interest, of why an international system based on gold delivered tolerable results in the nineteenth century:

> The growth of population and of invention, the opening-up of new lands, the state of confidence and the frequency of war over the average (say) of each decade seem to have been sufficient, taken in conjunction with the propensity to consume, to establish a schedule of the marginal efficiency of capital which allowed a reasonably satisfactory level of employment to be compatible with a rate of interest high enough to be psychologically acceptable to wealth-owners.[31]

This, as we can see, is a version of the favorable conjuncture argument. The spontaneous forces making for expansion in the nineteenth century (when?) were sufficiently strong to offset the gold standard's flawed adjustment mechanism. Keynes stated this proposition more precisely in the first draft of his Clearing Union plan. Here he argued that there were only two periods when the use of commodity money in international trade worked – the silver inflation period of the sixteenth century and the gold standard of the late nineteenth century when "the system of international investment pivoting on London transferred the *onus* of adjustment from the debtor to the creditor position." This system of unlimited capital mobility only worked because credit balances flowed into the development of new resources, unlike in the interwar years, where speculative flows dominated investment flows. "To suppose that there is a smooth adjustment which preserves equilibrium if only we trust to methods of *laissez-faire* is a doctrinaire delusion that disregards the lessons of historical experience without having behind it the support of sound theory."[32]

9. The last prewar piece of evidence comes from a letter Keynes wrote to a German correspondent, W. Luck, on October 13, 1936. This came just after the Tripartite Monetary Agreement and conveys Keynes's (and

---

30 JMK, CW, VII: 349.   31 Ibid., 307.
32 JMK, CW, XXV: 21–2, 30–1.

the Treasury's) sense of the limits of what was possible and desirable at that moment:

1. In general I remain in favor of independent national systems with fluctuating exchange rates.
2. Unless, however, a long period is considered, there need be no reason why the exchange rate should in practice be constantly fluctuating.
3. Since there are certain advantages in stability . . . I am entirely in favor of practical measures towards de facto stability so long as there are no fundamental grounds for a different policy.
4. I would even go so far . . . as to give some additional assurance as to the magnitude of the fluctuations which would be normally allowed. . . . Provided there was no actual pledge, I think that in most ordinary circumstances a margin of 10 percent should prove sufficient.
5. I would emphasize that the practicability of stability would depend (i) upon measures to control capital movements, and (ii) the existence of a tendency for broad wage movements to be similar in the different countries concerned.[33]

KEYNES AND SCHACHT

There is one missing piece in the jigsaw: Hjalmar Schacht. In the 1930s, Keynes took no interest in Schacht's system of bilateral clearing agreements, which were designed to free the Nazi government's rearmament program from the balance of payments constraint. It therefore comes as something of a shock to find the early pages of volume twenty-five of the Collected Writings dealing with the origins of the Clearing Union plan full of appreciative references to the "Schachtian system." A little historical background is needed to explain Keynes's appreciation.

When British and German leaders first thought of economic life after the war, it was in terms of the economic and political systems they had built up in the 1930s, consolidated during the war and augmented by victory. They thought, that is, in terms of largely self-sufficient blocs (national or imperial) that traded with third countries on a restricted, reciprocal, basis.

In the 1930s, Britain's sterling area, which was larger than the Empire proper, was not seen as a "closed" system by Keynes or anyone else. Britain was the largest market for all sterling area countries. Without the need for exchange controls or formal embargoes on capital export, it was able to use its buying power to build up sterling balances in London that, by the outbreak of war, came to £500 million – down from their peak in early 1938. Britain was able to balance its accounts with the United States, and

---

33 JMK, CW, XI: 501.

thus maintain exchange rate stability between the pound and the dollar from 1933 to 1938, by running up debt to sterling area countries. After 1938, London was no longer such a safe haven. The withdrawal of short-term funds caused the sterling–dollar exchange to drop to $4.02, where it was fixed soon after the war started. After a slow start, and with considerable prodding from Keynes, the British authorities blocked off all escape routes of foreign exchange from London. Sterling balances were made inconvertible into hard currencies. Bilateral clearing agreements were negotiated with nonsterling neutrals in Europe and Latin America. By the summer of 1940, Britain had adopted the Schachtian system to fight the war. The closed area was open only at one point, but a crucial one: Britain was forced to pay out gold for its growing import bill with the United States. It did so for the first eighteen months of the war.

In the summer of 1940, Hitler was master of Western and Central Europe. As far as he was concerned, the war started in September 1939 was over, Britain's refusal to recognize this fact no more than an awkward detail. As part of his "peace offensive," he authorized his economics minister, Walter Funk, to think out loud about the shape of the postwar economic system. In a rare effort to make Germany's conquests more palatable to its victims, satellites, and European neutrals, Funk announced a "New Order" at a press conference in Berlin on July 25, 1940. It had two elements. Germany and Italy would use their combined productive power to reconstruct Europe after the war. Beyond this, Germany would set up a payments union managed by a central clearing office in Berlin. Within the Union there would be fixed exchange rates and free trade, with any trade imbalances being offset by the clearing office. Trade with outside countries would be regulated by barter agreements. European imports from the United States would exactly balance European exports to the United States. In any case, gold would no longer function as a means of payment, either within the Union or with other countries: America's gold stock would become redundant.[34] The plan was the work of able technocrats in the Reichsbank and Economics Ministry, who in turn might have been influenced by Britain's wartime sterling area arrangements. Hitler, of course, never took the Funk Plan seriously – a warning to historians that political leaders are rarely interested in the schemes of their experts.

The New Order dossier finally arrived on Keynes's desk on November 19, 1940, with a note from Harold Nicolson at the Ministry of Information

---

34 Dormael, *Bretton Woods*, 5–7; see also Harold James, "Post-War German Currency Plans," in Christoph Buchheim, Michael Hutter, and Harold James, eds., *Zerrissene Zwischenkriegszeit: wirtschaftshistorische Beiträge* (Baden-Baden, 1994), 205–18.

asking for his comments on a suggested broadcast designed to discredit it. Keynes immediately wrote back that the proposed broadcast was hopeless: It was no use trying to outflank Funk by offering Europe the blessings of the gold standard. In fact, the Funk plan was "excellent and just what we ourselves ought to be thinking of doing. If it is to be attacked, the way to do it would be to cast doubt and suspicion on its *bona fides*."[35] Following a request from the Foreign Office, Keynes drafted some notes on Britain's economic peace aims for use by the foreign secretary, Lord Halifax. In these, he concentrated on the fraudulence of Funk's reconstruction proposals.[36] Keynes's draft did the rounds of Whitehall, ending up on Churchill's desk on January 30, 1941. Suitably watered down, it became the Foreign Office draft.

Much more important than this propagandist exercise was Keynes's acceptance of the fundamental postulates of Funk's permanent system:

I have assumed [he wrote in a covering note] that we shall continue our existing exchange controls after the war, and that we do not propose to return to *laissez-faire* currency arrangements on pre-war lines by which goods were freely bought and sold internationally in terms of gold or its equivalent. Since we ourselves have very little gold left and will owe great quantities of sterling to overseas creditors, this seems only commonsense. . . . The virtue of free trade depends on international trade being carried on by means of what is, in effect, *barter*. After the last war *laissez-faire* in foreign exchange led to chaos. Tariffs offer no escape from this. But in Germany Schacht and Funk were led by force of necessity to evolve something better. In practice they have used their new system to the detriment of their neighbors. But the underlying idea is sound and good. In the last six months the Treasury and the Bank of England have been building up for this country an exchange system that has borrowed from the German experience all that was good in it. If we are to meet our obligations and avoid chaos in international trade after the war, we shall have to retain this system. But this same system will serve to protect the impoverished European countries and is an essential safeguard against a repetition of what happened last time.[37]

In a letter he wrote to Ashton-Gwatkin of the Foreign Office on April 25, 1941, Keynes expanded on these initial observations, as follows:

(i) Capital exports would be restricted to the case where the capital exporting country had a favorable trade balance with the capital importing country. "Whatever one might wish, something of the sort seems to be inevitable, since we shall no longer have a cushion of gold or other liquid assets, by means of which the immediate effects of unbalanced capital movements can be handled."
(ii) Large elements of multilateral clearing would exist within the Sterling Area, but payments agreements would be required to handle relations between the area and

35 JMK, CW, XXV: 2.   36 Ibid., 12–16.
37 Ibid., 8–9.

the outside world. "Unquestionably [this] would involve a discrimination against the United States if she persisted in maintaining an unbalanced creditor position. Again, whether we like it or not, this will be forced on us. We shall have no means after the war out of which we can pay for purchases in the United States except the equivalent of what they buy from us."

(iii) The exchange rate between sterling and the dollar should be fixed by agreement, but the rate at which it was fixed would no longer be so important. "For, with a proper system of payments agreements which would prevent an unbalanced situation from developing, there would be no longer much object in depreciating the exchange. The method of depreciation is a bad method that one is driven to adopt failing something better. The currency system I have in view would be that something better. If United States inflates more than we do, we might even *appreciate* sterling."

(iv) The postwar sterling area could be extended to countries like Holland and Belgium. But even within the closed area it would still be necessary to guard against an "unbalanced position" of a member country. "There would have to be some arrangement by which an unbalanced position up to an agreed figure would have to be cared for by credit arrangements. But, if the maximum were reached, then the unbalanced debtor would have to restrict its purchases until it was in balance again."

(v) The essence of the system was "trading goods against goods." If Argentina bought maize from Britain, it would have to spend its sterling in Britain or in the Sterling Area. Britain's role as the world's largest importer would give it a huge bargaining power to negotiate payments agreements with outside countries.

(vi) "The difficulty is to know quite how far it is safe to go in the direction of a complete freedom of transactions within the sterling area." If Britain found itself with an adverse balance of payments as a result of countries like Argentina using their export earnings to Britain to buy too many goods from other sterling area countries then "we should have to insist that the Argentine seller of maize must spend his sterling in the United Kingdom."

(vii) The necessity for some such plan as the above arises essentially from the unbalanced creditor position of the United States. It is a necessary condition of a return to free exchanges that the United States should find some permanent remedy for this unbalanced position. Sooner or later one can only suppose that she will have to do so. But it would be very optimistic to believe that she will find the solution in the immediate postwar period, even if she tries to mitigate her task by making large presents for the reconstruction of Europe.[38]

Keynes's letter to Ashton-Gwatkin was a first, very uncertain, bash at his own Clearing Union plan, which he drafted that autumn. It is essentially what his Clearing Union might have looked like *without the United States in it*. The crucial point was the priority given to commercial planning. If trade between the sterling area and the United States was to be on a barter (bilateral clearing) basis, monetary issues like the sterling–dollar exchange

---

38 Ibid., 16–19.

rate and creditor versus debtor adjustment became secondary. It was the inclusion of the United States in the Clearing Union that would make them primary.

It would be a mistake to believe that Keynes was *advocating* a "Schachtian" world for Europe after the war, only one managed by Britain, not Germany. This is to ignore the context in which these ideas were put forward. Until America entered the war at the end of 1941, Keynes could not assume that America would play any part in constructing a new international economic order, one which would provide a "permanent remedy" for its "unbalanced position." The Atlantic Charter was some months ahead; Russia was not yet involved in hostilities. If Britain "won the war" in these circumstances, it would be left responsible for the "economic reorganization of Europe"; or more realistically, it would be left *a deux* with a presumably post-Nazi Germany. An economic settlement would therefore of necessity have to build on the "Schachtian" arrangements of the 1930s, as developed during the war itself; hence, too, the importance Keynes attached to the continuing "*economic* leadership [of Germany] in central Europe."[39]

At the same time, Keynes never thought of Schachtian devices merely as a *pis aller*. Even an "ideal system" which included the United States would not be a return to the gold standard, free trade, and unlimited capital mobility. Equally striking was his refusal to contemplate floating currencies that, on most assumptions, would have provided a complete answer to the problem of short-run payments imbalances. In his reading of interwar history, currency manipulation and tariffs alike were weapons in the "blind struggle" of countries to escape from the shackles of the gold standard, with a tendency to produce war.[40] The Schachtian system (in its "good" sense) avoided this by ensuring that "goods exchanged for goods" not gold.

Keynes's hostility to currency depreciation as an adjustment mechanism also reflected a theoretical unease that comes out in a letter he wrote to Henry Clay on December 5, 1941. He admitted that, if domestic prices and costs were "sticky," currency depreciation could stimulate exports and retard imports. But "the measure of these effects is likely to be much complicated by possible alterations in the terms of trade. A small country in particular may have to accept substantially worse terms for its exports in terms of its imports

---

39 Ibid., 9.
40 JMK, *The General Theory of Employment, Interest and Money*, CW, VII: 348–9. Hubert Henderson agreed: "Of the various expedients which different Governments employed in the 1930s, none produced more unfortunate results than deliberate exchange depreciation. It was the least helpful to countries which tried it, and the most harmful to other countries." Dormael, *Bretton Woods*, 129.

if it tries to force the former by means of exchange depreciation."[41] These lines of thought led Keynes to favor what would now be called wide bands (5 percent or 10 percent) round a central rate in his Clearing Union plan.

Despite some support for "clean" floating by Dennis Robertson, the doctrine that exchange controls were superior to currency depreciation became Treasury and Bank of England orthodoxy. It owed less to Keynes than to general reflection on interwar currency experience, though Keynes may have sharpened these reflections.

ARTICLE VII

Between May and July 1941, Keynes was in Washington negotiating details of Lend–Lease. They do not concern us except insofar as they reveal America's commitment to "creditor voluntarism." Keynes had arrived with an ingenious plan, designed to preserve for Britain a modicum of financial independence. Britain would limit its requirements under Lend–Lease to the bare minimum needed for survival, provided the United States took over responsibility for three months of pre-Lend-Lease orders, by repaying down payments, and meeting the balance owing, out of Lend–Lease appropriations.[42] This would replenish Britain's war chest, which could be used for buying non–American goods and would not cost the United States a penny. Morgenthau flatly refused. He insisted on a smaller war chest and a larger control over British procurements. Eddie Playfair, the British Treasury official attached to the Washington Embassy, summed up the problem: Morgenthau would have responded better to a begging letter. But "Maynard . . . is inclined to ask as of right what they are only prepared to give as a favour."[43]

Keynes had another shock when Acheson handed him, on July 28, a draft of the Lend-Lease Agreement, Article VII of which pledged Britain, in "consideration" for Lend–Lease, to end all discrimination against American goods and to formulate measures for the achievement of this aim. Article VII ruled out a continuation both of the wartime Schachtian sterling system and the prewar Ottawa Preference system. Keynes's explosive reaction had been amply documented. But Britain was trapped, unless it was prepared to scale down its war effort sufficiently to risk imminent defeat or a forced peace with Germany. The Clearing Union Plan was Keynes's attempt to set out the conditions that would enable Britain to meet American requirements.

41 T 247/116.   42 JMK, CW, XXIII: 74–7.
43 E. Playfair to S. G. Waley, May 16, 1941, T.175/121.

THE UPSHOT

Keynes wrote the first draft of his Clearing Union scheme in September 1941, drawing both on his prewar plans for an "ideal standard" and on Britain's de facto wartime system. He was persuaded by James Meade to temper his advocacy of controlled trade. On December 14, 1941, Morgenthau instructed his director of monetary research, Harry Dexter White, to draw up a plan for an Inter-Allied Stabilization Fund. Finalized three months later, White's plan provided for a Reconstruction Bank and a Stabilization Fund. The latter was modeled on the Exchange Equalisation Funds operated by both Britain and the United States in the 1930s. But instead of each country operating its own stabilization account as under the Tripartite Agreement, there would be a pooled fund. The two plans, endlessly redrafted, were exchanged in August 1942 and simultaneously published on April 7, 1943. In October 1943, a "Joint Statement by Experts of the United States and Associated Nations" accepted the White framework. After further modifications, the "Joint Statement" was published in April 1944. This was the prelude to the Bretton Woods Conference itself, with the Final Act signed by the representatives of forty-four nations on July 22, to universal acclamation, followed, over the next few months, by general ratification.

Keynes's Clearing Union was intended as a comprehensive alternative to Britain's discriminatory trading system of the 1930s. The main condition Keynes set for a return to "a liberal economic system" was the "creation of international credit" by a World Bank in which all central bank members of the Union would keep accounts for settling international balances. Every member country account would start off with a stock of reserves proportioned to its importance in world trade – equivalent to the "caches of gold certificates," now called "bancor," which Keynes had advocated in 1933. Just as a country's domestic banking system creates deposits by means of overdraft facilities, so the World Bank would provide member states with automatic overdraft facilities equal to their "quotas." Accounts in debit would be cleared, or settled, by automatic transfers (up to the agreed quotas) from accounts in credit. Interest would be charged on credit and debit balances above a quarter of the member states' quotas, and there were to be agreed provisions for revaluation and devaluation of currencies and other measures. The aim of these was to exert a symmetric pressure toward balance of payments adjustment. Because the country members' quotas were set at half the prewar value of their foreign trade – a formula that favored the British – the total resources of the Clearing Union would be very large – up to $40 billion. The principle of automatic creditor adjustment was to be applied to a large range of activities. The Clearing Union was to be an all-encompassing institution – an embryo world government run on formulaic principles. It was meant to finance not just short-term imbalances, but relief, reconstruction, investment, buffer stocks, even a world police force. Members would bind themselves to pursue liberal trade policies. The credit mechanism built into the Clearing Union was a straightforward application of Keynes's liquidity-preference theory of the rate of interest. The basic political thinking behind it was a desire to multilateralize hegemonic functions that Britain had performed before World War I, but which it did not trust or *want* the United States to perform.

The White Plan for an International Monetary Fund comes out of a very different intellectual atmosphere. Fixed exchange rates were to be virtually immutable; members' quotas represented subscribed capital not credit; the total of quotas, worked out according to a different formula, was designed to limit the Fund's resources to $5 billion, and the American liability to $2 billion. The Fund's short-term lending facility was seen as supplementary to the normal settling of international balances through transfers of gold and foreign exchange, and was not intended to be automatic. Keynes saw it as a combination of the Tripartite Agreement and U.S. Stabilization Fund principles.[44] The wider functions envisaged for the Clearing Union were dropped or hived off to separate institutions: an International Bank for Reconstruction and Development (which formed part of the Bretton Woods Agreement) and an International Trade Organization (which foundered). White's plan did not foresee "global" liquidity-preference as a problem. And it rested unashamedly on a hegemonic outlook, with the dollar as the key currency.

The Bretton Woods Agreement reflected the American position. During the negotiations, the Americans made some concessions to the British view: The resources of the Fund, and America's liability, were somewhat increased (from $5 billion to $8.8 billion and from $2 billion to $2.75 billion, respectively); adjustment of exchange rates in situations of "fundamental disequilibrium" was allowed, if the Fund agreed; domestic policies resulting in "fundamental disequilibrium" were immune from criticism; the "scarce currency clause" allowed members to introduce exchange controls against the "scarce" currency; and an indefinite "post-war transitional period" was agreed before the System became operational. However, no attempt was made to define "fundamental disequilibrium," nor who should decide when it existed; neither the right to devalue nor access to quotas was to be

---

44 JMK, "The Berle Memorandum," Feb. 18, 1943, T.160/1281/F 188885/1.

unconditional. On the central issue of creditor versus debtor adjustment, the British made little progress. As White put it: "We have been perfectly adamant on that point. We have taken the position of absolutely no . . . (to the British demands)."[45]

Thus, the agreement did not alter the fundamental realities of prewar monetary relations. Keynes and the British had not succeeded in binding the United States to the principle of involuntary creditor adjustment. The Agreement upheld, in modified form, the principle of compulsory debtor adjustment; the modification consisting in extending the escape clauses that had existed under the gold standard, and subjecting their exercise to agreed rules. Once Britain had failed to win Keynes's main point, belief that the system would help it overcome the "dollar gap," either in the short term or long term, rapidly faded. The Bank of England was adamant that Britain should retain exchange controls and the Sterling Area; the Imperialists, led by Beaverbrook, insisted on maintaining the Ottawa Preference System. British support for the Fund idea cooled noticeably in the six months leading up to the Bretton Woods conference: All the pressure came from the United States to conclude an agreement, while the British dragged their feet as opposition developed in the Cabinet.[46] In the United States, the New York bankers were unreconciled to what they saw as the transfer of control over American foreign lending from the private sector to the Washington administration. They supported the so-called key currency proposal put forward by Professor John H. Williams, Harvard economist and vice president of the Federal Reserve Bank of New York, which aimed to stabilize the exchange rate between the two major reserve currencies, the dollar and sterling, by means of a large bilateral grant or loan to Britain. Williams saw this as the key to a general return to a gold-exchange standard. With the retirement of Morgenthau, the discrediting of White, and the general fading of the New Deal after Roosevelt's death in 1945, the "key currency" approach, rather than the multilateralism of Bretton Woods, came to dominate U.S. monetary policy. In particular, it provided "a substantial part of the intellectual underpinning" of the Anglo-American Loan agreement of 1946 and the Marshall Plan of 1947.[47]

Keynes continued to support his own handiwork, but even his enthusiasm cooled once the interpreters got to work. No sooner was the Agreement signed than Keynes and White had a major row over the conditions under which a country would have the right to impose exchange controls. By

---

45 Dormael, *Bretton Woods*, 171.   46 See ibid., chaps. 11, 12.
47 James, *International Monetary Cooperation*, 66.

September 1944, Keynes himself was expressing doubts about whether Britain should ratify the Agreement.[48] In December, he favored the suggestion of "responsible" American opposition that "the Fund should be postponed until we can see our way more clearly."[49] In April 1945, he was "particularly interested" in Edward Bernstein's suggestion that "the transition period might never in fact be formally brought to an end." This, he thought, might be the "best way" of resolving the problem that had arisen.[50] Whether Britain would have ratified the Agreement at all had acceptance not been made a condition of the American Loan of 1946 remains an open question.

CONCLUSION

The British started by championing the principle of a symmetry of compulsion; they were reduced to arguing for the principle of a symmetry of discretion. Having started the process with an ambitious plan for a world economic government, Keynes spent his waning energies fighting for a postponement of the coming into operation of the system, escape clauses designed to preserve British monetary independence, and eleemosynary American help on a bilateral basis. As for the United States, its insistence on creditor voluntarism greatly limited the resources it was willing to make available to Fund and Bank unconditionally. It set about reconstructing a liberal economic system, on a dollar basis, outside the Bretton Woods framework.

It would be wrong to conclude that nothing had changed. The 1950s and 1960s were not like the 1920s and 1930s. Exchange rates were gradually stabilized, and currency convertibility slowly reestablished. This promoted trade liberalization, which in turn fueled economic growth. But this favorable evolution had little to do with the Bretton Woods Agreement. The crucial shift that separated the postwar from the prewar years was the ending of America's political isolation. This came three years after the Agreement – with Marshall Aid, OEEC, NATO, and parallel initiatives in East Asia. Had it not been rescued by the Cold War, the Bretton Woods Agreement might have remained a historical curiosity – like the Funk Plan and other long-forgotten schemes for monetary union. In the face of the perceived communist threat, the United States took responsibility for underwriting the security of much of the noncommunist world. This released American money on a scale never imagined by the architects of the Bretton Woods system and lubricated the liberalization of trade and payments which

48 Dormael, *Bretton Woods*, 228; JMK, CW, XXVI: 134.
49 JMK, CW, XXVI: 147.   50 Dormael, *Bretton Woods*, 237.

Bretton Woods itself could never have achieved. But the cost of a largely discretionary system was a hubris that ultimately destroyed it.

The ultimate irony is that although the United States "won" the battle of Bretton Woods, the Cold War "compelled" it to run down its excessive credit balances via the Marshall Plan and later other foreign aid and military defense programs. In other words, the United States acted "as if" it had accepted the creditor compulsion principle of Keynes's "bancor" plan. American actions were twice blessed in the sense that for the first time there was no severe recession after war in American history, and that the war-devastated nations of Western Europe and Japan could rebuild their economic systems at a rate that would not have been possible had America continued to accumulate surplus balances.

Despite their irrelevance, the Bretton Woods institutions – the International Monetary Fund and the World Bank – survived the objects they were set up to serve. The IMF's central function, support of fixed nominal exchange rates, was rendered superfluous by the collapse of the fixed exchange rate system between 1971 and 1973. The World Bank's function has been marginalized by the resumption of private capital flows. Although Milton Friedman has called for the abolition of the IMF, its short-term future seems relatively secure as crisis manager, guru to marketizing economies, and lender of last resort. These remnants of the Grand Design may still have a part to play in the monetary arrangements of the next century.

6

Bretton Woods and the European Neutrals, 1944–1973

JAKOB TANNER

In July 1944, when the Bretton Woods conference took place, though the war was not over, there was no doubt who would win it. The efforts of the wartime coalition (the United Nations) concentrated on building up a new postwar order, one able to combine peaceful interaction between states, social change, and economic growth. The conference at Bretton Woods aimed at an international financial system under the umbrella of the *Pax Americana* that would be able to guarantee the stability of a restored and improved version of the pre-1914 gold standard and, beyond it, to increase the scope for autonomous national economic policies in every country that joined the system. The two main institutional pillars of the new order were fixed exchange rates and – in the long term – free currency markets based on current account convertibility. In order to meet these two contradictory goals, the architects of the Bretton Woods System decided to introduce a gold–dollar standard. This system combined a sufficient built-in flexibility for the specific economic goal of every member state and a standardized procedure for realignment of the exchange rates in the case of "fundamental" asymmetries in the balance of payments.[1]

In this context, the European neutrals and nonbelligerent countries had to adjust their policies. This chapter analyzes the way this group, which encompasses Sweden, Switzerland, Portugal, Spain, and Turkey (albeit with a somewhat different and peculiar status), coped with new problems. Special attention is focused on Switzerland, the only country which preserved the

---

1 The founding and development of the Bretton Woods financial order and institutions are described in *Proceedings and Documents of the United Nations Monetary and Financial Conference*, Bretton Woods N.H., July 1–22, 1944 (Washington, D.C., 1948); *World Bank and International Monetary Fund: Basic Documents/Weltbankgruppe und Internationaler Währungsfonds: Gründungsdokumente*, ed. Martina Ernst et al., on behalf of the Landesverbandes Berlin der Deutschen Gesellschaft für die Vereinten Nationen, vol. 2 (Berlin, 1988).

convertibility of its currency (the Swiss franc) throughout the war and which played an important role for both the Axis Powers and the Allies. Whereas the political decision process which ended up with the Bretton Woods System confronted the neutral states with analogous challenges, the economic growth of the postwar period brought other factors to the fore. Apparently, neutrality did not help in dealing with currency problems of the reconstruction period. Already by the beginning of the 1950s, neutrality had lost its importance as a decisive determinant in an explanatory model of economic policy. Since the 1960s, a trade-off between transnational market integration and state sovereignty can be observed. The support of globalization by the national states, which saw a part of their power in economic policy eroding, makes this development paradoxical.[2]

FROM THE STARTING POINT IN 1944 TO THE BREAKDOWN IN 1971–1973

As Robert Solomon pointed out, this new international monetary system was composed of a set of arrangements, rules, practices, and institutions under which payments were made and received for transactions carried out across national boundaries. Nonetheless, the new order was "not fully international" (since the Soviet Union and the People's Republic of China, among other countries, did not participate). "It was 'broader than monetary,' and less formal than a fully coherent system."[3] Therefore the notion "international monetary system" proved to be a semantic approximation of the modus operandi of the "system." As a consequence, an explanatory model is obliged to differentiate between the blueprint and the working version of the Bretton Woods System.

It was also due to this pragmatic construction that, after some initial difficulties, the international monetary system of Bretton Woods worked as a quite effective monetary framework for a rapid socioeconomic recovery and subsequent accelerated economic growth which was the outstanding feature of the postwar period up to the 1970s. The European neutrals took part in

2 Eric Helleiner, *States and the Reemergence of Global Finance: From Bretton Woods to the 1990s* (Ithaca, N.Y., 1994), 91ff.
3 Robert Solomon, *The International Monetary System, 1945–1981*, 2d. updated and expanded ed. (1977; reprint, New York, 1982), 5; see also Harold James, *International Monetary Cooperation Since Bretton Woods* (Washington, D.C., 1996); Margaret Garritsen de Vries, *The IMF in a Changing World, 1945–1985* (Washington, D.C, 1986); Fred L. Block, *The Origins of International Economic Disorder: A Study of United States International Monetary Policy from World War II to the Present* (Berkeley, Calif., 1977); Kenneth W. Dam, *The Rules of the Game: Reform and Evolution in the International Monetary System* (Chicago, 1982); Armand van Dormael, *Bretton Woods: Birth of a Monetary Order* (New York, 1978); Hans Aufricht, *The International Monetary Fund. Legal Bases, Structure, Functions* (London, 1964); Richard N. Cooper, *The Economics of Interdependence* (New York, 1968).

this general development. The success must be interpreted in the context of other institutions, especially the Marshall Plan/European Recovery Program (ERP) and the Organization for European Economic Cooperation (OEEC, later transformed into OECD). It was connected with a significant power shift toward the United States as the now dominant protagonist in international affairs. Since the U.S. dollar was the major reserve currency in the newly created system, the United States had "enormous power in the fund"[4] and was able to finance its growing deficit in the balance of payments in the 1960s by printing money. This advantage was directly linked to the productivity lead of the United States and the hegemonic position of the former "Arsenal of Democracy" in the new world order. Europe was divided by the rising superpowers, and the neutral or nonbelligerent countries of the wartime period (Switzerland, Sweden, Spain, Turkey) were integrated in its western half. The more both parts of the Old World became internally stabilized by the antagonistic structure of the bipolar Cold War competition, the more the neutrals had to find a new place in the Western Hemisphere that was not compatible with equidistance between East and West.

In the first years, the rapid economic recovery of Western Europe was paralleled by a severe dollar shortage that declined according to the extent the United States financed its military expenditures by deficits and lost its productivity lead due to massive American direct investments in Europe already in 1950.[5] At the end of that decade, monetary diagnoses varied considerably. Those countries such as Switzerland or the Federal Republic of Germany that had balance of payments problems up to the early 1950s very soon held that international liquidity was sufficient and that the Americans should restrict their surplus expenditure. On the other hand, the countries with deficits continued to argue that the dollar gap was of dangerous proportions.[6] This debate coincided with the introduction of convertibility. In December 1958, fourteen Western European countries, later followed by fifteen others, made their currencies externally convertible on current account.[7] On this basis, the 1960s saw the take-off of financial globalization. Both currency convertibility and the abolishment of multilateral monetary controls kicked off short-term capital movements which produced severe destabilizing effects. In order to preserve their policy autonomy, the states experiencing disequilibrating speculative capital outflows continued to maintain

---

4 Block, *Origins*, 179.   5 Cooper, *Economics of Interdependence*, 81ff.
6 Henner Kleinewefers, *Inflation und Inflationsbekämpfung in der Schweiz* (Frauenfeld, 1976), 87–8.
7 John Keith Horsefield, ed., *The International Monetary Fund, 1945–1965: Twenty Years of International Monetary Cooperation*, 3 vols. (Washington, D.C., 1969), 2: 277.

some unilateral capital controls and to build up extensive offsetting financing networks.[8]

Already in the early 1960s, the Bank for International Settlements and the International Monetary Fund tried likewise to neutralize these threats to the system. In the spring of 1961, the BIS initiated the Basel convention in which reciprocal currency agreements were put into action.[9] These procedures were considered to be temporary and should be replaced by more permanent techniques for dealing with the problems of international financial disequilibria.[10] In February 1962, the Swap-credit-network was consolidated with a new agreement. In October 1961, the London Gold Pool was created by the Federal Reserve System, the Bank of England, the central banks of the five member states of the European Economic Community (EEC) and the Swiss National Bank. But these measures did not address the "underlying problems in the Bretton Woods system, problems which stemmed from the heavy reliance on the dollar as the main source of international liquidity; from the reluctance of countries to change par values until the last minute; and from the delays in adjusting domestic policies, particularly among countries with persistent deficits." In this situation, the IMF launched the idea of the General Agreements to Borrow (GAB), which were based on the Articles of Agreement of July 22, 1944.[11] When the basic concept was approved, the Managing Director of the IMF, Per Jacobsson, stated: "We have saved the monetary system for the next generation!"[12] While the question whether international liquidity was sufficient remained controversial, the GAB was put into operation in 1962 as part of Jacobsson's "pragmatic package of measures aimed at strengthening the Fund's resources in the aftermath of convertibility."[13] In the following

---

8 Helleiner, *States and the Reemergence*, 96ff.

9 According to Fred Block (*Origins*, 177–81), the American Robert Roosa, Undersecretary of the Treasury, played a decisive role in strengthening international financial cooperation. The Basel Agreement is described in P. Rushing, "The Reciprocal Currency Arrangements," *New England Economic Review* (Nov.–Dec. 1972): 3–15; Horsefield, ed., *International Monetary Fund*, 1: 483; Fred Hirsch, *Money International* (London, 1967), 243; Erin E. Jacobsson, *A Life for Sound Money: Per Jacobsson, His Biography* (Oxford, 1979), chap. 8, "The General Arrangements to Borrow," 358–85.

10 Horsefield, ed., *International Monetary Fund*, 1: 483.

11 Horsefield, ed., *International Monetary Fund*, 3: 194ff; Dam, *Rules of the Game*, 142–8; Block, *The Origins*, 178–9. Both authors emphasized the diverging positions among the participating countries. Whereas the United States and Britain advocated enhanced international liquidity, several European countries (France, Germany) did not see any need for action. See Michael Ainley, *The General Arrangements to Borrow*, IMF Pamphlet Series, no. 41 (Washington, D.C., 1984), 4.

12 Jacobsson, *Life for Sound Money*, 385.

13 This is a quote form Per Jacobsson's address at the IMF Executive Board, Feb. 10, 1961. See Ainley, *General Arrangements*, 6. Horsefield, ed., *International Monetary Fund*, 1: 502–3; Joseph Gold, *The Fund and Non-Member States. Some Legal Effects*, IMF Pamphlet Series, no. 7 (Washington, D.C., 1966); Joseph Gold, *Membership and Nonmembership in the International Monetary Fund. A Study in International Law and Organization* (Washington, D.C., 1974); Joseph Gold, *International Capital Movements Under*

years, the rise of the Euro-dollar market made clear that neither the United States nor the most important European national economies were willing to impose new regulations on the rapidly growing transnational financial markets. This expansion was driven also by increasing tensions which pro-voked a crisis after 1968 and finally led to the collapse of the Bretton Woods System in the years between 1971 and 1973.[14]

The following section deals with the attitude of the neutral countries to the creation of the Bretton Woods institutions, and aims at explaining why they applied for membership and how they were integrated in the sys-tem. This group of countries (Sweden, Switzerland, Portugal, Spain, and Turkey) was not invited to the conference at Bretton Woods and could join the new body only after January 1, 1946. In the eyes of the Allied Powers, neutrality was considered to be an excuse for rather than a solution to the main difficulties of the postwar period. Moreover, the neutrals' loss of credibility was aggravated by the interrelated facts that neutral countries were relatively small and were characterized by a comparatively high quota of foreign trade. They had therefore to cope even harder with the ten-sion between national economic policy and transnational economic inter-dependency, which was reflected by deficits and surpluses in the balance of payments.

A historical analysis demonstrates that being neutral is not a fixed approach to foreign policy. Although neutrality was (and is) in some countries, es-pecially Switzerland, deeply rooted in the mentality of the population, this status can be very flexible and it depends also on the interests of powerful "neighbors" and other nations which may interfere in an indirect way in the foreign policy of small countries.[15] So the group of neutral countries underwent considerable changes in the years since 1945. Turkey, for ex-ample, entered the war on the side of the Allies in February 1945 and was no longer a neutral country just a few months before the end of the war. In 1949, Portugal was a founding member of NATO, thereby leaving the group of European neutrals. On the other hand, Europe saw the emergence

the *Law of the International Monetary Fund*, IMF Pamphlet Series, no. 21 (Washington, D.C., 1977); Joseph Gold, *Legal and Institutional Aspects of the International Monetary System. Selected Essays*, ed. Jane B. Evensen and Jai Keun Oh, 2 vols. (Washington, D.C., 1979–84); Joseph Gold, "The General Arrangements to Borrow of the International Monetary Fund," in Wolfram Engels, Armin Gutowski, and Henry C. Wallich, eds., *International Capital Movements, Debt and Monetary System/Internationale Kapitalbewegungen, Verschuldung und Währungssystem: Essays in Honour of Wilfried Guth* (Mainz, 1984), 135–69.

14 Victor Argy, *The Postwar International Money Crisis: An Analysis* (London, 1981), 60ff; Dam, *Rules of the Game*, 175ff.

15 Jakob Tanner, "Die internationalen Finanzbeziehungen der Schweiz zwischen 1930 und 1950," *Schweizerische Zeitschrift für Geschichte* 47, no. 4 (1997): 492–519.

of new neutrals: In 1948, Finland had no other choice than to accept a Friendship and Mutual Assistance Pact with the USSR, which made it a de facto neutral. In the same year, Yugoslavia, which was a neutral up to 1940 and then occupied by the German Wehrmacht, moved away from the Eastern bloc and started to be "bloc-free." Austria became a neutral in 1955, officially designed on the model of Switzerland.

Despite a severe shortage of currency reserves and economic difficulties, most of the neutral countries were eager to join the Bretton Woods institutions. Sweden became a member in August 1951, Spain in September 1958 (with the introduction of external convertibility). Portugal, now part of NATO, had to wait for another one and a half years and was accepted in March 1961. Countries that had not been neutral before the Cold War era had joined the Bretton Woods institutions even earlier: Finland and Austria entered in 1948.[16] Austria, which had lost all its currency reserves by the end of the war, was forced to maintain a strict regime of foreign exchange control which contradicted some of the basic assumptions of the Bretton Woods Order and was only gradually relaxed in the 1950s.[17]

In this group of neutral countries, Switzerland must be treated as a special case due to its strong and freely convertible currency.[18] In the long run, the competitive advantage of the Swiss financial center was based on a combination of an old banking tradition with a protective legal framework (banking secrecy) and a highly developed banking system. After the outbreak of World War II, the most competitive big banks became more and more international, a development that was accelerated by the deregulation of financial markets after 1945. Because of this liquid capital market, Switzerland was expected to become an efficient financial supporter for countries under

16 Both countries made their application in 1947; in the case of Austria, this was eight years before the State Treaty of 1955, while in the case of Finland it coincided with the treaty with the USSR of 1948. Horsefield, ed., *International Monetary Fund*, 1: 163, 196, 257, 443, 474.

17 Hanns Abele and Ewald Nowotny et al., *Handbuch der österreichischen Wirtschaftspolitik* (Mainz, 1982), 18.

18 See Werner Rings, *Raubgold aus Deutschland: Die "Golddrehscheibe" Schweiz im Zweiten Weltkrieg* (Zurich, 1985); Jakob Tanner, *Bundeshaushalt, Währung und Kriegswirtschaft: Eine finanzsoziologische Analyse der Schweiz zwischen, 1938–1953* (Zurich, 1986); Markus Heiniger, *Dreizehn Gründe: Warum die Schweiz im Zweiten Weltkrieg nicht erobert wurde* (Zurich, 1989); Gian Trepp, *Bankgeschäfte mit dem Feind: Die Bank für Internationalen Zahlungsausgleich im Zweiten Weltkrieg: Von Hitlers Europabank zum Instrument des Marshallplans* (Zurich, 1993); Marco Durrer, *Die schweizerisch-amerikanischen Finanzbeziehungen im Zweiten Weltkrieg: Von der Blockierung der schweizerischen Guthaben in den USA über die "Safehaven" – Politik zum Washingtoner Abkommen (1941–1946)* (Bern, 1984); Marc Perrenoud, "Banques et diplomatie suisses à la fin de la Deuxième Guerre mondiale: Politique de neutralité et relations financières internationals," *Studien und Quellen*, ed. Schweizerisches Bundesarchiv, nos. 13–14 (Bern, 1987–8), 7–128; Linus von Castelmur, *Schweizerisch-alliierte Finanzbeziehungen im Übergang vom Zweiten Weltkrieg zum Kalten Krieg: Die deutschen Guthaben in der Schweiz zwischen Zwangsliquidierung und Freigabe (1945–1952)* (Zurich, 1992).

reconstruction and also for the World Bank.[19] The state and private sectors contributed 2.4 billion Swiss francs to the economic reconstruction of the heavily destroyed European economies.[20]

This relatively generous help from Switzerland after the war resulted from a mixture of commercial self-interest and informal "reparation" for strongly criticized war profits. After 1942, Switzerland was confronted with growing reproaches. The closer the victory of the Allies, the harsher the criticism the neutral country had to endure because of its profit-oriented and security-driven industrial and financial cooperation with the Third Reich. At first Switzerland found itself together with other neutrals. With Sweden, Spain, Portugal, and Turkey, all countries that did not belong to the United Nations camp, Switzerland fell under suspicion as a go-between that had engaged in dubious dealings with the enemy. In the summer of 1941, the Allied economic war was extended to the international financial market and consequently to the neutral countries, and Switzerland in particular. By freezing all their assets in June 1941 and by putting suspicious firms on blacklists, the Allies made the neutrals in general an important target of an economic war effort.[21] After the turning point of the war in 1943, the strategy of the Allied powers relied upon two complementary aims: the final destruction of the German war potential and the construction of a stable peace. These measures resulted in an economic espionage program named *Safehaven*, which was drawn up by American agents. At the same time, Britain proposed that the neutral countries should be warned that assets from Germany or territories occupied by Germany were bought and traded at their own risk. One of the major concerns of the Allies at that time was the looted gold the German Reichsbank had shipped to Switzerland.[22] Already in 1942, the British had broadcast warnings to Switzerland. On January 5, 1943, the first declaration making reference to the looted gold, which was supported by the United Nations, was issued. A year later, in February 1944, this warning was renewed in unmistakable language.[23]

In view of the close Swiss economic involvement with Germany, the attention of the Allies was focused more and more on the gold and financial transactions. These topics were discussed in the third commission of the

19 See Hans Bachmann, *Die Konventionen von Bretton Woods: Internationaler Währungsfonds und Internationale Bank für den Wiederaufbau: Mit Übersetzungen der Vertragstexte* (St. Gallen, 1945).
20 Walter Spahni, *Der Ausbruch der Schweiz aus der Isolation nach dem Zweiten Weltkrieg* (Frauenfeld, 1977), 476.
21 Durrer, *Die schweizerisch-amerikanischen Finanzbeziehungen.*
22 Independent Commission of Experts Switzerland – Second World War (ICE), *Switzerland and Gold Transactions in the Second World War* (Bern, 1998).
23 Arthur L. Smith, *Hitler's Gold: The Story of the Nazi War Loot* (Oxford, 1989), 64–5.

Bretton Woods conference ("Other means of international financial co-operation"). When the conference met in July 1944, there were already reports that Germany had begun to transfer its assets abroad to find a "safe haven." So the Allied Powers proposed an international action to discourage neutral nations from allowing enemy countries to transfer or conceal assets outside the reach of the probable winners. If such a German operation was successful, a number of the Allies feared that another generation of Nazis would employ the hidden resources to launch another quest for world dom-ination. Before the delegates met at Bretton Woods, the United States had already begun to discuss the "safe haven" problem with neutrals, and, with encouragement from the French and Polish delegations, the United States successfully sponsored resolution VI calling on neutral nations to take ap-propriate measures that would prevent the disposition of looted gold and the concealment of enemy assets.[24]

THE BRETTON WOODS CONFERENCE AS A CHALLENGE
FOR SWITZERLAND

At the Breton Woods conference, grave reproaches were heaped on Switzerland. A secret report on the conference, written by the journal-ist Walter Bosshard from the *Neue Zürcher Zeitung*, dated August 3, 1944, mentioned the skeptical, if not openly hostile, attitude of many delegates to-ward the Swiss. The proposals made "in respect of the problematic German, Italian and Japanese financial assets in neutral countries as well as questions concerning gold reserves, securities and objects of art were unmistakably directed against Switzerland . . . as the country of refuge for vast quantities of assets of German origin, stolen gold and currency, securities unjustly ac-quired, as well as objects of art from occupied territories." Bosshard spoke of "so-called factual evidence" but had to admit that "this documentary evidence did not shed a very good light on the activities of certain Swiss banks and financial institutions and proves at the same time how efficiently the Allies' economic espionage worked."[25]

---

24 Alfred E. Eckes, Jr., *A Search for Solvency: Bretton Woods and the International Monetary System, 1941–1971* (Austin, Tex., 1975), 153.
25 B. (Walter Bosshard), Bericht über die Finanz- und Währungs-Konferenz von Bretton Woods, N.H., 1.–23. Juli 1944, Vertraulich und nicht zur Veröffentlichung bestimmt, New York, Aug. 3, 1944, in Schweizerische Gesandtschaft in den USA an das EPD, Washington 7. 8. 1944, Swiss Federal Archives E 2001 (D), -/3, vol. 499, pp. 24–5. See also Madeleine Herren, " 'Weder so noch anders': Schweizerischer Internationalismus während des Zweiten Weltkrieges," in "Die Schweiz und der Zweite Weltkrieg," special issue of *Schweizerische Zeitschrift für Geschichte* 47, no. 4 (1997): 621–43, 642ff.

The proposed measures to deal with the enemies' assets ranged from blocking and certification to the restitution of stolen gold, currency, works of art, and other items. The board of the Swiss National Bank stated that some of the above points "had already been realized." They did not, however, wish to comment on the other mainly political issues, in spite of the fact that in their aide-mémoire of August 23, 1944, the Allies issued further clear warnings to Switzerland.[26] The small neutral state was called upon in its "own interest" to refrain in the future from all further gold transactions with Germany and its allies.

Although the British were opposed, saying that this question had little bearing on topics that the conference was summoned to consider, resolution VI gained widespread approval. It committed the United Nations "to do their utmost to defeat the methods of dispossession."[27] One further measure was to propose that an Allied mission should be sent into Switzerland for direct negotiations, which took place in the beginning of 1945 and was, according to its head Lauchlin Currie, referred to as the "Currie Mission."[28] In February, all German assets in Switzerland were frozen. One year after this mission, negotiations in Washington followed concerning the restitution of stolen gold and the confiscation of the German assets in Switzerland. They ended with a compromise. The financial agreement of May 1946 contains the obligation of dividing the liquidated German assets with the Allies in favor of the Inter Allied Reparations Agency signatory states. In addition to that, Switzerland agreed to pay 250 million Swiss francs for the purpose of reconstruction in Europe.[29] In return, the Allies ended the blacklists; furthermore, the United States released the frozen assets by means of a certification procedure.[30] This was an important step toward the normalization of relations between the United States and the politically isolated neutral.

Switzerland was also involved in the debates in Bretton Woods, because the headquarters of the Bank for International Settlements (BIS) was located in Basel.[31] The BIS was an agency that had been created in 1930 to manage the payment of German reparations from World War I. In the interwar period, this bank became an important forum for central bank cooperation, bringing together the representatives of central banks and large American banks. Arthur L. Smith stated that "the close working relationship that the

26 Aide-mémoire Erwerb feindlichen Goldes durch die Schweiz vom 23. 8. 1944, Archive Swiss National Bank, B3/117.8 I.
27 *Proceedings and Documents*, 939.
28 Durrer, *Die schweizerisch-amerikanischen Finanzbeziehungen*.
29 ICE, *Switzerland and Gold Transactions*, 185ff; due to changing conditions, the agreement was fulfilled in a quite different way. See von Castelmur, *Schweizerisch-alliierte Finanzbeziehungen*.
30 ICE, *Switzerland and Gold Transactions*, 188.   31 Trepp, *Bankgeschäfte mit dem Feind*.

BIS enjoyed with Swiss banks, especially the Swiss National Bank headed by Ernst Weber, a member of the BIS directorate, virtually made Swiss banking policies at times indistinguishable from those of BIS."[32]

As a result of growing criticism because of the presumptive collaboration of the BIS with Nazi Germany, its future became one of the most controversial items of the conference at Bretton Woods. Due to a Norwegian initiative, the very existence of the BIS was threatened. In his report, Bosshard wrote that many of the financial experts attending the conference had the opinion that "Swiss neutrality was only a cover up behind which all sorts of dubious business was transacted."[33] Despite some resistance from Keynes and J. W. Beyen (leader of the Dutch delegation and himself a former president of the BIS), the conference approved a resolution calling for liquidation of the BIS "at the earliest possible moment." Bosshard's comment was that this decision "can . . . hardly be stopped."[34] The fact that the proposal was not carried out was due above all to delaying tactics, the outbreak of the Cold War, and the still indispensable role of the BIS in achieving co-operation between the central banks. The Bretton Woods resolution in fact contained no specific date by which the BIS should be liquidated.

Bosshard's report from August 1944 criticizes the Swiss government for having missed the opportunity of sending a "competent personality" to the conference who could have made clear the country's position. He then quoted a representative of the Bank of England who said, according to Bosshard's paraphrase, "Switzerland will never accept the proposals of Bretton Woods as they contain conditions which are too contrary to our economic and financial tradition." In addition, he stated that "our country was offered the unique possibility of becoming the center of the financial black market of Europe, even the whole world." With a similar argument, Dutch representatives contended that "by keeping Switzerland apart, this country would become a haven for foreign capital and consequently a 'black stock exchange.'"[35]

Bosshard then observed that conviction was gaining ground that "after this war neutrality in the past sense will no longer be acknowledged and at the very most will further be tolerated as "humane neutrality."[36] There were, however, strong forces at work to undermine the reputation of Switzerland in this area, too. In general, the question was asked "whether our country is at all interested in international organizations." This question was prompted by

32 Smith, *Hitler's Gold*, 60.
33 Bosshard, *Bericht über die Finanz- und Währungs-Konferenz*, 24.
34 Ibid., 23.   35 Ibid., 27.
36 Ibid., 28.

the "total silence of our government to date."[37] After a few harsh opinions on the directors of the SNB ("The elderly men of the Board still hold opinions of the nineteenth century and often did not know themselves what they wanted"), Bosshard came to the interesting conclusion "that Switzerland can play a unique role in the building up of Europe if it succeeds in overcoming the difficulties in obtaining raw material." The future lay in particular in "the production of high quality products" and is to be won independent of the IMF and the World Bank.[38]

In this aloof manner, he met the General Director of the SNB, Paul Rossy, who, already at the end of May 1944 when the Bretton Woods conference was about to take place, stated informally that Switzerland "had no great interest in being a party to the future agreements on currency stabilization and the world bank." But in the longer term, the financially efficient and solvent neutral country would in any event be forced to join. In order to receive favorable conditions, Switzerland should first "show marked reserve to the outside world."[39] The fact that the United Nations concentrated on currency matters rather than on the all-embracing economic questions was interpreted by Paul Rossy as a maneuver of camouflage, because it is "much easier to feign unanimity and positive work in dealing with the broad public in the impenetrable monetary matters instead of dealing with economic problems which are more understandable."[40]

Nonetheless, Switzerland was highly interested in the objectives of the Bretton Woods Conference, but tried to cooperate on a bilateral basis. Consequently, the Federal Council came to a negative decision, when, for the first time, it officially discussed entry into the IMF and the World Bank on January 17, 1947.[41] Four reasons were decisive. The first reason lies in the mentality of the Swiss population and elite. At the end of the war, there was a considerable gap between the harsh criticism from the outside and Switzerland's self-image as a small, neutral country that had survived as a democratic country in the "eye of the hurricane." This incongruity between self-perception and external stereotype was not transformed in internal political debate. The war experience rather strengthened Swiss confidence about solving the important problems of the future through their own efforts. A correlate of this "special case" (*Sonderfall*) attitude was a preference

---

37 Ibid.   38 Ibid., 32–3.
39 Notice on a discussion between Paul Rossi and the diplomat Daniel Secrétan, May 31, 1944, p. 1, Swiss Federal Archives, Bern, E 2001 (D), -/3, Bd. 499.
40 Ibid., 2.
41 See Franz Augstburger, Bernd Decker, and Hanspeter Hofstetter, *Die Institutionen von Bretton Woods und die Schweiz* (Zurich, 1992). Typescript located at the Nachdiplomstudien Entwicklungsländer, Eidgenössische Technische Hochschule (NADEL/ETH), Zurich.

for bilateral agreements and the rejection of joining international organizations.[42] Second, Switzerland feared that the IMF could force the country to publish important information on the financial system and the banking system. This seemed to be incompatible with the *ordre public* of the small state that supported its credit institutions in legal terms with a strong banking secrecy. Third, the government assumed that the IMF could be tempted to declare the Swiss currency in short supply on the basis of a generally expected surplus demand of Swiss francs. This would have allowed other countries to take up foreign exchange restrictions as regards Switzerland without having permitted the country to resort to corresponding retaliatory measures. In the fourth place, the Federal Council believed there were no sound reasons to switch from the "bilateral conception that had proved for our country all in all to be worthwhile, to an at least very insecure multilateral solution." If Switzerland joined the convention of Bretton Woods, "we should have to lose control of our capital wealth in the form of payments and credits and have no more possibilities to negotiate in international affairs about the provision of services in return." And an international organization would then be in charge of the Swiss franc, which would be equivalent to a loss of national autonomy.[43] This asymmetrical evaluation of the war time and the present situation fostered in the Swiss population as well as in governmental circles the conviction that it would be best to continue to be neutral and to solve the problems of the foreign policy and economy independently, on its own. For this reason, Switzerland preferred, unlike the other neutral European countries, to join neither the UN nor the Bretton Woods monetary system.[44]

But as the Swiss franc still was directly connected with the gold and therefore also indirectly with other currencies, the Confoederatio Helvetica (the official name of the country) depended to a high degree on the world market. Even if the formal outside position had some competitive advantages for Switzerland, the country shared the fate of the international monetary system.[45] National independence, which was the lodestar of foreign policy, was therefore of a rather phantasmagoric quality. This was the reason why Switzerland's absence in the most important international organizations was combined with pragmatic participation in economic and financial

42 Peter Hug and Martin Kloter, eds., *Aufstieg und Niedergang des Bilateralismus: Schweizerische Aussen- und Aussenwirtschaftspolitik, 1930–1960* (Zurich, 1999); Hans Ulrich Jost, *Europa und die Schweiz, 1945–1950: Europarat, Supranationalität und schweizerische Unabhängigkeit* (Zurich, 1999).
43 Protokoll der Bundesratssitzung vom 17. Januar 1947: Vereinbarung von Bretton Woods. Beitritt der Schweiz, in Swiss Federal Archives, Bern.
44 *Die Schweiz und die Bretton Woods-Institute/La Suisse et les Institutions de Bretton Woods* (Bern, 1991).
45 Henner Kleinewefers, *Inflation und Inflationsbekämpfung in der Schweiz* (Frauenfeld, 1976), 78ff.

cooperation programs. Thus Switzerland played a relatively important role in the OEEC and in the foundation and the financial performance of the European Payments Union.[46]

The 1960s proved to be a decade of transition in the development of the international monetary system. The restrictions introduced in the immediate postwar period were softened and a globalization process began.[47] In this situation, Switzerland became a major target of short-term capital movements. This was the main reason why the IMF aimed at integrating Switzerland, despite its neutrality, in the bargaining process which led to the General Arrangements to Borrow (GAB).[48] Switzerland for its part was also interested in cooperation with the IMF, and in 1963 the Federal Council (the Swiss government) prepared an agreement with the IMF to support the GAB financially. It was approved a year later, on June 11, 1964. Switzerland placed 865 million Swiss francs at the disposal of the IMF. Switzerland also played a considerable role in the Swap-Agreement of 1962. Together with other Neutrals, Switzerland also joined the Settlement of Investments Disputes in 1968 (signature) and 1971 (entry in force).[49]

Even without being a member of the Bretton Woods Institutions, Switzerland profited substantially from the rapid recovery of the European economy, as did the neutrals which participated formally in the institutions of the international monetary system. Economic prosperity made it profitable to support the efforts of other countries, which were damaged severely by the war, with credits and bilateral financial aid. This proved to have considerable synergetic effects: It helped the Swiss export industries to gain new markets and to combine market expansion with modernization of the production facilities, and it was a decisive factor behind the ability of the Swiss National Bank to continue to base its monetary policy upon a strong currency. Thus, the Swiss franc remained one of the most stable currencies of fixed value. It was, together with the U.S. dollar, the only monetary unit which in the period between the end of World War I and the collapse of the Bretton Woods system, had only once – in the Swiss case in 1936 – been devalued. Between the end of World War II and 1971,

46 See Jacob Julius Kaplan and Günther Schleiminger, *The European Payments Union* (Oxford, 1989).
47 Helleiner, *States and the Reemergence of Global Finance.*
48 See Gold, *Membership and Nonmembership*, 458–61; Gold *Non-Member States*, 33–40; Gold, *Selected Essays*, 1: 460–2; Gold, "General Arrangements to Borrow," 164–6; Ainley, *General Arrangements to Borrow*, 23–4.
49 *Worldbank and International Monetary Fund: Basic Documents*, 121–2. Sweden entered in 1967, Finland in 1969, and Austria in 1971.

the Swiss franc:dollar ratio changed only insignificantly (between 4.29 and 4.37).[50]

While the policy of the Swiss National Bank had still focused during the early postwar years on monetary policy objectives and therefore on the external value of the currency, a gradual reorientation took place in the 1950s. The stabilization of the price level in the Swiss national economy received more attention and became a more important target in the politics of finance, without however, challenging the priority of fixed exchange rates in currency policy.[51] But in the 1960s, due to the fixed exchange rates, the Bretton Woods system was connected with a growing money inflow; the Swiss banks were "swimming" in money and the capital markets were characteristic by a distinctive liquidity. The result was an inflation in Switzerland, imported by the mechanism of autonomous money supply.[52]

At the same time, the Swiss franc was undervalued until 1971.[53] The transition to floating exchange rates was therefore connected with a strong rise in the value of the Swiss franc, which thereby became even more popular as a refuge of foreign capital. Massive capital flight waves into the hard currency were the consequence. The Swiss franc had been revalued between December 1973 and December 1977 by 50 percent in terms of comparative purchasing power.[54] For this reason, Swiss export industries abruptly and permanently lost the protection that had been provided by an undervalued rate.[55] The adverse interaction of monetary trends and developments in the industrial sphere of the national economy explains why in the economic crisis of 1974–5 Switzerland achieved, in international comparison, an impressive stabilization record and at the same time experienced a massive collapse in investment and employment.[56]

This irregularity of the Swiss development, which can be traced back to the dominant position of the financial center in a highly internationally oriented country, shows that the category "neutral countries" during the course of the postwar era had largely lost its explanatory value. During the war years, neutrality mattered in terms of economic transactions. And during the formation period of the new international monetary order of Bretton

---

50 Kleinewefers, *Inflation und Inflationsbekämpfung*, 86.
51 Union Bank of Switzerland, ed., *Die Schweizer Wirtschaft: Daten, Fakten, Analysen, 1946–1986* (Zurich, 1987), 177.
52 Kleinewefers, *Inflation und Inflationsbekämpfung*, 47.
53 René Erbe, *Helvetia-schrumpf Dich krank! (oder die Folgen des überbewerteten Schweizerfrankens)* (Basel, 1976), 24.
54 OECD, *Switzerland*, Apr. 1978, 6.
55 Kleinewefers, *Inflation und Inflationsbekämpfung*, 96, 64.
56 See OECD, *Switzerland*, Apr. 1978.

Woods, neutral status confronted the other neutral countries with analogous problems. The Allies often addressed the group as a whole and developed strategies of economic warfare intended to prevent the Axis Powers from using the neutral countries as an operational basis for arms dealing, foreign exchange, and capital flight. Even if Switzerland had played a special role within the camp of the neutrals during the war and therefore had been harshly criticized by the United States and the other Allied Powers, the country still saw itself confronted with structural problems similar to those of other neutral countries. This common ground of perception and action dissolved in the following years. In the Cold War period, neutrality was reduced to a mere concept of foreign policy, which did not have an impact on the development of the national economy. In this sense, the question raised implicitly in the title of this essay – whether the European neutrals should be considered as a group of countries with similar problems in the area of currency – has proved to be a good starting point for this analysis. In the final state – in the early 1970s – this group became more and more heterogeneous; neutrality has lost its usefulness as an analytical category as well as its explanatory power.

7

The 1948 Monetary Reform
in Western Germany

CHARLES P. KINDLEBERGER AND F. TAYLOR OSTRANDER

The initial purpose for writing this essay was to disabuse many scholars in the United States of the idea that the monetary reform in Western Germany on June 20, 1948, was the work of Ludwig Erhard, at that time chairman of the Sonderstelle Geld und Kredit (Special Unit on Money and Credit) and director of the Economic Administration of the bizonal Wirtschaftsrat (economic council) appointed by the British and American occupation powers.[1] That attribution is mistaken, called by many German analysts a "myth" or a "legend" (Sauermann 1979, 316). Christoph Buchheim has recently asserted that everything contained in the ultimate reform laws was included in a paper that Erhard wrote late in 1943 and early in 1944 (Buchheim 1993, 84), but we believe this stretches matters. Erhard himself is reported to have said, in response to claims that German experts had produced the reform, that "practically all suggestions made by German experts ... have been rejected ... by inexperienced and technically unqualified personnel."[2] This goes too far in the other direction.

Erhard's role in June 1948 was in removing price controls and rationing, not in one fell swoop and completely, as sometimes alleged, and even he

We are grateful for information, papers, and documents to Werner Abelshauser, Jörg Baumberger, Knut Borchardt, Christoph Buchheim, Comerica Incorporated (Detroit), the Detroit Public Library, Theodore Geiger (and the National Policy Association), Carl Holtfrerich, J. Burke Knapp, Gail Makinen, Horst Mendershausen, Nadia Soboleva of Yale University, Mrs. J. Kipp Tenenbaum, and the Truman Library.

1 Jean Edward Smith notes in his biography of General Lucius D. Clay, commanding general of the Office of Military Government for Germany (U.S.) (OMGUS), that "Erhard ... became the father of West Germany's economic miracle" (Smith 1990, 455). Later, however, he states, "Erhard ... often took credit for the currency reform. Erhard did lift controls shortly afterward, but his role in the currency changeover has been greatly exaggerated" (484).

2 Brackmann 1993, 278, quoting a telegram of July 9, 1948, to the U.S. Department of State by Maurice W. Altaffer, U.S. consul general in Bremen, reporting on a session of the Wirtschaftsrat. The reference to the "personnel" is to the 25-year-old Tenenbaum, deputy to Jack Bennett, director of the OMGUS Finance Division.

warned against such precipitous action in a speech to the Bizonal Economic Council on May 10, 1948 (Erhard 1963, 36). But legends have power in history; what was originally *Allied* monetary reform became, within a few years, *German* monetary reform (Wandel 1979, 321).

We have some limited personal interest in the start of the so-called Colm-Dodge-Goldsmith report ("A Plan for the Liquidation of War Finance and the Financial Rehabilitation of Germany"), a secret report conveyed to General Lucius D. Clay, American military governor, on May 20, 1946. Taylor Ostrander, then heading the Price Control Section of the Office of Military Government for Germany (U.S.) (OMGUS) in Berlin, was involved in recommending to General Clay the names of Gerhard Colm and Raymond W. Goldsmith, two Americans who had emigrated from Germany and were working then as economists in the U.S. government in Washington. Clay recommended to the War Department the appointment of a commission consisting of Colm and Goldsmith, adding Joseph M. Dodge, to make a study of monetary reform for Germany. Dodge, a Detroit banker and Clay's close financial adviser, was then serving as director of the OMGUS Finance Division.

Of greater importance than the legendary role of Erhard in currency-reform history or how the Colm-Dodge-Goldsmith mission got under way is a series of questions in economics and finance, interesting in themselves and of possible relevance to other experience with financial disorder:

(a) Is it desirable and feasible to reduce the money supply to the level of controlled prices or, alternatively, to allow prices to rise, free of control, to an equilibrium level with the money supply? If compromise that relies on both is chosen, should mild reduction in money and higher prices or radical amputation and lesser rising prices be preferred?

(b) Should reduction of the money supply be decisive, once and for all, or only partially, with a part blocked and the possibility of later release as economic recovery proceeds?

(c) How should debt – public, private, both securities and contractual – be handled, all alike to the extent feasible or differentially, depending on the type?

(d) Timing: Should a reform be undertaken as soon as possible after a war and the recognition of suppressed inflation, or is it better to wait until economic recovery has gotten under way and government finances have recovered from wartime deficits? Some time must elapse, to be sure, to provide for the printing of a new currency and to draw up necessary regulations. The wait in the western zones of Germany, while seeking four-power agreement, was not a policy choice. Would it have been better, however, to have moved in 1945 or 1946, rather than in 1948?

(e) If one assumes that the economy is moving to a free (or freer) market, should rationing and price controls be removed sooner or later, and all together in one fell swoop, or carefully and piecemeal?

(f) What ancillary steps are required? Restoring a central bank, banks in general, government budgets, and the tax structure, with attention in the last both to revenue and to incentives for the public to work and to save?

(g) How much consideration should be given to equity of loss or sacrifice, to burden sharing, as between capitalist owners of debt on the one hand and those of real assets on the other, between rich and poor, not to leave out the middle class?

(h) Would monetary reform in West Germany have been possible if the country had not been occupied? Few Germans thought so. Is the task of monetary reform so far-reaching in the problems it poses for a nascent democracy with representative interests that an autocratic despot from outside, especially a benevolent one, has a much greater chance of pulling off drastic reform successfully?

(i) Was the Marshall Plan, which got under way about the same time as monetary reform, or the prospect of aid under the Marshall Plan a significant contributor to the success of the reform and to the *Wirtschaftswunder* (economic miracle)?

In dealing with such questions as economists, we tend to slight a series of other important issues of the time, largely political: as to whether four- instead of three-power reform had been possible; the question of the currency conversion in a Berlin shared by four occupying powers and its relation to the blockade of the city by the Soviets, the airlift, and the East–West split in the Cold War.[3] Nor do we treat the important economic issue of the exchange rate for the new currency.

Technical financial questions, to be sure, are inherently political. Those treated below evoked political forces among the occupying powers, both in Berlin and in their respective capitals, between Germans and the occupying powers, and among German groups. It is, in fact, difficult sometimes to determine whether a given German, such as Ludwig Erhard, should be regarded as an expert or as a politician.

---

3 Tenenbaum characterized Berlin as the Allies' knottiest question and treated it in some detail (Tenenbaum ca. 1957, chap. 13, 62–75). See also Gottlieb 1956–7, 398–417, and 1960. Christoph Buchheim reports that General Clay made a last proposal for four-power monetary reform in mid-January 1948, well after the bizonal arrangement had been decided, but backed off when Soviet General Vassily Sokolovsky showed interest (Buchheim 1998, 127).

We take as given the chaotic position left by German war finance that made little or no attempt to sell bonds to the public but relied on "silent financing," in which debt was piled up in the banking system. To quote the Colm-Dodge-Goldsmith report:

> Between 1935 and 1945, currency in actual circulation increased from about 5 to 50 billion RM (including Allied Military Marks), and bank deposits grew from about 30 billion to over 150 billion RM. During the same period the Reich debt expanded from 15 billion RM to 400 billion RM, not yet counting war damage and other war-connected claims of 300 to 400 billion RM. In contrast, Germany's national real wealth has decreased by one-third, from about 370 billion RM to 250 billion RM; her capacity to produce – at least in the near future – has been reduced to about one-half the prewar level. (Colm, Dodge, and Goldsmith 1946, Summary I)

These estimates, with details furnished in the several appendices to the report, relate, of course, to late 1945 or early 1946. Somewhat later data, especially those of the revisionist economic historian Werner Abelshauser, paint a less dismal picture. Net losses in plant and equipment because of war damage and reparation removals of capital equipment were merely 5 percent because of substantial rates of investment during the war, and because the average quality of the capital stock had been improved. The structure of the labor force had been altered by war casualties, but the skill levels of those surviving, plus those of expellees and refugees from the East, were above prewar. Abelshauser writes of "hidden reparations" in goods and services supplied to the occupation forces that, in his estimate, far exceeded the food imported into Germany "to prevent disease and unrest such as might endanger the occupation forces" (Abelshauser 1984, 11–15). There were bottlenecks: the damaged transport system, inability to import materials for industry, and the like, but Abelshauser regards these as relatively unimportant and thinks that the German economy was recovering rapidly, or at least steadily, before 1948. He, Mathias Manz, an economics student in the French zone, and Henry Wallich, a Yale economist, later a governor of the Federal Reserve Board, all thought that official German statistics understated the level of output before monetary reform and hence overstated recovery after it.[4] Even their adjusted figures, however, show a quantum leap in recorded output after June 20, 1948 (Ritschl 1985).

With perhaps adequate capital and labor, and output recovering slowly from abnormally low levels, there was still far-reaching economic disorder.

---

4 Wallich 1955, 148. Tenenbaum asserts that production just before reform was 50 percent of prewar, not 40 percent as the official statistics read (Tenenbaum ca. 1957, chap. 7, 6).

Prices had been fixed in 1939 at the level of October 1936, with only limited adjustments by German authorities during the war and permitted by Allied authorities after it. At the end of 1946, the consumer price index in the American zone was 120 percent of 1936, with the money supply up 500 percent for bank deposits and 1,000 percent for currency.[5] Bare necessities were handled by ration cards but were often insufficient,[6] and large portions of the population, except for farmers, coal miners, and employees of the occupation forces, were hungry. In the harsh winter of 1946–7, they were also cold. The economy was highly inflated, but the inflation was suppressed.

Edward A. Tenenbaum opens his unfinished draft history of the German mark with two chapters on suppressed inflation and goes on in chapters 5 and 7 to deal with its consequences to a degree rare in academic literature, although the subject was treated authoritatively in a special report of the American military governor in June 1947 that described Germany's two-year-old "stagnant inflation": The discredited reichsmark showed little sign of cumulative change, yet "money and the price system have become more and more meaningless," economic activity was increasingly dependent on "compensation trading" (a form of barter, of disputed legality), and price controls and other market policies faced severe challenge (OMGUS 1947).[7]

Tenenbaum's chapter 5, of which we have only his summary, deals with "Rationing, Price Control, Black and Gray Markets." The theme of chapter 7 on "Production and Distribution Costs" is distortion, hoarding, corruption, deterioration of quality, misallocation of natural resources and labor – a catalog of economic horrors. In chapter 8 on "Labor and Food," the account becomes even darker: absenteeism, diversion of labor to repairs and plant construction, as against production for the market, coal consumed by the mine in wage payments – *Deputat Kohle* – and private compensation or barter, coal miners stopping work to glean potatoes after the harvest, and the familiar story of urban folk traveling by train to the countryside to exchange personal and household possessions for potatoes and butter. One could add milk fed to pigs instead of to children, who, along with the elderly, bore the brunt of the hunger. Tenenbaum notes that the average German's

---

5 Tenenbaum ca. 1957, chap. 8, 14. For a series broken down by category for Octobers 1945, 1946, and 1947 and May 1948, see table 1 in Mendershausen 1949, 649. Based on 1938 as 100, the cost-of-living index for three American zone Länder goes only to 112 in October 1946, 126 in October 1947, and 131 in May 1948.

6 Count Christian von Krockow opens his account in *Mein Kopfgeld* by telling of buying ink. He was asked whether he had brought a bottle. When he said yes, the shopkeeper told him there was no ink (von Krockow 1988, 39).

7 This special report, entitled "Price Control, Compensation Trade, and Inflation," drafted by Ostrander, was prepared by OMGUS Economics Division. Originally confidential, it was later declassified.

overweight was reduced in these years but recovered after monetary reform (Tenenbaum ca. 1957, chap. 8, 32–3).

For a terse summary of the situation, applied generally to Europe in the harsh winter of 1946–7, see the second and third paragraphs of Secretary George C. Marshall's commencement address at Harvard University on June 5, 1947, taken largely from Undersecretary William L. Clayton's notes on his trip to Europe at the end of April (*Foreign Affairs*, May/June 1997, 160).

Postwar planning was a preoccupation in many countries during World War II, most notably, perhaps, in the United Kingdom. Germany was not exempt from the temptation despite a 1942 order from Hitler not to indulge in it. One memorandum (Denkschrift), of 268 pages, entitled "Kriegsfinanzierung und Schuldenkonsolidierung" (war finance and debt consolidation), was written by Erhard at the end of 1943 and in early 1944, taking off from the huge Reich debt that had piled up in deficits. It was, however, less a plan for consolidating the Reich debt than one for establishing a new economic order. It was written for the Reichsgruppe Industrie (RI). Erhard wrote it in Nuremberg in a one-man institute, financed by a grant of 60,000 reichsmarks from the RI arranged by his brother-in-law, who held a high position in Berlin. The memorandum was distributed to the RI and to the members of the so-called Stahl Kreis (Stahl circle). Rudolph Stahl was deputy to the head of the RI. One copy went to Otto Ohlendorf of the Reichswirtschaftsministerium (Economic Ministry), who was gingerly exploring postwar questions (Brackmann 1993, 191–200),[8] and one to Carl Goerdeler, former mayor of Leipzig and conservative politician, who was executed for his role in the July 1944 attempt on Hitler (Abelshauser 1984, 4–5). Erhard's wartime memorandum was finally published in facsimile in 1977 on the occasion of his eightieth birthday.

The monetary aspects of postwar reconstruction seem not to have been the focus of the memorandum. Much of it was taken up with relaxing restrictions on consumer-goods industries with which Erhard had been associated in RI and the Stahl Kreis. The financial essence dealt largely with disintermediation, forcing households to give up cash and take over Reich debt in a new form of certificates that bore no or only low interest, were without term, and restricted in transferability (Herbst 1977, 318).

8 Ohlendorf was executed in 1951 for his participation in atrocities on the eastern front in 1941.

The notion of certificates survived in modified form in the Colm-Dodge-Goldsmith report and in the final reform law.

Despite his start as an economist and a politician focusing on economic questions, Erhard is generally regarded in the literature as a politician as distinct from an expert. Experts were busy throughout Germany during the war but especially afterward. Monetary theorizing was at its peak from 1945 to 1948 in Germany, with never so much debate (Tenenbaum ca. 1957, chap. 12, 2). Hans Möller, late professor of economics at the University of Munich and a leading member of the Rothwesten group, discussed below, published 36 of the 218 currency reform proposals collected by Wolfram Kunze; Kunze noted another 24 proposals for which texts were not available, for a total of perhaps 250 in all, not 1,000 as sometimes thought (Möller 1961, 6). Appendix Q to the Colm-Dodge-Goldsmith plan, by Heinz Sauermann, states that the commission examined thirty plans produced by German experts (Sauermann 1955, 195). Unfortunately, we have been unable to locate a copy of the appendix volume to determine which they were. Since appendix Q is only seven pages in length, however, it is clear that Sauermann did not provide much detail.[9]

INITIAL U.S. AND U.K. EXPLORATIONS

Sometime during the war, the U.S. War Department asked two distinguished economists, Howard S. Ellis, author of a book on German monetary theory, and Gottfried Haberler, an Austrian who had come to Harvard University from the League of Nations Secretariat, to prepare plans for German postwar finance.[10] These plans seem not to have played any role in Frankfurt or Berlin nor to have been published (Wandel 1979, 322). In April 1945, J. Burke Knapp, working briefly on German economic affairs in the Department of State, wrote a memorandum for Ambassador Robert Murphy, political adviser to General Clay, objecting to the lack of specificity in annex 14

---

9 Möller believes that Gerhard Colm spoke to Walter Eucken, who sent OMGUS a plan of reform in April 1946; it is listed in the compendium as plan 19, the Eucken Gutachten, Freiburg (Möller 1961, 202). Possibly this was a polished version of a clandestine wartime memorandum that Eucken had shown to Captain Henry S. Reuss and Ostrander in September 1945; but he had not offered them a copy. In his history Tenenbaum refers continuously to plan G, calling it the work of Adolf Weber as modified by Munich experts (Tenenbaum ca. 1957, chap. 12, 5). Plan G is identified in the Möller-Kunze collection as no. 34, the Entwurf (draft) of the Arbeitsgemeinschaft für Bayern (working group for Bavaria), based on a 1944 paper by Weber and elaborated in a University of Munich seminar in May 1945 (Möller 1961, 407). Elsewhere, however, Möller records a sketch of plan G by Erwin Hielscher and Richard Oechale, no. 3 in the compendium, worked on in Munich before the middle of July 1945 and published in that city in November. These are probably overlapping versions of the same proposal.
10 Wandel 1979, 321, quoting Manuel Gottlieb as his source. See also Ellis 1934.

(on finance) in J.C.S. 1067, the Joint Chiefs of Staff policy directive to the U.S. military governor in Germany, stating that the stability of the mark would have to be dealt with, since collapse of the currency would wreak havoc with the rest of military government objectives (Knapp 1945). Manuel Gottlieb, a young economist in the Finance Division, is said to have proposed a currency conversion in September 1945 with a ratio of one unit of new money to RM 10 (Wandel 1979, 322). In October, Captain Henry S. Reuss, chief of price control in U.S. military government in Frankfurt, later a distinguished congressman specializing in economic questions, submitted a terse proposal, written in military style, calling for a ten to one reduction of money to be undertaken by December 31, 1945, or, if this proved impossible, relieving military government of responsibility for reestablishing and overseeing the German price control machinery in the American zone.

The pace picked up in November. The Colm–Dodge–Goldsmith letter of transmittal to General Clay states that the recommendations in the report responded to the questions raised by the U.S. member of the Finance Directorate at the Allied Control Council in ACC document DFIN/PC of November 15, 1945, but we have not learned what these questions specifically were. On November 21, Dodge visited Adolf Weber at the University of Munich and received his recommendation that 95 percent of the Reich debt be written off. Dodge further invited a group of financial experts, including Möller, Sauermann, Otto Pfleiderer, and Fritz Terhalle, to a meeting November 27–9 to discuss the currency question (Wandel 1979, 322–3). A Dodge memorandum of December 6, entitled "Program for Immediate Action to Reduce the Inflationary Potential," stirred up debate (Brackmann 1993, 224 n.191). Additionally, the Frankfurt chamber of commerce convened a large group of experts, fifty according to one report (Sauermann 1955, 195), twenty-six according to another (Sauermann 1979, 308). Günter Keiser, an economics expert and a Social Democrat from Hamburg, in the British zone, presided. The meeting produced a general declaration in favor of monetary reform but no agreement on details beyond German readiness to take responsibility (1955, 195).

In mid-January 1946, Goldsmith, then a State Department delegate to a conference on reparations in Paris, went to Berlin on a visit, where he looked up Ostrander, a friend and colleague from price control work at the National Defense Advisory Commission (NDAC) in Washington in 1940–1.

Samuel Katz, a new member of the OMGUS price control staff, was present when Goldsmith and Ostrander discussed the vast excess of reichsmarks, the danger of open inflation, and whether or not a study by outside consultants could be of help to OMGUS. Goldsmith was interested. Gerhard Colm's name was suggested.

Captain Charles David Ginsburg and Don D. Humphrey, then working with General William H. Draper, Clay's economic adviser, had also been at NDAC in Washington in 1940–1, and Goldsmith and Ostrander had worked with them. Ginsburg and Humphrey were probably also involved in forwarding to Dodge and General Clay the suggestion that Colm and Goldsmith should undertake such a study. Ostrander and Goldsmith were asked to draft a cable that Clay sent to the War Department, proposing a commission of Colm, Goldsmith, and Dodge to prepare a report on German monetary reform.

The proposal quickly received War and State Department approval. Colm and Goldsmith assembled a staff in Washington, including Lloyd Metzler, Horst Mendershausen, Robert Eisenberg, Jerome Jacobson, and Gerald Matchett (in the order listed in the report), and started work in Berlin at the beginning of March 1946.[11] The first draft was completed by April 5, followed by a month of consultations with German experts, a second draft by May 14, and the final report submitted to General Clay on May 20.[12]

The report's letter of transmittal stated that seventeen listed appendices would be forthcoming in a single volume. To our knowledge only five are publicly available: appendix O on recent foreign experiences with monetary and financial reform, by Metzler, dated June 10, 1946 (Metzler 1979, 365–72), and four more published by Möller: D on the German government budgets and the tax structure, by Gottlieb; E on the present status of financial institutions, by Jacobson; H on the analysis of size distribution of deposits of selected banks, by Mendershausen and Matchett; and N on facts and considerations concerning the rate of exchange, by Metzler. All of these appear in English (Möller 1961, 429–76).

The report called for three steps: (1) the conversion of reichsmarks into a new currency at the ratio (sometimes called in German discussions a *Quote*)

---

11 Sauermann, in his introduction to the first publication of the Colm-Dodge-Goldsmith plan, calls these men the "closest coworkers" and lists among a "wider group" Manuel Gottlieb, Frederick Dirks, F. Williams, A. L. George, Heinz Sauermann, F. Taylor Ostrander, and Robert J. Myers (Sauermann 1955, 194).

12 The Colm-Dodge-Goldsmith report, issued as a secret OMGUS document, had limited distribution, though its main proposals were known to German members and experts of the Sonderstelle Geld und Kredit and the Rothwesten Konklave. In March 1950, in response to a request by Heinz Sauermann, it was declassified by U.S. High Commissioner John J. McCloy. Its first unclassified publication was in 1955, with Sauermann's German translation. A "Preface" in the English version only, written after 1948 by Colm, Dodge, and Goldsmith, gives their brief commentary on the monetary reform (Colm, Dodge, Goldsmith 1955, 204–7).

of one new unit for RM 10, with similar downsizing for bank deposits, mortgages, public debt other than that of the Reich, and private debt, but not amounts in contracts such as rents, pensions, or insurance. The Reich debt was to be canceled in full, but new government obligations in sharply reduced amounts would be issued to banks holding Reich debt (but experiencing a 90 percent reduction in deposit liabilities) to keep them from going bankrupt; (2) a mortgage of 50 percent of the value of real assets, land, buildings, plant, and equipment, with the proceeds turned over to a fund for the equalization of war losses (*Lastenausgleich*); and (3) a progressive capital levy, above a substantial exemption to leave most property owners unaffected, to be applied on gains in wealth between 1935 and 1945. The rates suggested ran from 10 to 90 percent, payable over ten years, with the money added to the fund for the equalization of the burdens of war losses.

The State Department accepted the report as a useful basis for proceeding. The War Department did not. It objected to steps two and three, the opposition coming, as Kindleberger remembers it, from Secretary of War Kenneth Royall, a lawyer from North Carolina, who couched his objections in terms of giving excessive powers to administrators and stifling initiative but who in reality had strong ideological objections to capital levies under any circumstances. Clay responded that he was unwilling to accept any further responsibility in the matter, since while the OMGUS view had been disapproved, no alternative course had been suggested. The disagreement within the U.S. government was finally resolved in the State-War-Navy Coordinating Committee (SWNCC, pronounced "swink"). It was agreed to turn steps two and three over to the future German government, when formed, to be enacted within a stipulated period. Clay responded that this imposed a heavy burden on a new government that would need to gain popularity and that the responsibility should be borne by military government (Brackmann 1993, 213–15; Clay 1950, 210).

A German account, following on Tenenbaum, observed that Clement Atlee, the British prime minister, initially objected to the Colm-Dodge-Goldsmith plan because British policy was to socialize Germany, while the United States was trying to devolve responsibility onto the Germans (Wandel 1979, 325; Tenenbaum ca. 1957, chap. 13, 5). A French reaction to the plan was that it did too well by the Germans, making them suffer less than the French (Tenenbaum, ibid.). In one statement, the British and French saw the currency problem as not pressing, since they covered their occupation costs with Allied military marks (Benz 1988, 19).

Colm, Dodge, and Goldsmith also addressed a series of policy issues and logistical procedures. The former concerned timing, the impact on wealth distribution, whether or not part of the monetary overhang should be blocked for possible later release to finance growth, the need for some form of central bank, and the speed with which price and rationing controls could be lifted. On detailed procedures, they suggested the terms of a mortgage on real property and progressive taxes on wartime increases in wealth and called for a covering law, plus the convening of a group of German financial and legal experts to draw up the laws and regulations for carrying out the proposed measures.

Michael Brackmann states that the Colm–Dodge–Goldsmith report was the first American plan for monetary reform and the last (Brackmann 1993, 212). In his capacity as liaison officer, along with British and French colleagues, Tenenbaum was said to have, at the beginning of April 1948, an "outline" of what the Allies wanted (ibid., 262; Möller 1976, 447). No such outline is mentioned in his unfinished history, but in the daylong meeting he and one British representative had with the Sonderstelle Geld und Kredit on November 20, 1947, Tenenbaum's unscripted discussion conformed closely to the spirit and most of the letter of the Colm–Dodge–Goldsmith report (Sonderstelle 1947 passim). Tenenbaum, aged twenty-five and less than half the age of the chairman, Erhard, dominated these discussions, which roamed over a wide number of issues in currency reform. He more than held his own in debate, answering questions, emphasizing the importance that the bizonal authorities attached to German cooperation.[13]

Lord Annan, a British intellectual and former military administrator, has written, "No doubt Germany's recovery could not have begun without the currency reform imposed by British initiative" (Annan 1995, 234). There is no doubt that a number of early German plans were produced in the British zone of occupation, and there were some early British proposals for open inflation.[14] The Detmold memorandum of November 17, 1945, has been called "the first official German plan" (Buchheim 1993, 95).[15] But Annan's statement raises questions about two phrases: "imposed by British" and

---

13 Mrs. Tenenbaum has kindly furnished us with a stenographic transcript of her husband's first meeting with the Sonderstelle Geld und Kredit on November 20, 1947, which was not saved by him but given to him by Erwin Hielscher in 1969 in the course of a social visit.

14 British officials in London, where Colm and Goldsmith stopped briefly en route to Berlin, favored dealing with the excess money supply by "controlled inflation," letting German prices rise by as many as four times. Later, at the Finance Directorate of the Allied Control Council, the British raised this to five times. Moreover, even after agreement by the Western Allied governments on the Colm–Dodge–Goldsmith plan, the British, at the Finance Directorate in September 1946, insisted on a 50–100 percent rise in prices as a "precondition" of currency reform (Hoppenstedt 1997, 197, 202, 214).

15 Brackmann states that "already in 1945, the British authorities had instructed the combined finance committee to prepare studies in consultation with German experts" (Brackmann 1993, 197).

"British initiative." The currency reform of June 20, 1948, was imposed by the three Western Allies: British, French, and American. "British initiative" is ambiguous without more context. It may refer to temporal primacy, in which case Lord Annan has a point. More significant, however, is where the ideas came from, whose ideas prevailed, and whether or not German recovery would have been as far-reaching if British policies, many of them socialist, had been the basis of the reform.

BASIC IDEAS

After the Bizonal Agreement of December 1946 between Britain and the United States was amended in July 1947 to divide aid to the bizone 50–50 rather than on the basis that each power help (largely help feed) its own zone, monetary reform began to move forward in earnest. The German bizonal authorities were encouraged to set up the Sonderstelle Geld und Kredit under the chairmanship of Erhard.[16] In its turn, the Sonderstelle called on German experts to draw up their own reform plan, which became known as the Homburg plan after the group met in Bad Homburg (Möller 1961, Plan 36). The Homburg plan was completed on April 18, 1948. Two days later a group of German economists and jurists assembled in an isolated military installation in Rothwesten, near Kassel, to settle with the Allies the final design of the currency reform and, as recommended in the Colm-Dodge-Goldsmith plan, to draw up the rules and regulations for its implementation.

The Rothwesten Konklave lasted forty-nine days, with twenty meetings (Möller 1976, 446). British, French, and American liaison officers traveled back and forth from Berlin and zonal headquarters to attend the meetings. Tenenbaum took the leadership of the trizonal liaison group partly because, as he explained, he was the only person attending who was fluent in English, German, and French, and also, it would appear, because he had command of the issues (Tenenbaum ca. 1957, chap. 13, 22).

German politicians, including Erhard, met with the group at Rothwesten on May 14 in a meeting described by Möller as dramatic because of wide disagreement on the German side, both among the experts and between experts and politicians (Möller 1976, 449). It is noted by Tenenbaum, if

---

16 Other members of the Sonderstelle were Erwin Hielscher, vice chairman, Günter Keiser, Otto Pfleiderer, Karl Bernard, Fritz Cahn-Garnier (replaced by Walter Dudek in November), Heinrich Hartlieb, and Victor Wrede. Experts were co-opted, among them Hans Möller, Heinz Sauermann, and Edward Wolf. A number of outsiders were brought in from time to time, also sworn to secrecy, notably, Walter Eucken, Fritz Terhalle, Otto Veit, and Adolf Weber (Brackmann 1993, 244–5, n.83).

his mention of meeting with fifty German politicians refers to the same occasion, as "an unfortunate expedient" (Tenenbaum ca. 1957, chap. 13, 19). Meeting in small groups, however, the German experts produced twenty-two documents, consisting of laws, announcements, proclamations, and instructions to banks (Möller 1976, 451). The final reform law followed the Colm–Dodge–Goldsmith plan more closely than it did the Bad Homburg, which was regarded by Tenenbaum as "inconsistent," a mixture of mild and radical measures (Tenenbaum ca. 1957, chap. 12, 68), and by unnamed OMGUS lawyers as "pure farce" (Brackmann 1993, 266). The Homburg plan did contain, however, some suggestions for burden sharing and a capital levy, both of which had been stripped from the OMGUS plan by the War Department.

As already noted, the Colm–Dodge–Goldsmith plan adopted the ratio or quota of RM 10 to 1 unit of new currency for bank notes (but not coin), bank deposits and savings accounts, private debt, and public debt other than that of the Reich, and strongly opposed blocking, as it "would only postpone the final solution, leave uncertainty, and invite constant pressure for deblocking." One German economist wanted to reduce the money supply to 40 percent of the existing RM amount but block three-quarters of this.[17] In the final reform, there was some yielding on blocking, favored by most German economists, presumably on the ground that deblocking would enlarge the money supply as recovery got under way. First econometric calculations, according to Tenenbaum, indicated that RM 10 to 1, or RM 100 to 10, was likely to be too mild and inflationary, and that 7 new for 100 old would be better, 5 best. He records that some of his colleagues thought 5 new for 100 old was disloyal to the Colm–Dodge–Goldsmith report, but in 1948, in Washington, Colm agreed with Tenenbaum on the lower number (Tenenbaum ca. 1957, chap. 13, 27). The Homburg plan called for 10 new for 100 old, but in the negotiations at Rothwesten a compromise was reached, providing ten new units, five of which would be blocked, with a decision reached on them in ninety days. In October 1948, one of the five blocked DM was freed, three and a half canceled, and one-half temporarily blocked further. This action produced a final ratio of six and a half, not ten or five or seven, to one hundred (Buchheim 1998, 131).

All these ratios were thought of in terms of amounts above initial small quantities exchanged for everyone at one new unit per RM, called in German *Kopfgeld* (head money). Colm, Dodge, and Goldsmith had suggested that this distribution be set at fifteen new units for each head

17 This was the proposal of Wilhelm Lautenbach (Möller 1961, plan 26, 333–4).

of a family, plus ten more for each dependent. This was too radical for most of the German experts, whose ideas typically ran in terms of fifty or sixty new units as the initial individual allocation. The Allies finally yielded on this, despite the fact that fifty new units for sixty million Germans came to DM 3 billion. This was done, according to Jack Bennett, director of OMGUS Finance Division, because, if the Allies had disallowed DM 50, German politicians would have had a field day (Brackmann 1993, 265). In the end, the figure was set at DM 60, with DM 40 immediately available and DM 20 available in four weeks.

Reich debt posed a problem as cancellation threatened banks with bankruptcy. The solution was to cancel it in full – underlining the fact that Germany had lost the war, which had been financed recklessly – but, as noted earlier, to issue a new form of security in varying amounts depending on the position of a given bank. Since bank deposits had been reduced by 90 percent, these issues were not enormous. The U.S. War Department interfered again at the last minute, trying to modify the treatment of Reich debt on the ground that cancellation set a bad precedent for other countries' debtors. Trizone military government got around this by leaving Reich debt denominated in reichsmarks, which ceased to be a valid currency (Tenenbaum ca. 1957, chap. 13, 20, 40). Americans in OMGUS were not impressed by the argument that cancellation of Reich debt would mean the failure of many banks (Brackmann 1993, 226).

German experts at Rothwesten were on the whole agreeable to cancellation of Reich debt but felt differently about private debt. The Homburg plan wanted Reich debt treated like its version of public debt, 80 percent canceled, 15 percent blocked, and 5 percent free. Some Germans even argued for keeping private debt intact at RM 1 equals DM 1. Tenenbaum and the French liaison officer, Le Fort, insisted on 90 percent cancellation. Keeping private reichsmark debt intact, Tenenbaum argued, would lead to bankruptcies on the part of some debtors, especially of the coal mines, which had been borrowing RM 2 billion in addition to the subsidies from the British occupation authorities, to close the gap between the controlled price of RM 15 per ton and costs of more than RM 30 (Tenenbaum ca. 1957, chap. 13, 44).

In discussion of private debt in the November 1947 session of the Sonderstelle Geld und Kredit, various cases were brought up: loans to buy goods that were hoarded, intact working farms, mortgages on buildings destroyed by bombing. None of these seemed to move Tenenbaum to depart from a uniform rule of 90 percent write-down on private debt (Sonderstelle 1947 passim).

Timing of the currency reform and timing of any removal of price controls and rationing are perhaps separate issues. Many experts wanted reform as soon as possible. Others preferred to wait until recovery of output had gone some distance and even until a German government had been established and its finances straightened out. The Colm-Dodge-Goldsmith plan urged against waiting for these eventualities, recommending as soon as possible but after the 1946 harvest.

In the event, the matter was not one for choice. There was a long delay over whether or not the Soviet zone would join in the reform, conforming to the Potsdam Agreement requirement that the four occupation zones be treated as a single economic unit. When this was provisionally agreed, there was an extended Allied Control Council (ACC) debate over whether or not to print some of the new currency in the Reichsdruckerei (government printing office) in Leipzig in the Soviet zone, as well as in the American sector in Berlin. The Western Allies, perhaps mostly the Americans, were fearful that printing in Leipzig would be difficult to supervise, given the strong Soviet incentive not to allow their access to the new currency to be subject to four-power control, as had occurred in Vienna to its perceived economic cost.

Once the decision had been made to go ahead on a Western basis, sometime after July 1947 and before the end of September, there was an additional inescapable delay in getting a new currency printed in the United States. This was done in "Operation Bird Dog," estimated in the Colm-Dodge-Goldsmith report as requiring four to six months, actually taking six to nine. That the printing was being undertaken was not kept secret and was noted by the Soviet commander, Marshal Vassily Sokolovsky, in the ACC in December 1947. The delivery of the currency to Germany and the timing of the reform, however, were tightly held. Twenty-three thousand steel cases, weighing in all 1,035 tons, were shipped from New York marked for Barcelona via Bremen and delivered by 800 army trucks, without public notice, to the vault of the Reichsbank in Frankfurt, where they were stored until the distribution to the Land and other banks between June 11 and 15, 1948 (Benz 1988, 17). It was said by Tenenbaum to have been the greatest logistical triumph since the Allied landing on Normandy beaches in June 1944 (Tenenbaum ca. 1957, chap. 13, 16).

It is perhaps not fair to compare the speed of the conversion – mostly in a couple of days from June 20, 1948 – with the scheduled time for the switch from national currencies to the euro in the European Monetary Union (EMU), as agreed at Maastricht, which runs from 1999 to 2002, with the introduction of the currency planned to take several weeks in the last year

(Currie 1997, 29 box). Converting several national currencies into the euro is surely more complex than converting the RM into the DM. The speed of the latter was nonetheless remarkable.

The Colm-Dodge-Goldsmith report set forth the need to end controls on the German economy but held that this could be done through minor changes in existing machinery (Colm, Dodge, and Goldsmith 1946, 21–2). A Socialist reform plan developed in England in December 1945 by E. F. Schumacher, originally German and later an economic adviser to British military government in Berlin, and Walter Fliess called for more price controls, rationing, holding the line on wages, salaries, and pensions, and punishing black marketeers severely; in other words, a continuation of repressed inflation (Möller 1961, plan 15, 158–72). The prominent Hamburg economist Günter Keiser took the view that monetary reform would not solve the bottlenecks of food and coal, that decontrol should proceed slowly, and was sharply attacked for this by Wilhelm Röpke, who even called the position, in print, Nazi (Brackmann 1993, 250–1).

In a speech to the Bizonal Economic Council on April 21, 1948, Erhard said:

> We regard total abolition of controls, with currency reform or after, as neither possible nor practical. Indeed, we shall have to proceed circumspectly when deciding which markets, and in what sequence, free competition and decontrolled prices are introduced. (Erhard 1963, 36)

It can be argued that the decontrol that Erhard announced on June 20, 1948, was circumspect, but it was not complete. Buchheim says that Erhard decontrolled the prices of "almost all" finished manufactured goods (Buchheim 1998, 22). Mendershausen's summary is that "all comprehensive price, rationing, and allocation controls" were withdrawn. However, he produced a table showing seventeen categories of goods and services remaining under maximum prices in the fall of 1948, four still under fixed maximum and minimum prices, and eighteen free from all controls (Mendershausen 1949, 663–4). As a broad generalization, finished goods and fresh foodstuffs were freed, basic foodstuffs, fuels, metals, medicines, and rents were not. The freeing process went on, however. By the middle of July, 90 percent of controlled prices were free, and much of the remaining rationing was treated loosely by shopkeepers or altogether ignored (Brackmann 1993, 278). Rationing of some items was lifted slowly: potatoes in October 1948, sugar in April 1950, gasoline in 1951, and coal in 1953 (Benz 1988, 27). Delay in decontrol in the French zone led Röpke to raise an economic question, whether currency reform or decontrol was the more effective in stimulating output. No conclusive answer emerged, as production rose 22 percent in the bizone between June and August 1948 and 23 percent in the French zone (Buchheim 1993, 117; Buchheim 1998, 135).

Prices rose with decontrol, and with them popular unrest. The consumer price index rose 18 percent above the level of the first half in the second half of 1948, finished goods 14 percent, and industrial materials 26 percent (Brackmann 1993, 277; Buchheim 1993, 118). In November, the trade unions threatened a general strike because prices had been allowed to rise but not wages, and a Socialist proposal in the Wirtschaftsrat for a vote of no confidence in Erhard was defeated, but not resoundingly – 52 votes to 43. In the same month, polls showed that 70 percent of the German people wanted price controls reintroduced, putting Erhard under strong pressure (Buchheim 1993, 119). He weathered it successfully, helped partly by the introduction of credit restrictions by the Bank deutscher Länder (BdL), which were eliminated in May 1949 when prices began to stabilize with the help of deliveries under the Marshall Plan (Holtfrerich 1995, 437).

The Colm-Dodge-Goldsmith report called for a series of steps auxiliary to the currency reform itself: the establishment of a central bank, cleaning up of the government budget, raising some taxes on what has been called "undue enrichment" but lowering others to stimulate incentives to work and save, and the establishment of a group of banking experts and lawyers to work out the regulations for the currency reform, as undertaken at Rothwesten. The complexity of the planning and the unfolding experience that called for four laws in all, issued from June to October, pose problems for economists who believe in free banking, see no need for central banks, and advocate extremely limited government. To caricature this attitude, some come close to suggesting that the German economy could have been started on its way to its *Wirtschaftswunder* by a simple drastic reduction in the money supply and a single decree abolishing all controls on everything. We note the establishment of the Bank deutscher Länder in March 1948, transformed in 1957 into the Deutsche Bundesbank. The Americans, according to one source, wanted to have a separate central bank for each Land, or province, but the British insisted on amalgamating the Land banks into a single Bank deutscher Länder (Holtfrerich 1988, 139).[18] The BdL played a

18 In a memorandum of May 29, 1946, F. R. Klopstock of the Foreign Research Division of the Federal Reserve Bank of New York, commenting on the Colm-Dodge-Goldsmith report and some other OMGUS papers, observed that Dodge wanted a central bank for each Land, with an overall Länder Union Bank. The latter would be administered by an Allied Control Board, which among other duties such as centralizing the financing, clearing, and recording of export and import transactions would control the issue of public loans to prevent extravagant borrowing by national or local governments (Klopstock 1946, 9–10).

significant role in the currency exchange, among other functions. Equally, the Rothwesten Konklave produced twenty-two sets of laws, ordinances, regulations, and instructions vital to the reform exercise. The case for the need of government in critical action of this sort was set out powerfully in a letter to the *New York Review of Books* by Tenenbaum's widow, criticizing Milton and Rose Friedman's *Free to Choose* for its treatment of the episode. She wrote:

> The Friedmans' whole book is a diatribe against government interference and bureaucracy, yet in Germany after World War II reconstruction of the economy could not have occurred without a sound currency and massive aid from the Marshall Plan, both accomplishments of the U.S. bureaucracy so despised by the Friedmans. (J. K. Tenenbaum 1980, 52)

We come penultimately to the question of burden sharing, embodied in the great bulk of German proposals for reform and in the Colm-Dodge-Goldsmith steps two and three. As Germans, Colm and Goldsmith had experienced the inflation of 1918–23, when the middle class with financial assets lost heavily relative to those with property and equities, a redistribution of wealth that, along with the Versailles Treaty and the unemployment of the early 1930s, contributed to the rise of National Socialism. We have noted that the U.S. War Department vetoed a mortgage on real assets and progressive taxes on substantial wartime increases in wealth, on ideological grounds, but it did accept that the matter be turned over to the Germans with a deadline for action. One of us mistakenly thought that the Germans had followed through with these measures, and on this basis called the reform as a whole "one of the greatest feats of social engineering of all time."[19] The less brilliant history of the *Lastenausgleich* and of the taxes on substantial gains in wealth, after the formation of the German government, requires a lowering of the hyperbole in this statement.

The German bizonal authorities did not enact these burden-sharing measures by the end of December 1948, as called for in the first reform law. While most German reform plans called for burden sharing, and in Tenenbaum's view almost all Germans favored it (Tenenbaum ca. 1957, chap. 13, 48), the politicians paid it only limited attention and were not bothered by the American veto (Buchheim 1993, 95). In Buchheim's judgment, the weak proposals on the issue in the Homburg plan – which, for example, allowed wealth taxes to be paid with canceled Reich debt and unconverted reichsmarks (105) – led the Germans at Rothwesten not to put up much of a fight

---

19 See Kindleberger 1993, 407. The characterization was repeated by Samuel Katz in a discussion session summarized in Cairncross and Cairncross 1992, 33.

for the Lastenausgleich and wealth taxes (Tenenbaum ca. 1957, chap. 12, 52). The German authorities acted not by the end of 1948, as called for in the law, but provisionally on August 8, 1949, in the Immediate Assistance Act and in the form of an annual 3 percent tax on increases in wealth rather than the drastic 10 to 90 percent numbers of Colm, Dodge, and Goldsmith. At this level, it was more like an income tax than a capital levy. Anticipated to produce DM 2.8 billion a year, it yielded only DM 1 billion. After the Federal Republic of Germany was established in September 1949, the law was finally enacted in August 1952 and many times amended. By its end in 1979, it had produced DM 42 billion for distribution to nine million people with claims of war losses. Brackmann states that the unsettled status of the *Lastenausgleich* (and the mortgage?) hung like a Sword of Damocles over German politics (Brackmann 1993, 275).

Kurt Schumacher, the fiery Socialist leader, spoke out in 1947 and 1948 against the lack of effective *Lastenausgleich*, which lack favored the owners of great properties at the expense of owners of monetary assets. As late as 1955, the *Neue Rheinzeitung* is quoted as saying that the Federal Republic of Germany was founded on the Allied monetary reform and not on the Grundgesetz (Basic Law) (Renger 1988, 87–91).

We have not found a discussion of the mortgage on real assets and its success or failure. Tenenbaum noted that the appraisal of property proved difficult as many records had been destroyed, and different sorts of property were best served by different rates of mortgage (Tenenbaum ca. 1957, chap. 12, 52). One judges from these remarks that the 50 percent mortgage in the Colm-Dodge-Goldsmith recommendation – well below the 90 percent cancellation of financial assets and the maximum that they thought could be levied without some ill effects and also leave some room for errors in appraisal (Colm, Dodge, and Goldsmith 1946, 12) – was not efficiently applied and not an unmitigated success.

A decade after the reform, the German record in burden sharing was vigorously attacked by Tenenbaum. The German parliament, he wrote, failed, and the failure to achieve effective burden sharing left the country philistine and weakened the interest of youth in sharing (Tenenbaum ca. 1957, chap. 13, 61). Henry Wallich was also not impressed, claiming that the reform left severe inequalities, especially adverse for labor, old people, and pensioners (Wallich 1955, 16–17). And even at the time, in the summer and fall of 1948, there was considerable disapproval and protest: The view of trade unions, especially, was that Erhard's reform was too liberal and that more controls were needed, a call that, as noted, was temporarily heeded (Domes and Wolffson 1979, 341).

The issue is closely connected to that of timing. Tenenbaum holds that too much time was lost on the road to monetary reform and that the burden-sharing program could have been adopted intact in 1946 (Tenenbaum ca. 1957, chap. 13, 60). It is also tied up with whether or not a currency reform and accompanying measures could have been put through by the Germans if they had not been occupied by the victorious Allies. The failures in monetary reform of the United Kingdom, France, and Italy with participatory democracies were noted earlier, and there was partial success in small countries for which plans were prepared by governments-in-exile, far from the clash of local interests. Timing is one issue, another is whether or not the mistake – from the point of view of optimal social engineering – was that of the Allies, especially the United States, in handing the problem over to the Germans.

The history of monetary reform in Germany is replete with statements that it required occupation of the country by the Allies. One writer after another says that the Germans could not have carried it out by themselves. General Clay's angry response to the War Department when it turned down steps two and three of the Colm-Dodge-Goldsmith plan was indicated above, with his insistence that leaving burden sharing to a new German government would put it through the ringer. Different writers use different reasons why, though Germans must be consulted, the Allies must take responsibility. For one thing, there was at the time no German government (Buchheim 1998, 117); for another, even if there had been, the parliamentary process would have been close to impossible to carry through, presumably because of the clash of interests.[20] While an ex-Reichsbank president of the early 1930s, Hans Luther, thought that either the Allies or the Germans could handle the task of reform, a later Bundesbank president, Otmar Emminger, wrote, "Only an occupation authority could undertake such a drastic monetary reform" and that other countries (victorious and unoccupied) could not reduce the money supply and were left with a *Klotz am Bein* (shackled leg).[21] Some felt that the Germans could not keep secrets, though this is a libel against the experts and even the politicians of the Sonderstelle and at Rothwesten (Wandel 1979, 321). Möller thought that monetary reform could not be carried out by a German regime because of its *Schärfe und Kompromisslosigkeit* (harshness and inability to compromise) (Möller 1976, 437). Tenenbaum writes that currency reforms

---

20 Brackmann 1993, 258, quoting the lawyer Karl Bernard, president of the Central Bank Council of the Bank deutscher Länder from 1948 to 1957.
21 Möller 1961, plan 35, the Luther Report, representing a temporary solution (*Zwischenlösung*). Luther was president of the Reichsbank from 1930 to 1933. See also Emminger 1986, 23.

are inherently conspiratorial, given to parliaments only as an ultimatum (Tenenbaum ca. 1957, chap. 13, 17–18).

Perhaps it is less inflammatory to suggest that in complex financial matters that may roil economic and political behavior there is something to be said for a form of benevolent despotism, whether of independent central banks, treasuries that spring currency devaluations after denying that they will, or outsiders who take responsibility for monetary reform. Town meetings are an attractive form of decision making in political terms but occasionally end in stalemate.

The picture of young Tenenbaum pushing the currency reform through the German experts and politicians at Rothwesten and earlier reminds one of a Belgian description of Assistant Secretary of the Treasury Harry Dexter White ramrodding the Bretton Woods Agreements through, leaving little or almost no role for John Maynard Keynes, Undersecretary of State Dean Acheson, or the hundreds of self-important representatives from all over the world (Van Dormael 1978, chap. 16).

The "despots" in the German case were the Western Allied military commanders, especially General Clay of OMGUS, but their on-the-scene deputy at Rothwesten was Edward Tenenbaum. His superior, Jack Bennett, once or twice laid down the law to the Rothwesten group,[22] but Tenenbaum was really in charge there. According to some colleagues who knew him – though not those of his Finance Division – he was not a particularly warm or outgoing man, though he was bright, very bright, acknowledged widely to have been the leader of the Allied team that pushed *Allied* monetary reform to completion at Rothwesten.

Wandel calls Tenenbaum hyperbolically "the father of the deutsche mark" (Wandel 1979, 323). Tenenbaum himself says in his history that he "originated" the name, deutsche mark, "for purposes of four-power discussion," and that it was selected for the new currency in competition with a long list of other candidates such as taler, batzen, neumark, warenmark, arbeitsmark (Tenenbaum ca. 1957, chap. 12, 5). He was apparently not overconfident of the success of the deutsche mark, for Mrs. Tenenbaum has told us that in 1948, just after returning to Washington, her husband "thought the currency reform produced at Rothwesten was a flop and that inflation would follow."[23]

---

22 Brackmann states that the Germans wanted to start the discussion with the *Lastenausgleich*, but Bennett insisted that it be separated and left to the Germans for later (Brackmann, 1993, 267). The British did not regard Bennett highly, thinking him doctrinaire and obstinate (Holtfrerich 1995, 431).

23 Ostrander memorandum of a telephone conversation with Mrs. Tenenbaum, Sept. 17, 1997.

Commenting on an early draft of this paper, Horst Mendershausen objected to regarding Tenenbaum as the father of the deutsche mark, saying that he preferred to think of Colm, Dodge, and Goldsmith (and one should add the German economists they consulted) as the fathers and Tenenbaum as the midwife.[24]

The fact that the German public regarded monetary reform as legitimate, despite its imposition by foreign occupying powers, attests to its undoubted success, albeit less than complete in the matter of burden sharing. This success and the understandable concern for legitimacy help explain the public's inevitable movement to transform an Allied accomplishment into an ostensible German one.

Cause and effect are difficult to connect in macroeconomic events such as sudden recovery followed by rapid growth. Often there is a series of necessary conditions but no *causa causans*. Some revisionists deny the importance of any single event or policy, as Abelshauser has insisted, first, that recovery was well under way before monetary reform (Abelshauser, 1984, 15); second, that Marshall Plan aid was too small and too late to contribute substantially to recovery;[25] third, that Erhard's policy of decontrols, *Sozialmarktwirtschaft* (social market economy) in the coinage of Alfred Müller-Armack of the University of Münster, stood in the way of an even better performance.[26]

There were candidates for roles in producing economic recovery in western Germany in addition to the monetary reform (itself the inspired work of Colm, Dodge, and Goldsmith and the Germans they borrowed from), the Marshall Plan, and the free-market economy. One was the good harvest of 1948 following the disastrous one of 1947 as a result of dry weather in the summer of 1946 and the wet and cold winter that followed. Another was the Korean War starting in June 1950, which brought about a shift in production priorities and a stimulus to heavy industry. Wallich focuses on currency reform, the lifting of controls, and sound monetary and fiscal policies (Wallich 1955, 15–16). Two well-placed American officials with different experiences took separate views. General Clay thought that the Marshall

---

24 Mendershausen letter to Kindleberger of Aug. 25, 1997.
25 Abelshauser 1991, 400. He quotes a June 1950 Erhard editorial that "the Marshall Plan has not made the *least* [italics in the original] contribution to the revival." This statement is preceded, however, by "This is not to say that recovery and economic growth would automatically materialize."
26 Abelshauser 1984, 1, gives as a reason that Erhard freed consumer industries first and kept controls on basic activities, whereas he should have done the opposite.

Plan got too much credit for the economic recovery that his administration had prepared; his successor, High Commissioner John J. McCloy, was an enthusiastic supporter of the Marshall Plan (Schwartz 1991, 178, 181).

Our interest is less in the economic recovery as a whole than in the effects of monetary reform. Admittedly, a substantial part of the spectacular recovery in the hours and days that followed the Basic Law introducing the new currency came from bringing hoarded goods out and up from back rooms and cellars, goods that had been kept out of sight for use in private compensation trade, Deputat wages, and black markets. Hoarding with a view to waiting until money was worth having had been under way since at least the fall of 1947, and the few available data on the illicit activity show that it was substantial.[27] In his April 21, 1948, speech to the Economic Council in Frankfurt, Erhard said that it should be easy with monetary reform to enforce a reduction of domestic stockpiles, and so it proved (Erhard 1963, 40). In the same speech, he also observed that currency reform and the Marshall Plan should work together. This is less persuasive for the early years.

We agree with the conventional wisdom that the Allied currency reform kick-started the German recovery, that market decontrol, after initial complications subsided, was a desirable adjunct, and that when the flow of aid had grown, the Marshall Plan helped substantially.

One can perhaps go further. Brackmann, whose concluding statements attaching importance to early German wartime planning we disagree with, offers the bold statement that monetary reform was responsible for advancing and consolidating democracy in Germany (Brackmann 1993, 283). This surely overstates its long-run importance, as comparison with democratic Britain, France, and Italy, which failed to reform their currencies, indicates, and underestimates the contributions of many other Western Allied programs, including denazification, the Nuremberg trials, establishment of representative bodies, support for education, and possibly decentralization. But monetary reform and the boost it gave to economic recovery did give defeated Germany hope for the future. We regret that burden sharing did not go further in rooting democracy more firmly.

We take exception to Secretary Royall's view that capital levies are transnationally infectious, as we do to the dictum of Governor Emmanuel

---

27 The Hesse Statistical Office showed that thirty-four firms with RM 18 million of inventories in 1936 had RM 47 million by 1945, accumulated during the war, and RM 60 million by 1946. Whereas stocks of raw materials and semifinished goods were sufficient to supply only two months' production in 1936, by 1947 they were enough for twelve months' output – at, of course, a level of less than half, this while the inventory of finished goods was below that of 1936 (Buchheim 1993, 92; Buchheim 1998, 98).

Monick of the Bank of France and Finance Minister René Pleven that a permanent amputation of money in circulation must be "unpopular, unfair, arbitrary, and ineffective" (Kindleberger 1993, 388–9). Unpopular, perhaps, and requiring despotic power to put through. Arbitrary, perhaps, and mistakes would inevitably be made. Unfair, not necessarily with burden sharing, which should at least be attempted. Ineffective seems wrong in the case of Germany. It is sad for social science that democracies sometimes fail in drastic and therapeutic financial surgery. It is consoling, however, that a successful operation, even one that fell short in fairness as in the German case, can strengthen democratic institutions and habits.

REFERENCES

Abelshauser, Werner. 1984. "The Economic Policy of Ludwig Erhard." Fiesole, Italy: European University Institute (EUI). Working paper no. 80.

――――. 1989. *Wirtschaftsgeschichte der Bundesrepublik*, 5th ed. Stuttgart.

――――. 1991. "American Aid and West German Recovery: A Macroeconomic Perspective." In *The Marshall Plan and Germany: West German Development within the Framework of the European Recovery Program*, edited by Charles S. Maier. New York and Oxford: Berg.

Albrecht, Karl. 1970. *Das Menchliche hinter dem Wunder: 25 Jahre Mitwirkung am deutschen Wirtschaftsausbau*. Düsseldorf and Vienna: Econ Verlag.

Annan, Lord Noel. 1995. *Changing Enemies: The Defeat and Regeneration of Germany*. London: Harper/Collins.

Benz, Wolfgang. 1988. "Die Währungsreform – Legende und Wirklichkeit: Eine Einführung." In *Mein Kopfgeld: Die Währungsreform, Rückblicke nach vier Jahrzehnten*, edited by Heinz Friedrich. Munich: Deutscher Raschebuch Verlag, no. 10901.

Borchardt, Knut, and Christoph Buchheim. 1991. "The Marshall Plan and Key Economic Sectors: A Microeconomic Perspective." In *The Marshall Plan and Germany: West German Development within the Framework of the European Recovery Program*, edited by Charles S. Maier. New York and Oxford: Berg.

Borchardt, Knut, and Otto Schötz, eds. 1931, 1981. *Wirtschaftspolitik in der Krise*. Baden-Baden: Nomos.

Brackmann, Michael. 1993. *Vom totalen Krieg zum Wirtschaftswunder: Die Vorgeschichte der westdeutschen Währungsreform 1948*. Essen: Klartext Verlag.

Buchheim, Christoph. 1993. "The Currency Reform in West Germany in 1948." In *German Yearbook of Business History, 1989–1992*.

――――. 1998. "Die Errichtung der Bank deutscher Länder und die Währungsreform in Westdeutschland," in *Fünfzig Jahre Deutsche Mark: Notenbank und Währung in Deutschland seit 1948*, Deutsche Bundesbank, ed. (Munich, 1998). [*Fifty Years of the Deutsche Mark: Central Bank and Currency in Germany Since 1948*, Deutsche Bundesbank, ed. (Oxford and New York, 1999).]

Cairncross, Alec, and Frances Cairncross, eds. 1992. *The Legacy of the Golden Age: The 1960s and Their Economic Consequences.* London and New York: Routledge.

Clay, Lucius D. 1950. *Decision in Germany.* New York: Doubleday.

Colm, Gerhard, Joseph M. Dodge, and Raymond W. Goldsmith. 1946. *A Plan for the Liquidation of War Finance and the Financial Rehabilitation of Germany.* Office of Military Government for Germany (U.S.), Berlin. National Archives, Suitland, OMGUS Finance Division, 14–3/5.

———. 1955. op. cit. Reprinted in *Zeitschrift für die gesamte Staatswissenschaft* 111.

Currie, David. 1997. *The Pros and Cons of EMU.* London: The Economic Intelligence Unit.

Deutsche Bundesbank, ed. 1976. *Währung und Wirtschaft in Deutschland, 1876–1975.* Frankfurt am Main: Knapp.

Domes, Jürgen, and Michael Wolffson. 1979. "Setting the Course for the Federal Republic of Germany: Major Policy Decisions in the Bizonal Economic Council and Party Images, 1947–1949." In "Currency and Economic Reform after World War II," edited by Rudolph Richter. *Zeitschrift für die gesamte Staatswissenschaft* 135, no. 3 (September).

Dupriez, Leon H. 1947. *Monetary Reconstruction in Belgium.* New York: King's Crown Press.

Ellis, Howard S. 1934. *German Monetary Theory, 1905–1933.* Cambridge: Harvard University Press.

Emminger, Otmar. 1986. *D-Mark, Dollar, Währungskrisen: Erinnerungen eines ehemaligen Bundesbankpräsidenten.* Stuttgart: Deutsche Verlags-Anstalt.

Erhard, Ludwig. 1943–4, 1977. *Kriegsfinanzierung und Schuldenkonsolidierung, Faksimiledruck der Denkschrift, 1943–4.* Frankfurt, Berlin, and Vienna.

———. 1963. *The Economics of Success.* London: Thames and Hudson.

Feldman, Gerald. 1993. *The Great Disorder: Politics, Economics and Society in the German Inflation, 1914–1924.* New York: Oxford University Press.

Friedman, Milton, and Rose Friedman. 1980. *Free to Choose.* New York: Harcourt, Brace, Jovanovich.

Friedrich, Heinz, ed. 1988. *Mein Kopfgeld: Die Währungsreform, Rückblicke nach vier Jahrzehnten.* Munich: Deutscher Raschebuch Verlag.

Gottlieb, Manuel. 1956–7. "Failure of Quadripartite Monetary Reform, 1945–47." *Finanz-Archiv* 17.

———. 1960. *The German Peace Settlement and the Berlin Crisis.* New York: Paine-Whitman.

Herbst, Ludolf. 1977. "Krisenüberwendung und Wirtschaftsneuordnung: Ludwig Erhards Beteiligung an den Nachkriegsplanungen am Ende des Zweiten Weltkrieges." In *Vierteljahreshefte der Zeitgeschichte* 25.

Holtfrerich, Carl-Ludwig. 1988. "Germany, 19th Century to Present." In *Central Bank Independence in Historical Perspective,* edited by Gianni Toniolo. Berlin and New York: Walter de Gruyter.

————. 1995. "The Deutsche Bank, 1945–1957: War, Military Rule and Reconstruction." In Lothar Gall et al., *The Deutsche Bank, 1870–1995*. London: Weidenfeld and Nicolson.

Hoppenstedt, Wolfram. 1997. *Gerhard Colm: Leben und Werk, 1897–1968*. Beiträge zur Wirtschafts- und Sozialgeschichte 65. Stuttgart: Franz Steiner Verlag.

Kindleberger, Charles P. 1984, 1993. *A Financial History of Western Europe*. 1st ed., London: George Allen & Unwin; 2d ed., New York and London: Oxford University Press.

————. 1991. *The Life of an Economist: An Autobiography*. Cambridge, Mass., and Oxford: Basil Blackwell.

————. 1991, 1995. "The Economic Crisis of 1619 to 1623." *Journal of Economic History* 5, no. 1 (March). Reprinted in *The World Economy and National Finance in Historical Perspective*. Ann Arbor: University of Michigan Press.

Klopstock, F. R. 1946. "New Proposals for Monetary and Financial Reform in Germany." Federal Reserve Bank of New York memorandum.

Knapp, J. Burke. 1945. Memorandum to General Milburn from Robert Murphy, director, Political Division, OMGUS, initialed BK, deposited Hoover Institution November 1991.

Mendershausen, Horst. 1949. "Money and the Distribution of Goods in Postwar Germany." *American Economic Review* 39, no. 2 (June).

Metzler, Lloyd A. 1979. "Recent Experience with Monetary and Financial Reform," a reprint of appendix O to the Colm-Dodge-Goldsmith report. In "Currency and Economic Reform in West Germany after World War II," edited by Rudolph Richter. *Zeitschrift für die gesamte Staatswissenschaft* 135, no. 3 (September).

Möller, Hans. 1976. "Die Deutsche Währungsreform von 1948." In Deutsche Bundesbank, ed., *Währung und Wirtschaft in Deutschland, 1876–1976*. Frankfurt am Main: Knapp.

————, ed. 1961. *Zur Vorgeschichte der deutschen Mark: Die Währungsreformpläne. Eine Dokumentation unter Mitwirkung von Wilhelm Kunze*. Basel: Kyklos Verlag; Tübingen: J.C.B. Mohr (Paul Siebeck).

OMGUS. 1947. *Price Control, Compensation Trade, and Inflation*. Special Report of the Military Governor. Ostrander papers.

Pfleiderer, Otto. 1979. "Two Types of Inflation, Two Types of Currency Reform: The German Currency Miracles of 1923 and 1948." In "Currency and Economic Reform in West Germany after World War II," edited by Rudolph Richter. *Zeitschrift für die gesamte Staatswissenschaft* 135, no. 3 (September).

Renger, Annemarie. 1988. "At the End of the Thousand Years." In *Mein Kopfgeld: Die Währungsreform, Rückblicke nach vier Jahrzehnten*, edited by Heinz Friedrich. Munich: Deutscher Raschebuch Verlag, no. 10901.

Ritschl, Albert. 1985. "Die Währungsreform von 1948 und der Wiederaufstieg der Westdeutschen Industrie: Zur These von Mathias Manz und Werner Abelshauser." *Vierteljahreshefte für Zeitgeschichte* 33, no. 1.

Sauermann, Heinz. 1955. "Der Amerikanische Plan für die deutsche Währungsreform." *Zeitschrift für die gesamte Staatswissenschaft* 111.

———. 1979. "On the Economic and Financial Rehabilitation of Western Germany, 1945–1949." In "Currency and Economic Reform in West Germany after World War II," edited by Rudolph Richter. *Zeitschrift für die gesamte Staatswissenschaft* 135, no. 3 (September).

Schonfeldt, Gräfin Sybil. 1988. "Kaum ist ein bischen Silber um den Spiegel." In *Mein Kopfgeld: Die Währungsreform, Rückblicke nach vier Jahrzehnten*, edited by Heinz Friedrich. Munich: Deutscher Raschebuch Verlag, no. 10901.

Schwartz, Thomas. 1991. "European Integration and the 'Special Relationship': Implementing the Marshall Plan in the Federal Republic." In *The Marshall Plan and Germany*, edited by Charles S. Maier. New York and Oxford: Berg.

Shlaes, Amity. 1997. "Loving the Mark." In Annals of Money, the *New Yorker* (double issue of April 28 and May 5).

Smith, Jean Edward. 1990. *Lucius D. Clay: An American Life.* New York: Henry Holt.

Sonderstelle. 1947. "Stenographic Report of the Sonderstelle Geld und Kredit," session of November 20.

Tenenbaum, Edward A. ca. 1957. "The German Mark," an unfinished manuscript, deposited at the Truman Library, Independence, Missouri.

Tenenbaum, J. Kipp. 1980. "Free to Choose?" Letter to the Editor, *New York Review of Books* 27, no. 18 (November 20).

Van Dormael, Armand. 1978. *Bretton Woods: Birth of a Monetary System.* New York: Holmes & Meier.

Von Krockow, Graf Christian. 1988. "Nicht einmal Tinte." In *Mein Kopfgeld: Die Währungsreform, Rückblicke nach vier Jahrzehnten*, edited by Heinz Friedrich. Munich: Deutscher Raschebuch Verlag, no. 10901.

Wallich, Henry C. 1955. *Mainsprings of German Revival.* New Haven: Yale University Press.

Wandel, Eckhard. 1979. "Historical Developments Prior to German Currency Reform of 1948." In "Currency and Economic Reform in West Germany after World War II," edited by Rudolph Richter. *Zeitschrift für die gesamte Staatswissenschaft* 135, no. 3 (September).

8

The Burden of Power

Military Aspects of International Financial Relations During the Long 1950s

WERNER ABELSHAUSER

I

The objective of this chapter needs clarification. *Prima vista*, the title promises information on what extent military expenditures contributed to the financial imbalances that have been a dominant feature of international relations between major countries of the North Atlantic Treaty Organization (NATO) during the 1950s and early 1960s. A correlation between these two phenomena may, on the one hand, be obvious, but is, on the other hand, difficult to quantify without further detailed research. Taking this problem into consideration, the scope of this essay is more modest, and at the same time, more ambitious. Without neglecting the military origins of these financial problems, I am going to explain how monetary pressure on international relations, stemming from the burden of security, had far-reaching and unintended consequences on international politics in general and on the process of economic integration in Western Europe in particular. The decision on the foundation of the European Economic Community (EEC) and the European Atomic Energy Community (EURATOM) in autumn 1956 and the signing of the Treaties of Rome in March 1957 cannot be understood properly without taking into consideration that there had been a hidden agenda within international security policy. Paradoxically, it is for the same reason that after 1958 it was not the Franco-German alliance that provided for the basic elements of a European security system, but still the Americans, who succeeded in making West Germany their closest and most dependent partner in Europe. In both cases, international financial relations played a crucial role in triggering far-reaching political decisions.[1]

1 This argument is based on my study of economics and armament during the 1950s that was published by the Militärgeschichtliches Forschungsamt (MGFA) of the German Army: Werner Abelshauser,

197

The second point I would like to make is to challenge the common view of a strong correlation between military pressure and international financial obligations. It is a well-known fact and indeed not a great surprise that security-induced expenditures in general and the costs of maintaining troops abroad in particular were closely linked to international financial problems during the Cold War. However, empirical studies on this field are still rare, especially those with a historical perspective. Therefore, it is still an open debate whether military expenditures were the major cause of financial imbalances, or whether they opened – on the contrary – a wide field for diplomatic action in order to compensate international payments imbalances and other monetary problems which stemmed from other sources. It is not even clear whether military expenditures abroad really were mainly motivated by the threat of Soviet aggression. My reading of the records in Washington, London, and Bonn suggests a different perspective. By numerous statements of the National Security Council (NSC), the president of the United States was regularly informed that a short-term threat did not exist for two reasons: During the 1950s, the Soviet Union was neither prepared to take military strike action on a large scale nor did it regard global military action as its preferred option in order to win the global competition between the antagonistic political systems in East and West. Therefore, the NSC came to the conclusion that "it appears unlikely that, within the next five years, the USSR or Communist China will deliberately initiate war."[2] The NSC, like the German intelligence service "Organisation Gehlen," emphasized rather the *potential* threat in an impending "era of nuclear plenty" that could emerge in the long run from a potentially fast growing economic development – in particular in the field of heavy industries involving the military-industrial complex.

Britain's Field Marshall Bernard Montgomery also did not believe in the possibility of an "all out war" in Central Europe, but rather in the danger of being confronted with a number of local conflicts at the European periphery and in the Third World. In his own words: "The risk of test match has now far receded, but the risk of village cricket remains."[3] In his security report for Chancellor Konrad Adenauer, General Reinhard Gehlen repeated year after year that the Red Army was not yet prepared to launch a major attack

---

Wirtschaft und Rüstung in den Fünfziger Jahren, vol. 4/1 of *Anfänge westdeutscher Sicherheitspolitik*, MGFA, ed. (Munich, 1997).

2 National Security Council: Basic National Security Policy (NSC 5501, Jan. 6, 1955), National Archives (hereafter NA), Record Group (hereafter RG), 273.

3 Chief of staff to minister of defense, Sept. 26, 1957, Public Record Office (hereafter PRO), MD 13, 90.

during the next three or four years.[4] Gehlen's assessment was based on a quite exact knowledge of the organizational and infrastructural deficiencies of the Red Army in Germany, Czechoslovakia, and Poland, which made any fast and surprising move of Russian troops extremely unrealistic.

Against this background, the relatively high, although decreasing, level of military expenditures in the West (with the exception of West Germany, where defense costs were rising but from a relatively low level) also had to serve other, more or less classical, purposes in the field of international relations. Military resources were certainly part and parcel of the United States' hegemonial mission. They were needed for the maintenance of colonial positions in France and Britain, and they represented some kind of a *bilet d'entrée* to great-power status in the realm of diplomacy in general. Maintaining troops in Germany, therefore, served many purposes including, of course, military ones. Foreign troops had to fill the military gap in Central Europe that the demilitarization of Germany in the post-1945 decade had opened. For London, Paris, and Washington, Germany proved to be after all an ideal place for defending their own countries and interests in war and peace – and up to 1955–6 it had been inexpensive, as well. However, there was also no doubt that the North Atlantic Treaty Organization (NATO) had not only "to keep the Soviets out" but also the "Germans down." The purpose of maintaining troops in Germany, therefore, was not in the first place to provide security for Germany, but rather to give the Western European countries security against a potential revival of German revisionism and revanchism. Not to mention the nonmilitary purposes, which may give rise to doubts whether this chapter is dealing with military aspects at all. Against this background, it may be more reasonable to blame the burden of power rather than the burden of security for most of the militarily induced international financial problems within the political relations of the members of the NATO.

II

Notwithstanding this ambiguity, West Germany was desperately dependent on British and American troops on its soil. Playing also the role of "hostages," 250,000 GIs and 105,000 soldiers of the British Army of Rhine and the Royal Air Force (both in the mid-1950s) could alone prevent, in case of Soviet aggression, the Western nuclear powers from following any of the

---

4 Deutscher Industrie- und Handelstag (DIHT), Rotberg to Paul Beyer and Gerhard Frenzel, Aug. 20, 1952 (betr. Beurteilung der militärischen Situation), Archiv DIHT, BN, o. Sign.

Table 8.1. *Selected American and British Balance-of-Payments Figures, 1954–65*

	United States ($ million)				Britain (£ million)		
	Liquidity Balance[a]	Net Military Expenditure[b]	Total Reserve Assets	Gold Reserves	Current Balance[c]	Balance for Official Financing[d]	UK Official Reserves
1954	−1,541	−2,460	22,978	21,793	+117	+126	2,762
1955	−1,242	−2,701	22,797	21,753	−155	−229	2,120
1956	−0,923	−2,788	23,666	22,058	+208	−159	2,133
1957	+0,621	−2,841	24,832	22,857	+233	+13	2,273
1958	−3,348	−3,135	22,540	20,582	+360	+290	3,069
1959	−3,648	−2,805	21,504	19,507	+172	+18	2,736
1960	−3,677	−2,753	19,359	17,804	−228	+325	3,231
1961	−2,252	−2,596	18,753	16,947	+47	−339	3,318
1962	−2,864	−2,448	17,220	16,057	+155	+192	2,806
1963	−2,713	−2,304	16,843	15,596	+125	−58	2,658
1964	−2,696	−2,133	16,672	15,471	−362	−695	2,315
1965	−2,478	−2,122	15,450	13,806	−43	−353	3,004

[a] 1954–9: gross liquidity balance; 1960–5: net liquidity balance.
[b] Direct expenditures minus military sales.
[c] Visible and invisible trade balance.
[d] Total sum (current balance + capital transfers + net investment and other capital transactions + balancing item) that has to be met by (or contributes to) official financing.

Source: Hubert Zimmermann, *Money and Security: Troops, Monetary Policy, and West Germany's Relations with the United States and Britain, 1950–1971* (Washington, D.C., and New York, 2002), 249 (offset agreements).

numerous strategies of "liberation by devastation" offered by the strategic "New Look," which naturally would have had a fatal impact on Germany's security. Therefore, both sides had a vital interest in stationing British and American troops in Germany.

Maintaining troops in Germany was, however, embedded in one of the most fundamental problems of international relations from the 1950s to the 1970s, namely, the increasing pressure on the currencies of the United Kingdom (UK) and, after 1958, of the United States (see Table 8.1). A major recipient of the vast sterling and dollar outflow was West Germany – and that is true not only for military reasons. Monetary problems, therefore, assumed an increasingly important role in British-German relations from the early 1950s as well as in American-German relations from 1959. For the United States and for Britain, a stable balance of payments was a necessary precondition for keeping up their roles as suppliers of international liquidity. Military expenditure abroad, of which troop stationing was

Table 8.2. *Cost of American and British Troops in Germany,*
May 1955–May 1956 (million DM)

	United States	United Kingdom
Work force	641.1	493.8
Accomodation	379.4	165.4
Communication	52.6	24.4
Transport	150.7	62.4
Services	160.7	40.2
Damages	75.0	25.0
Interests on Capital	11.6	22.7
TOTAL	1417.1	834.9
Including local foreign exchange cost	345.0	64.0
Cost of other troops		
France		614.0
Belgium		270.3
Denmark		4.7
Canada		5.1
TOTAL		3,200.0

Source: NA, RG 59, 740.5/3-2356.

a major component, was in either case a conspicuous negative factor (see Table 8.2).

Britain's financial policies in the 1950s were designed to help it escape its dependency on the United States and on the nations of the European Payment Union (EPU), and to achieve movement toward free convertibility. These objectives were undermined by recurring balance-of-payments problems and frequent waves of currency speculations against the pound, thus impeding the accumulation of sufficient reserves. Devaluation as a way out was ruled out after 1949 in order not to damage Britain's role as a world power, which to a large extent depended on the pound's stability. Until the mid-1950s, about 50 percent of all international financial transactions were still conducted in sterling. Britain had also been managing the reserves of numerous countries, which formed the Sterling Area. From the British Cabinet's point of view, therefore, the international value of sterling was "a matter of life or death to us as a country."[5] In the mid-1950s, Her Majesty's Government gradually became strongly committed to the rate of $2.80 per pound. It was to defend this rate until 1967 despite the ever higher costs of maintaining it. Nevertheless, the sterling remained fundamentally weak.

5 The Future of the UK in World Affairs (June 1, 1956), PRO, CAB 134/1315.

Generally speaking, this weakness was due to the permanent straining of British resources in the country's struggle to preserve its role as a world power, including the role of a colonial power, the capacity for worldwide intervention, the possession of nuclear weapons and the development of the H-bomb, and – as a consequence of all those costly ambitions – a relatively high level of armament expenditures and military forces that could not be justified solely by the potential military challenge of the Cold War. Fundamentally, troop maintenance on the Continent proved to be a drain on British reserves because of the need for conversion to pay for local services, civilian employees, allowances for soldiers, etc. Prior to May 1955, the local garrison's costs (in DM) of the British Rhine Army were comfortably covered by German payments. After that time, Britain had to fight a hard and humiliating struggle to retrieve support cost payments from the German Finance Ministry as compensation for the foreign-exchange losses Britain had to meet by stationing most of its European-based troops in Germany (see Table 8.3). But even if this German compensation had been taken into consideration, London had to cover average annual foreign-exchange costs caused by troop maintenance in Germany of about $180 million.

As early as March 1954, London was preoccupied with the bleak future of the British balance of payments after the end of German contributions and was looking for support from Washington, as for instance Anthony Eden did in a letter to John Foster Dulles: "Once the EDC [European Defence Community] is in force and the Germans are bearing their full share of defence expenditure we must face the certainty that after what may not be a long period we shall cease to receive any German contribution towards the costs of maintaining our forces in Germany. . . . At present level this would mean that we should have to finance an extra 80 million pounds in foreign exchange. This would present us with very great difficulties."[6] Being forced to make a choice between savings in conventional or nuclear armament, the prime minister clearly decided to stick to the latter, for "we would not expect, to maintain our influence as a world power unless we possessed the most up-to-date nuclear weapons."[7] The H-bomb was certainly not helpful in coping with Monty's "village cricket" scenario, but against the background of the latent sterling crisis the decision to update Britain's nuclear arsenal opened a financial dilemma, too. At the end of 1955, after the loss of $642 million (that is, one-quarter of all reserves), the economic situation came close to financial disaster. The British gold

6 Eden to Dulles, Mar. 6, 1954, PRO, T 312/53, Tel. 874.
7 July 7, 1954, PRO, CAB 128/27.

Table 8.3. *Support Cost and Offset Agreements Between Germany and the Stationing Countries,*
1955–65

Period	Legal Basis	Amount in DM
April 1952– April 1955	Occupation Costs	600m/month
1955–56	NATO Finance Convention Art. IV	3200m/year ($762m) UK: $140m US: $350m
1956–57	Support Cost Agreement	1500m UK: 400m (+524m/year to buy British weapons) US: 650m

1957–58	Support Cost
	Agreement
		1.200m
		UK: 588m +£75m deposit for settlement of
		    postwar debts +£30m deposit for arms
		    purchases + intention to buy "considerably"
		    more

1958–61	Support Cost Agreement	UK: 141, 2m/year +£50m deposit for arms orders +£22, 5m prepayment of debts US: $150m prepayment of debts
1961–63/4	Offset Agreement	UK: £54m (DM600m) for arms purchases US: $1425m (DM5700m) for military purchases
1963–65/6	Offset Agreement	UK: "as fully as possible" US: $1400m (DM5600m) for military purchases

Source: W. Abelshauser, *Wirtschaft und Rüstung in den Fünfziger Jahren (Anfänge westdeutscher Sicherheitspolitik 1945–56,* vol. 4/1) (Munich, 1997), chapter IV, passim (occupation cost and support cost agreements); Zimmermann, *Money and Security,* 252.

and dollar reserves were approaching the critical level between $1.5 billion and $2 billion, which almost automatically led to rising speculation against the pound. The chancellor of the exchequer, Harold Macmillan, closed his memorandum of January 1956 with the warning: "Time is running out."[8]

There was not much room left for maneuver. The Cabinet had explicitly assigned "top priority" to nuclear expenditures and according to Protocol No. II of the treaty on forces of Western European Union (WEU), Britain was obliged to maintain four divisions and the Second Tactical Air Force on the mainland of Europe.[9] However, Germany was adamant in its decision (and up to a certain point successfully so) not to continue the payment of

8 The economic situation (Jan. 5, 1956) C.P. (56) 17, note by the chancellor of the exchequer, C.P. (56) 32, PRO, CAB 129/79.
9 Treaty Series, 1955 (Oct. 23, 1954) Comnd. 9498.

occupation costs.[10] The way out of this dilemma seemed to lie in a change of NATO strategy that would allow the replacement of the expansive conventional forces with a nuclear strike capacity that Britain had to procure anyway. As with most of the big political decisions in NATO, the British proposal for a dramatic change in the alliance's strategic plans was also prepared by prior and secret Anglo-American cooperation. Growing British pressure on Washington to join London's desire for a new look in NATO's nuclear strategy fell on fertile grounds. The Eisenhower administration's military wing, represented by Secretary of Defense Charles E. Wilson and the head of the Joint Chiefs of Staff, Admiral Arthur W. Radford, early in 1955 became acquainted with the popular and attractive perspective "that [nuclear] weapons will replace men and money,"[11] and seemed to be thinking along the same lines as the British government – at least that's what the British ambassador believed.[12] Against the background of tighter U.S. budget problems – harbinger of the Triffin Dilemma yet to come – the Defense Department discussed internal plans to reduce American forces by 800,000 men, starting in 1956. The idea of relying more heavily on nuclear weapons became more and more attractive. There was, however, no lack of warnings; the United States could "suddenly wake up with alienated and disheartened Allies: it will take more for us to recapture their loyalty and our position of leadership if things are allowed to go this far."[13]

III

The Radford Plan, after being leaked to the public in an article in the *New York Times* dated June 14, 1956, hit U.S. relations with Germany and France like a bombshell. For the governments in Paris and Bonn, it was not difficult to understand the strategic consequences of the New Look – that France and Germany would be ground zero of a nuclear holocaust. Adenauer was particularly upset by this breach of trust. For his French colleague, Prime Minister Guy Mollet, the Radford Plan also indicated a *renversement* of the U.S. policy toward Europe. To the French, however, this did not come as

10 For more details, see Daniel Hofmann, *Truppenstationierung in der Bundesrepublik Deutschland. Die Vertragsverhandlungen mit den Westmächten, 1951–1959*, Beihefte 8 of *Dokumente zur Deutschland Politik*, Bundesministerium des Innern, ed. (Munich, 1997).
11 Edwin M. Martin, NATO Paris, to Ben T. Moore, State/RA, Aug. 13, 1954 (Subj.: New Look Paralysis), NA, RG 59, 740.5/8-1354.
12 Minutes of the meeting between Admiral Arthur W. Radford and Sir Roger Makins, June 22, 1956, NA, RG 59, 740.5/6-2256.
13 Martin to Livingston T. Merchant, EUR, Mar. 4, 1956 (Subj.: Conversation with General Gruenther), NA, RG 59, 740.5/3-455.

a surprise. France always had maintained a skeptical view toward the role of the United States in Europe. When in the autumn of the same year the Suez Crisis once more made clear that the Europeans could not rely on the Americans' willingness to defend European interests at all costs, France and Germany had to make their choices as to whether to accept being ranked as third-rate nations or whether they should instead make every effort to become nuclear powers themselves. Basically, the French had already made up their minds two years earlier when they demolished the European Defense Community (EDC), which had implied the renunciation of nuclear weapons by all participants. Now the German government did not hesitate to set the scene for a new look on the development of its future security policy. At its meeting on December 19, 1956, the Cabinet after a long debate on the consequences of the Radford Plan agreed on three points: to push ahead the buildup of the German Army, to speed up the process of European integration, and to produce nuclear weapons in Germany.[14] From the context of this Cabinet decision, it is obvious that the integration issue had been charged with a new meaning, changing its political appeal from the economy to the security aspect.

This new perspective of European integration, which was opened up by the political chain reaction following the initiative to solve the British monetary problem, lead to another unintended, yet far-reaching consequence. In 1956, the process of forming a Western European customs union had entered a state of stagnation. What began as a dynamic *relance européenne* after the EDC debacle was now confronted with strong opposition in France and Germany deriving from major economic interests. As late as the conference of the foreign ministers of the countries of the European Steel and Coal Community (ECSC), which took place in Paris on October 20–21, 1956, the diverging opinions and interests seemed to be paramount. But only two weeks later, Adenauer and Mollet were brushing aside all obstacles at an emergency meeting at the peak of the Suez Crisis in order to wave the flag of European solidarity and to take a first step in building up a new European defense community.[15] The German side considered both planned communities, the EEC and indeed particularly Euratom, as suitable places for organizing the production of nuclear weapons in a European context, if need be by France alone for the time being.[16] The chancellor's second

---

14 Minutes of the meeting of the Cabinet on Dec. 19, 1956, German Federal Archives, Military Branch (BA-MA), BM1/48957, 389.

15 Minutes of the talks at Hotel Matignon in Paris, Politisches Archiv des Auswärtigen Amtes (hereafter AA-PA), Büro StS, vol. 12.

16 Briefing for the Chancellor re: meeting with Guy Mollet, ibid.

thoughts are not difficult to guess, as Henri Spaak, the designated secretary general of NATO, told the British prime minister two months later: "If the French had [been] permitted to have a [nuclear weapons] program it might also be possible for the Germans to have a program in say five or ten years time."[17]

Consequently, this initial step was followed by others. In January 1957, the defense ministers of both countries signed a protocol on armament cooperation and a joint armament committee at the French military base, Colomb-Béchar, in the Algerian desert. In November, the French government, under the shock of the launch of *Sputnik*, decided to tighten up the relationship with Germany. On a conspiratorial trip to the German chancellor's home at Rhöndorf near Bonn, the French secretary of state, Maurice Faure, asked Adenauer to join France in a powerful initiative to produce nuclear weapons. Adenauer agreed, and in April 1958 a trilateral treaty was signed in Rome, with Italy as a third partner. This trilateral cooperation was, however, frozen after General Charles de Gaulle came to power in June 1958. De Gaulle preferred the formation of a three-power standing group within NATO rather than having France become the leader of the continental nations with Germany close behind. After the failure of this initiative for a NATO directorate, de Gaulle tried to return to the former nuclear alliance with Germany, accepting in his talks with Adenauer that it was "bon sense" that Germany could not renounce the possession of nuclear weapons in the long run.[18] But Adenauer did not join the French bandwagon. After de Gaulles's violation of the trilateral treaty, Germany had no other choice but to approach a close partnership with the Americans again. Under the rising pressure of the American monetary problems, the Eisenhower administration was also willing to move a bit in the direction of German nuclear interests.

The frustration of any European option on the nuclear field was complete – and did not only stem from French unpredictability. After the debacle of the Suez Crisis, the Foreign Office too had launched an initiative in European "nuclear" integration in order to overcome its dependency on the United States and, at the same time, to bridge the gap between its financial status and its political ambitions. To the foreign minister, it seemed clear that Britain could no longer sustain the defense burden that it was now carrying; but at the same time London's international standing would suffer if it sought relief by a unilateral reduction in defense expenditure. In

---

17 Record of Conversation at No. 10 Downing Street (Subj.: Euratom) on Jan. 15, 1957, PRO, FO 371/128308.
18 Minutes of the talks on Dec. 2, 1959, and July 29, 1960, BA, B 136/490.

a "Grand Design" for the Cabinet, Selwyn Lloyd tried to find a solution for Britain's dilemma:

A country which wishes to play the role of a great Power must ... have the power to use the whole range of thermonuclear weapons, including the megaton bomb. Although, if all goes well, Britain will shortly have the know-how of the megaton bomb and the possession of some kiloton weapons, Britain cannot by herself go the whole distance. If we try to do so we shall bankrupt ourselves. The choice is therefore clear.... If we are to be a first-class power with full thermonuclear capacity, it can only be done in association with other countries.... We should thereby enlist not only the resources and skill of our European neighbors, particularly the Germans, but also their finance.[19]

Unfortunately, Selwyn Lloyd's plan to convince the Cabinet failed, because it was based on the totally unrealistic assumption that the United States would agree on the proliferation of nuclear know-how for Continental Europe. Being in a position to frustrate any British "Grand Design" put forward without their prior approval, the Americans forced London to make a decision either "to go into Europe," taking the risk of American antagonism which could seriously damage the program, or to go on accepting American dominance within the "special relationship" between the two countries. The Cabinet preferred not to make an approach to any European country without prior consultation with the government of the United States and with the governments of the older Commonwealth countries.[20] However, in one respect Selwyn Lloyd's assessment was completely accurate. Without the Grand Design, Britain could no longer bear the burden of being a great power. In a memorandum on the economic situation of October 1957, the chancellor of the exchequer of the new Macmillan government, Peter Thorneycroft, warned his Cabinet colleagues: "We have been near to the edge of economic disaster. We are still near the edge."[21]

Within two months' time, Britain had lost £185 million. By the end of September, the reserves were down to £660 million, only two-thirds of the original amount from the end of 1954, despite the £200 million that London drew from the International Monetary Fund in 1956 and the £37 million the British gained by not paying interest on the American loan. In this difficult situation, Britain officially disclaimed its dubious demands on occupation

19 The Grand Design (co-operation with Western Europe), Jan. 5, 1957, PRO, CAB 129/84.
20 Co-operation with Western Europe: Minutes of a Cabinet meeting, Jan. 9, 1957, Cab 128/30; in *British Imperial Policy and Decolonization, 1938–64*, vol. 2, *1951–64*, ed. by A. N. Porter and A. J. Stockwell (London, 1989), 449.
21 The economic situation, note by the chancellor of the exchequer, Oct. 14, 1957, PRO, CAB 129/89.

law in Germany and asked NATO for help. According to Article 6 of Protocol II of the WEU treaty, a review of "the financial conditions on which the UK forces are maintained" was possible "if the maintenance of the UK forces on the mainland of Europe at any time [throws] too great a drain on the external finances of the UK."[22] In the end, it was Germany again which paid an annual financial aid of £12 million over the period from 1958–9 to 1960–1, but on a different legal and diplomatic basis. In addition, Bonn transferred more than £50 million in foreign currency as an advance payment for the procurement of weapons on a British government account at the Bank of England and renounced the interest. Bonn also repaid parts of the German postwar debts that otherwise would not have been due before 1962–4. Altogether Germany provided £200 million to help overcome Britain's financial problems without receiving an equivalent in terms of security (see Table 8.3). Nevertheless, London continued to withdraw battle troops and airmen from the Continent, although within the context of the support cost agreement of October 1958 the British had to commit themselves to keeping 55,000 men in Germany during 1958 and 45,000 men until 1961.

IV

The cure of the sick man from the River Thames was only the prelude to a far more important drama played on the international financial stage since the late 1950s – now starring Washington as the main protagonist. There had always been deficits in the U.S. budget of the 1950s, but in 1958 the traditionally high American trade surplus with Europe, which had balanced capital export and government expenditure abroad, shrank considerably. Suddenly the balance of payments revealed huge deficits. At the same time, the drain on the U.S. gold stock was growing to record levels. From the outset, raising the price of gold, implying a devaluation of the dollar, was ruled out as contradicting basic postwar American policy. Subsequently, Washington intensified its efforts toward trade liberalization as well as toward an improvement in sharing foreign aid and military burdens, particularly in relation to Europe. Germany was a major recipient of such policies. The foreign-exchange cost of American forces in Germany had risen sharply throughout the 1950s, in particular after the termination of occupation and support cost payments: from $250 million in 1953–5 to

---

22 Treaty Series, 1955 (Oct. 23, 1954), Comnd. 9498.

$686 million in 1959. It seemed as if troop stationing in Germany con-
tributed to about 20 percent of the deficit.[23] As the gold losses continued,
despite the recovery of the trade balance, there was obviously an urgent
need for taking measures. Again the question of withdrawing U.S. forces
from Europe came on the agenda. There was discussion of negotiating on
a bilateral basis with the European countries, especially Germany, for the
payment of the cost of maintaining U.S. forces abroad. After the London
gold crisis in October 1960, even the "lame duck" Eisenhower administration had to react immediately: The Anderson-Dillon mission to Bonn was
launched and pressed for full "offset" of the dollar drain.

The Germans were not unprepared, having just approved a big foreign
aid program amounting to $1 billion, of which more than a quarter would
be supplied by German industry. By doing so, Germany explicitly agreed to
share the burden of the West's politico-economic strategy toward the Third
World, which against the background of the Cold War also had strong
implications for the global balance of power. In addition, Bonn accepted a
larger share of NATO infrastructure costs and agreed on the prepayment
of postwar debts. As regards the demands for support costs, it definitely
rejected any kind of revival of occupation costs.

It was the newly elected Kennedy administration that finally broke the
deadlock. This time the Americans did not come empty-handed. They
offered the latest systems of high-tech weaponry short of nuclear arms.
Acquiring nuclear delivery systems was West Germany's closest possible
approach toward a more direct influence over the use of nuclear weapons
on its territory. Germany's intention was to use the strong reserve position
of the Federal Republic to enhance its military and political influence on
vital defense items. For John F. Kennedy, it was the other way round. He was
looking for a compromise in order to prevent Germany from joining France
on its way to nuclear independence: "If the French and other European
powers acquire a nuclear capability, they would be in a position to be entirely
independent and we might be on the outside looking in. We must exploit
our military and political position to ensure that our economic interests are
protected."[24] The situation that could be exploited emerged in August 1961
when the Berlin wall was built.

Now the Americans reinforced their troops in Germany by 45,000 men,
and the Germans provided for abundant funds to speed up both a further

---

23 Hubert Zimmermann, *Money and Security: Troops, Monetary Policy, and West Germany's Relations with
the United States and Britain, 1950–1971* (Washington, D.C., and New York, 2002), p. 107.
24 Remarks of President Kennedy to the NSC meeting, Jan. 22, 1963, FRUS XIII, 1961–3, 486.

buildup and the modernization of the German armed forces (Bundeswehr). Germany's defense budget was being increased by about DM 3 billion to DM 16.6 billion ($4.15 billion). The lion's share of the first offset agreement of October 24, 1961 (see Table 8.3) was used to purchase some of the most technologically advanced weapon systems, including nuclear-capable weapons such as sophisticated missile systems like Pershing (2 battalions = $126 million), Nike and Sergeant ($69 million), which were able to carry nuclear warheads, not to mention the notorious Starfighter interceptor. Further fields of cooperation opened up: co-production of common military equipment by German and U.S. sources, stocking up and maintenance support for Bundeswehr forces by U.S. military logistics systems, training of West German troops in U.S. military schools, joint usage of military facilities as well as joint research and development projects. Due to the huge amount of procurement ($1.425 million within two years), the Bundeswehr became a mainly American-equipped and dependent army for a long period of time. There was no space left for a French or British option in military cooperation. The offset problem afflicted German–American relations for many years to come – as was the case with German–British relations up to 1958 and beyond. Obviously, it was difficult to keep up the high level of U.S. procurements over a decade replete with changing budgetary problems and military requirements. In October 1965, when budgetary problems became apparent, the Bundesbank in a not quite serious recommendation came up with a "simple" solution for the British offset problem: German ministries should equip their Motor pools with Rolls Royce limousines instead of being forced to pay *à fonds perdue*.[25] The security argument also went far beyond the military aspects of the German–American relationship. It formed the background of many other "highlights" of German policy in the 1960s, including Chancellor Ludwig Erhard's fall from power in December 1966 and Bundesbank President Karl Blessing's famous letter of March 30, 1967. In this letter, Germany had been deprived of an important part of its monetary autonomy by Blessing's signing a pledge of nonconversion of dollars into gold by assuring the U.S. Treasury "that also in the future the Bundesbank intends to continue this policy and to play its full part in contributing to international monetary cooperation."[26] It was not until 1971 that the offset problem faded away. In the end, the offset problem did not lend to the withdrawal of foreign troops from Germany because

---

25 Memorandum department A21, Oct. 25, 1965, Bundesbankarchiv (BBA), A270/13168; cf. Zimmermann, *Money and Security*, 187.
26 For a detailed analysis see Zimmermann, *Money and Security*, chaps. 7–9.

Table 8.4. *Changes in Gross National Product (GNP) and Defense Expenditures, 1953–1958*

	Growth in Real GNP*	Defense Expenditures[†]
Belgium	14	3.6
Canada	15	6.1
Denmark	11	3.3
France	26	8.4
West Germany	37	3.6
Italy	29	4.4
Netherlands	25	4.9
Norway	12	4.1
United Kingdom	11	7.9
USA	8	11.2

*in percent.
[†] as a percentage of 1958 GNP.
· *Source:* Werner Abelshauser, *Wirtschaft und Rüstung in den Fünfziger Jahren (Anfänge westdeutscher Sicherheitspolitik 1945–1956*, vol. 4/1) (Munich, 1997), 111.

the matter was rendered irrelevant by the breakdown of the dollar gold system.

V

On account of all the facts reported so far, it seems obvious that occupation costs, support costs, offset payments, prepaid procurement, and other "militarily" motivated payments had little to do with the price for security that West Germany had to pay as an equivalent for defense services offered by foreign troops. The military argument served rather as a diplomatic lever for consolidating the mechanics of international financial balances that suffered from a typical postwar bias. Germany and other countries that were just recovering from war and regaining their former shares in the world market began to accumulate large surpluses at the expense of those countries that experienced a more modest development in foreign trade and, at the same time, suffered a great deal from the burden of power. During the 1950s, there was indeed a negative correlation between growth of GNP and growth of defense expenditures: the higher the rate of economic growth, the lower the burden of power (see Table 8.4). This burden of power was not the main reason for the imbalance of payments during the long 1950s, nor was it due to the burden of defending the West. Rather, it had been a question of defending power status within the Western alliance itself. The beauty of the military argument, therefore, lay in its emphasis on stability instead of on security. During the 1950s, West Germany alone reshuffled at least DM 70 billion ($16.66 billion) to countries with balance-of-payment problems via the military channel – either by providing for free goods and services for foreign troops in West Germany or by paying for local foreign-exchange costs in cash.[27]

Moreover, military aspects in the aforementioned sense do explain a great deal of the accidental character of the timing of the emergence of the EEC. International financial problems shaped a European security policy that opened up a new approach to the creation of a common market which had been blocked until then by the opposition of businesses and politicians in both countries. The EEC was finally born in order to pave the way for a European atomic energy community that was to be the first step toward a nuclear-based European defense community. Paradoxically, it was nevertheless the framework for European economic cooperation and not the vision of a close European armament and defense community that survived the political upheavals of the late fifties. The reason for the failure of the planned European – i.e., Franco-German – nuclear alliance had nothing to do with the constraints of international financial relations. On the contrary: General de Gaulle ignored the lessons of Realpolitik when he cancelled the second, and up to now last, attempt to organize a European defense union that could have given Western Europe a more effective focus for political integration. It is, however, an open question whether West Germany was really free to play the French card and thereby leave the Americans alone with the burden of power.

27 Cf. Abelshauser, *Wirtschaft und Rüstung*, 112–13.

9

Denationalizing Money?

Economic Liberalism and the "National Question" in Currency Affairs

ERIC HELLEINER

We live in an age when the ideology of economic liberalism is embraced by a growing number of governments in all parts of the world. Not since the early years of the twentieth century has this ideology dominated the global economic order to such an extent.[1] One of the most important thinkers behind the "neo-liberal" economic revolution of recent years was Friedrich Hayek. Among the more interesting of Hayek's ideas was his advocacy in 1976 of a world monetary system no longer centered around exclusive government-issued national currencies. In its limited form, this proposal would allow the co-circulation of foreign currencies alongside domestic currencies in each country's territory. In its more radical form, Hayek's reforms would do away with central banks and encourage private issuers of money to challenge the government's monopoly over currency. Hayek's advocacy of the "denationalization of money" – in both its limited and more radical approach – has attracted considerable attention in academic circles. Among policymakers, his proposal to allow co-circulation of currencies has also generated substantial interest, especially among those concerned with countries in the South and ex–Eastern bloc where "currency substitution" is widespread.[2]

I thank the Social Sciences and Humanities Research Council of Canada for assisting this research. I am also grateful for helpful comments to: Knut Borchardt, William Branson, Jennifer Clapp, William Clark, Benjamin Cohen, Marc Flandreau, Harold James, Don Moggridge, Lou Pauly, Robert Skidelsky, and David Wolfe. An earlier and shorter version of this chapter has appeared in E. Gilbert and E. Helleiner, eds., *Nation-States and Money* (London, 1999).

1 In referring to "economic liberalism" in this essay, I do not include what John Ruggie calls "embedded liberalism"; that is, the more interventionist forms of liberalism that became popular in the Keynesian age. See John Ruggie, "International Regimes, Transactions and Change," *International Organization* 36 (1983): 379–405. In monetary affairs, I consider the hallmarks of the economic liberal perspective to be a belief in stable money and a skepticism of discretionary monetary policy by governments.

2 The term "currency substitution" is used differently by different authors. In this essay, it refers to the use of foreign currency within the domestic territory of a country. For Hayek's ideas, see Friedrich

Most of the existing literature analyzing Hayek's monetary ideas focuses on their economic costs and benefits. In this essay, I aim to place Hayek's ideas in a more historical and political context. I begin by highlighting how different his proposals are from the international gold standard that existed in the last age when economic liberalism dominated monetary policymaking. Although the gold standard is often seen as a very cosmopolitan monetary order, I call attention to the fact that its establishment in the nineteenth and early twentieth centuries was usually associated with the consolidation of the very state-managed "national currencies" that Hayek now suggests we eliminate.[3] Indeed, I argue in the first section of the essay that this link between "nationalization of money" and the creation of the gold standard – often neglected in existing literature – helps to explain why the latter was able to garner political support in that age of nation-building and nationalism.

In the second section, I seek to explain why Hayek advocated the dismantling of the national currencies that his liberal predecessors helped to build. I suggest that his re-evaluation of the "national question" stems partly from an underlying individualism and cosmopolitanism in liberal thought. Equally important, however, was his reaction against the uses to which national currencies were put when mass democratic politics replaced the narrow elite politics which had been characteristic of the era of the gold standard.

In the final section, I evaluate the likelihood of his proposal attracting widespread political support in the contemporary age. Hayek and his followers usually cite states' desire to maximize seigniorage revenue as the key political barrier their proposal faces. But I suggest that they often overlook the way that the "national question" in currency affairs raises political issues relating to the coherence and identity of the nation as well as the nature of national citizenship. Thus, while liberals in the pre-1931 period could count on the support of many nationalists in their construction of the gold standard, Hayek's proposal is destined to be more controversial in an age when nationalism remains a potent force.

THE GOLD STANDARD AND THE "NATIONALIZATION OF MONEY"

Economic liberals traditionally supported the gold standard for a simple reason: It was the monetary order that seemed most closely associated with their cosmopolitan laissez-faire principles. In its ideal form, the gold standard

Hayek, *Choice in Currency* (London, 1976), *Denationalization of Money – The Argument Refined*, 3rd ed. (1976; reprint, London, 1990).

3 To be consistent with Hayek's language, I use the term "national currencies" in this article to refer to currencies which are homogenous and exclusive within the territorial boundaries of a nation-state.

would maintain international equilibrium, discipline government policy, and foster international trade and finance by providing fixed exchange rates and a common monetary standard. Moreover, it would accomplish these goals in an automatic fashion via the activity of self-regulating markets with a minimum of discretionary government involvement in the monetary sector.

The political prominence of liberal goals – as well as of the various domestic sectoral groups who would benefit from them[4] – undoubtedly played a key role in explaining why countries joined the gold standard in the nineteenth and early twentieth centuries. But the fact that the gold standard triumphed in an era of nation-building suggests that it satisfied not just liberal objectives but also more nationalist ones. Some historians, for example, have noted how countries saw joining the gold standard as a source of national prestige and a way to emulate the monetary system of the world's leading economic power, the United Kingdom.[5] For "late developers," adopting the gold standard was also a way to attract international investment by creating a more credible and stable standard of value.[6]

Equally significant was the goal of consolidating the national monetary system under state control. Before the introduction of the gold standard, countries usually had rather heterogeneous and often quite chaotic monetary systems over which the state exercised only partial control. Moving on the gold standard was often seen as the key monetary reform that could lead to a more unified and homogeneous monetary order controlled by the state, a project that appealed to nationalists for a variety of reasons outlined below. This feature of the gold standard has often attracted less attention in existing literature, perhaps because of the influence of the liberal ideal of the gold standard. But it deserves scrutiny in order to highlight a key contrast between most economic liberals during the era of the gold standard and Hayek: While the latter called for the denationalization of money, the former helped to "nationalize" money through their support of the gold standard. This aspect of the gold standard also calls attention to the tacit acceptance by most liberals of the nation-building aspirations and nationalism of that age, an approach that Hayek and his supporters do not emulate.

4 See for example Marcello De Cecco, *The International Gold Standard*, 2d ed. (London, 1984); Jeffry Frieden, "The Dynamics of International Monetary Systems: International and Domestic Factors in the Rise, Reign and Demise of the Classical Gold Standard," in Jack Snyder and Robert Jervis, eds., *Coping With Complexity in the International System* (Boulder, Colo., 1993).
5 Leland Yaeger, "The Image of the Gold Standard," in M. Bordo and A. Schwartz, eds., *A Retrospective on the Classical Gold Standard, 1821–1931* (Chicago, 1984), 657–9; Guilio Gallarotti, *The Anatomy of an International Monetary Regime: The Classical Gold Standard, 1880–1914* (Oxford, 1995), 143–7; Alan Milward, "The Origins of the Gold Standard," in J. B. De Macedo, B. Eichengreen, and J. Reis, eds., *Currency Convertibility* (London, 1996).
6 Milward, "Origins."

The gold standard consolidated national monetary systems and brought them under greater state control in several ways. To begin with, before adopting the gold standard, the dominant forms of money in domestic circulation were usually "full weight" silver and gold coins whose assigned value was equivalent to the value of the metals they were made of. Under this kind of coinage system, changes in the official gold-silver exchange rate or changes in world market prices of these metals could cause considerable disruption to the domestic monetary system as one or other of the dominant coins quickly disappeared from circulation. States sought to prevent this disruption by controlling cross-border movements of coins or by adjusting the official gold-silver exchange rate, but controls were usually ineffective and it proved difficult to set appropriate silver-gold ratios in times when the market exchange rate between the two metals was fluctuating rapidly.

The gold standard eliminated this age-old problem of traditional monetary systems overnight. The central significance of the introduction of the gold standard in this respect was the creation of a subsidiary "token" silver coinage; that is, a coinage where the face value of lower denomination coins no longer derived from their metallic content but from a value assigned by the state vis-à-vis gold.[7] To maintain their value, the supply of the token coins became closely managed by the state. In most countries (and of course particularly those who joined the gold-exchange standard), these token coins quickly came to comprise most of the coinage and few full-weight gold coins were actually used in domestic payments. This transformation of the coinage did much to reduce monetary chaos since it ended the risk of a sudden disappearance of a large portion of the coinage.

The fact that the gold standard brought the domestic coinage under this more homogenous and managed order often acted as the central reason for countries to join the gold standard. In his important though often neglected study, Neil Carothers pointed out that the United Kingdom (UK), the United States, and many continental European countries introduced the gold standard during the nineteenth century "primarily due to the impelling need for a stable and convenient small change currency."[8] Faced with sudden shortages of low denomination silver coins when the gold-silver price ratio changed dramatically, countries joined the gold standard and created a token silver currency as a way of preventing low denomination money from disappearing from circulation.

---

7 In some countries, monetary authorities had transformed some lower denomination silver coins into token coins before the introduction of a gold standard. But in these instances, the introduction of the gold standard was still significant in transforming *all* silver coins into a token form.
8 Neil Carothers, *Fractional Money* (New York, 1930), 137.

Angela Redish points out that governments were unable to contemplate this coinage reform until industrial minting technology enabled such coins to be produced in a fashion that was difficult to counterfeit during the nineteenth century.[9] If this supply-side innovation was a precondition for monetary reform, the move to the gold standard was also encouraged by a demand-side change. The need for a solution to the problem of small change only became particularly pressing when more and more of the population came to depend on monetary transactions for their livelihood. The rapid spread of the money economy and its penetration into daily life took place at different speeds in different countries during the nineteenth century under the pressures of industrialization and the emergence of national scale markets. But everywhere that this process took place, the poor became more vulnerable to the sudden disappearance of small change (on which they relied heavily) that was a constant risk associated with the old full-weight coinage systems. And as this vulnerability increased, shortages of small change triggered waves of popular protest and domestic petitions calling for a more adequate and reliable low denomination money. In the age of the nation-state, these protests and petitions met with a more receptive audience than they would have before the nineteenth century. They were, after all, made by people who were now considered "citizens" with a voice in the affairs of the nation. It was in response to these demands that the gold standard was frequently introduced.[10] In these contexts, the creation of the gold standard can be seen as an effort to find a monetary order more appropriate to an emerging market-based national economy and national polity.

The introduction of state-managed token subsidiary coins via the gold standard also enhanced the orderly nature of the monetary order in a second way. Under a coinage system with full-weight coins, an internal exchange rate existed between the value of gold and silver money. When the relative value of the two fluctuated frequently, considerable accounting difficulties and transaction costs were experienced. Indeed, to cope with changing relative values of coins – often further complicated by the presence of foreign coins (see below), widespread counterfeiting, and the failure to withdraw old and worn coins – abstract units of account were often used

9 Angela Redish, "The Evolution of the Gold Standard in England," *Journal of Economic History* 50 (1990): 789–805; "The Persistence of Bimetallism in Nineteenth-century France," *Economic History Review* 55 (1995): 717–36.

10 See, e.g., Carothers, *Fractional Money*; Jaime Reis, "First to Join the Gold Standard, 1854," in Jorge Braga De Macedo, Barry Eichengreen, and Jaime Reis, eds., *Currency Convertibility* (London, 1996).

to value the various forms of money in circulation. The introduction of the gold standard ended this confusion by creating a single standard that ensured all coins now existed in a fixed relationship to each other over time. Supporters of the gold standard often called attention to this benefit of the new monetary structure. For example, in his 1805 *Treatise on the Coins of the Realm* that paved the way for the introduction of the gold standard in the United Kingdom, Charles Jenkinson noted that a monometallic standard was essential for this reason in a country such as the United Kingdom which had a rapidly expanding commercial activity.[11] Commercial cities such as Amsterdam, he noted, had also encountered the transactions costs associated with multiple standards in the past and had them addressed through the creation of "bank-money" for leading merchants. But as the first economy with commercial activity spread out evenly across the entire nation, the United Kingdom, he argued, required a single homogenous standard available to all. The gold standard, in other words, was seen by Jenkinson as a necessary feature of the new "national-scale" commercial economies emerging in the nineteenth century.

A third way that the new state-managed token coins of the gold standard contributed to the consolidation of a homogeneous monetary system was that they encouraged the disappearance of foreign coins from domestic circulation. In a monetary system dominated by full-weight coins, it was common for foreign coins to circulate alongside domestic ones, and in some countries the majority of the currency in circulation was of foreign origin. But as coins everywhere increasingly assumed a "token" form, they were less likely to be accepted abroad. Their value no longer depended on its intrinsic metallic content but rather on some knowledge of the trustworthiness of the government that issued them as well as the prospect that the holder could redeem these coins into gold with that government. The introduction of the gold standard also encouraged public authorities to make active efforts to remove foreign currencies from circulation since their circulation could complicate the government's need to manage carefully the supply of token coins in domestic circulation. In addition, the role that foreign coins had often played supplementing an inadequate domestic small denomination coinage also was less useful once a modern subsidiary silver coinage was produced under the gold standard.[12]

The introduction of the gold standard was thus often the key development that ended the circulation of foreign coins, including various famous

---

11 Charles Jenkinson, *Treatise on the Coins of the Realm* (1805; reprint, London, 1880), 136–8.
12 See, e.g., David Martin, "The Changing Role of Foreign Money in the United States, 1782–1857," *Journal of Economic History* 37 (1977): 1009–27.

"cosmopolitan" coins such as the Mexican dollar.[13] While this development sometimes provoked complaints from international merchants and travelers,[14] it appealed to policymakers seeking both to reduce the transactions costs associated with a heterogeneous domestic coinage and to enhance their control over the domestic monetary system. It also had some symbolic appeal. The circulation of foreign coins was often seen by nationalists as something that "hurt national pride" or that was "humiliating" to the nation.[15] Not only was the existence of foreign coins seen as infringing on the sovereignty of a country, but it also raised symbolic concerns as imagery on coins increasingly took on nationalist overtones in the nineteenth and early twentieth centuries.[16]

Finally, while the discussion above focused on changes in the coinage, the introduction of the gold standard also came to be associated with a homogenization of the banknote circulation. As paper money began to be issued in greater quantities during the nineteenth and twentieth centuries, it often initially contributed to the heterogeneity of the money in circulation as many institutions – from various levels of government to a multitude of private banks – began to issue notes. Not only did the denominations and appearance of these different forms of paper money often vary considerably, but so too did their "quality" and thus the degree of their acceptance across the economic space of each country. The introduction of the gold standard was frequently the moment when states moved to consolidate the issuing of notes by granting monopoly note issue rights to the national central bank.

This link between the gold standard and note issue monopolies was not present in all cases during the nineteenth century; many countries on the

---

13 A. P. Andrew, "The End of the Mexican Dollar," *Quarterly Journal of Economics* 18 (1904): 321–56. This is not to suggest that all countries who joined the gold standard eliminated foreign coins from domestic circulation. Some countries allowed the full-weight gold coins of other nations to continue to circulate domestically, particularly if they did not produce such coins themselves. In most of these cases, however, few of these coins were actually in circulation. Some others also allowed foreign token coins to circulate domestically up until World War I, such as the member countries of the Latin Monetary Union (LMU) and the Scandinavian Monetary Union (SMU). They did so partly for reasons of convenience but also for broader political reasons associated with French imperial goals and influence in the case of the LMU and "pan-Scandinavian" sentiments in the case of the SMU. In these instances, however, it is important to note that foreign token coins now circulated domestically only under the terms of these international agreements which regulated their production and acceptance in each participating country. See for example Henry Parker Willis, *A History of the Latin Monetary Union* (Chicago, 1901); Axel Nielson, "Monetary Unions," *Encyclopedia of the Social Sciences* 10 (1933): 595–601.

14 George Knapp, *The State Theory of Money*, trans. H. Lucas and J. Bonar (1905; reprint, London, 1924).

15 Quotations from Reis, "First to Join," 161; Government of Canada, *House of Commons Debates*, 1st Parliament, 2d Session (1869; reprint, Ottawa, 1975), 464.

16 Eric Helleiner, "National Currencies and National Identities," *American Behavioral Scientist* 41 (1998): 1409–36.

gold standard in that era continued to have multiple note issues and other countries had a monopoly note issue without being on the gold standard. But the association between the gold standard and note issue consolidation became an increasingly common one after the United Kingdom's 1844 Bank Act granted the Bank of England monopoly note issue as part of an effort to make the gold standard operate more smoothly. The link between the gold standard and the consolidation of the national note issue grew particularly strong after World War I. At the Brussels (1920) and Genoa (1922) international economic conferences, resolutions were passed calling for the creation of central banks with monopoly note issues in all countries who had not yet created them as part of the effort to restore the international gold standard in that era.

Some economic liberals in the nineteenth century opposed the monopolization of the note issue, preferring to see a competitive system of note issue (although interestingly, few extended this argument to the issue of coinage). But the influence of this "free banking" school dwindled in the years leading up to World War I and then collapsed after 1918. The dominant position in economic liberal circles for most of the nineteenth century, and especially by the 1920s, was that countries on the gold standard should each create a central bank with a monopoly note issue for a straightforward reason: It was necessary to ensure that the supply of notes was regulated in a manner in keeping with the automatic self-regulating principles of gold standard. Whether this control was to be exercised along the rigid lines advocated by the Currency School in 1844 or along the more flexible lines suggested by the 1919 Cunliffe Committee, central banks with a monopoly note issue came to be seen as central to the smooth operation of the international gold standard. After World War I, they also were seen as important in facilitating a rapid restoration of currency stability as well as international cooperation in the monetary realm.

The link between the gold standard and a central bank with monopoly note issue held different appeal to those whose focus was less internationalist and more focused on the domestic task of national monetary consolidation. After all, it was not just liberals during the 1920s but also nationalists in Eastern Europe, Latin America, the British Dominions, and parts of Asia who welcomed the Brussels and Genoa resolutions.[17] To them, the creation

17 See, e.g., De Cecco, *International*, ii; Marcello De Cecco, "Central Bank Cooperation in the Interwar Period: A View from the Periphery," in Jaime Reis, ed., *International Monetary Systems in Historical Perspective* (London, 1995), 131; Paul Drake, *The Money Doctor in the Andes: The Kemmerer Missions, 1923–1933* (Durham, N.C., 1989); Maxwell Fry, *Money and Banking in Turkey* (Istanbul, 1979), 279–80; A. F. W. Plumptre, *Central Banking in the British Dominions* (Toronto, 1940); Ahmad Minai, "Economic Development of Iran: Under the Reign of Reza Shah, 1926–1941," Ph.D. diss, American

of a central bank with monopoly note issue represented simply one more way in which the move onto a gold standard was associated with the consolidation of the national monetary system under state control. A central bank with monopoly control over the note issue not only helped to reduce transaction costs within the nation (particularly for the poor and illiterate who had difficulty discriminating properly between "good" and "bad" private notes). It also gave the state a valuable source of seigniorage revenue as well as a tool to influence more effectively the nation's internal economy and its economic relations with the outside world (since the gold reserves of the country came under centralized control). In Marcello De Cecco's words, adopting the gold standard thus "was in most cases a giant step towards dirigisme."[18]

In addition, it should not be forgotten that the monopolization of the bank note under state control often had symbolic value for nationalists. Eric Hobsbawm explains how governments across the world launched extensive initiatives to "mass produce tradition" of a nationalist kind in the last third of the nineteenth century as a means of maintaining legitimacy in the face of domestic challenges to their rule.[19] Elaborate images on state-issued bank notes played a major role in these initiatives. The images included national landscapes, important events and personalities in the history of the nation, and portrayals of the everyday life of citizens and the economic progress of the nation. Policymakers recognized that images on notes were particularly effective tools of propaganda – more so than flags or anthems – because they were encountered so regularly in the context of daily routines in an age when the use of money was becoming increasingly pervasive. As one of the "most mass-produced objects in the world," bank notes also were seen as able to convey images to vast numbers of citizens in an age when the state had difficulty communicating with them through other means such as newspapers or schooling.[20]

The introduction of the gold standard thus encouraged a more consolidated and rationalized national currency to emerge under state control. This feature of the gold standard helps us to understand why the gold standard had particular appeal in an era of nation-building and nationalism. Although economic liberals saw the gold standard in primarily economic and

University, 1961, 159; Russell Ally, "The South African Pound Comes of Age," *Journal of Imperial and Commonwealth History* 22 (1994): 109–26.

18 De Cecco, *International*, ii.
19 Eric Hobsbawm, "Mass-Producing Tradition: Europe, 1870–1914," in Eric Hobsbawm and Terence Ranger, eds., *The Invention of Tradition* (Cambridge, 1983).
20 Quote from Virginia Hewitt, *Beauty and the Banknote* (London, 1994), 11. For a more extended discussion of these issues, see Helleiner, "National Currencies."

internationalist terms, nationalists saw it in a more domestic and political manner as useful for their goals of strengthening the state's power and its control over the economy, cultivating a sense of collective national identity, and consolidating the internal economic coherence of the nation.[21] The latter goal was particularly significant for nation-builders during the nineteenth and early twentieth centuries. The transaction costs and uncertainties associated with heterogeneous monetary systems were usually very significant for public authorities in areas such as tax collection as well as for private economic actors seeking to operate in the emerging economic space of the nation.[22] The more consolidated monetary order associated with the gold standard reduced them, often in a dramatic manner, thus both creating a more efficient public sector capable of mobilizing national resources and fostering the growth of a smoothly functioning national market economy. For this reason, the gold standard was often seen as a particularly "modern" monetary order well-suited to the age of nation-building.

HAYEK'S RE-EVALUATION OF THE "NATIONAL QUESTION"

If economic liberals in the nineteenth and early twentieth centuries were able to find support for the construction of the gold standard among many nationalists of their era, proponents of Hayek's proposal seem unlikely to repeat this experience. In calling for the "denationalization" of money, they can expect to arouse the opposition of nationalists who see national currencies as an essential part of a political fabric of a nation. Why then would Hayek and his supporters advocate the dismantling of the very national currencies that his liberal predecessors helped to build? What explains this re-evaluation of the "national question" in currency affairs?

The Cosmopolitanism and Individualism of Economic Liberalism

In part, Hayek's proposal stems from the strong cosmopolitanism and individualism in his thought and his concomitant hostility to collectivist ideas such as nationalism. Indeed, in *The Denationalization of Money*, he made

---

21 This domestic political goal also helps to explain the way in which the international gold standard emerged in what Gallarotti (*Anatomy*) notes was a rather decentralized and diffused fashion. Since a key goal in joining the gold standard was an inward-looking political one, policymakers often had little sense that they were also creating what came later to be seen as an organized "international economic regime."

22 Eric Helleiner, "One Nation, One Money: Territorial Currencies and the Nation-State," ARENA Working Paper no. 17 (Oslo, 1997); Eric Helleiner, "Historicizing Territorial Currencies: Monetary Space and the Nation-State in North America," *Political Geography* (forthcoming).

clear that it was not just national currencies he opposed but even national economies themselves: "There is indeed little reason why ... territories that happen to be under the same government should form distinct national economic areas."[23]

Hayek's individualistic and cosmopolitan sentiments were in fact not so different from those of his nineteenth-century predecessors. These kinds of sentiments have always been held central to the worldview of economic liberals, and they were important in leading some economic liberals of that era to oppose monopoly note issue in favor of "free banking," as we have already seen. Similarly, although other economic liberals in the pre-1931 era found themselves frequently allied with nationalists in supporting a monopoly note issue and the gold standard, they showed only limited interest in the latter's objectives. To be sure, many liberals certainly welcomed the more orderly and "scientific" domestic monetary order that was ushered in by a monopoly note issue and the gold standard.[24] But their interest in the relationship between the consolidation of national currencies and the broader political project of nation-building was usually limited. Indeed, whereas nationalists usually saw the goal of nation-building as an end in itself, most economic liberals hoped the construction of a coherent national economy was merely a temporary way station en route to the construction of universal global community.[25]

A key attraction of the international gold standard was that it seemed to help them to reach this cosmopolitan goal. Although the gold standard consolidated the domestic monetary system, for most liberals its more attractive feature was the fact that it constructed a world monetary system that would help maintain international equilibrium and foster the growth of international trade and investment. To many liberals, the gold standard in fact created a monetary order which had a de facto global currency: gold.[26] Indeed, most economic liberals did not find much significance in the fact that the gold standard rested on the foundation of *national* currencies with their distinctive imagery, names, and units of account. In Karl Polanyi's words, "If the nation was deemed by them an anachronism, national currencies were reckoned not even worthy of attention. No self-respecting economist of the liberal age doubted the irrelevance of the fact that different pieces of paper

---

23 Hayek, *Denationalization*, 114.

24 See, e.g., Emily Rosenberg, "Foundations of U.S. International Financial Power: Gold Standard Diplomacy, 1900–1905," *Business History Review* 59 (1985): 169–202.

25 Eric Hobsbawm, *Nations and Nationalism Since 1780*, 2d ed. (Cambridge, 1992), 43.

26 See, e.g., Bamberger's view that "a world monetary union would be superfluous if all countries based their currencies on gold" (quoted in Gallarotti, *Anatomy*, 19).

were called differently on different sides of political frontiers." They were, after all, simply "different tokens representing the same commodity."[27]

In keeping with their cosmopolitan sentiments, various economic liberals called for the creation of a truly universal currency at different times during the nineteenth and early twentieth centuries. The most prominent initiative came at the high point of the influence of economic liberalism during the 1860s when a proposal was made for the introduction of a universal coin that could circulate in all nations. Not only would this coin reduce transaction costs associated with handling various distinct national currencies, but it would also help people to transcend national identities by making people, in Walter Bagehot's words, "think they were of one blood."[28] The initiative garnered a remarkable degree of support from liberals across the world from Europe to Asia and the Americas, helped perhaps by the fact that many countries were contemplating currency reforms anyway as a result of the dramatic changes in the silver–gold price ratio in this period.

That the initiative ultimately failed is often attributed to the lack of British leadership, the wariness of the U.S. Congress, or the decision of Germany after unification to consolidate its coinage system on a basis that was not easily reconcilable with that of other nations. But underlying these circumstances was the fact that this liberal initiative – in contrast to the construction of the gold standard – worked against the nationalist aspirations of the age. The German decision after unification, for example, highlighted the fact that the goal of domestic national monetary consolidation took precedence over that of global monetary integration (in addition to reflecting Bismarck's suspicions of French interest in the universal coin proposal).[29] In the United Kingdom and United States, the proposal ran into opposition from nationalists who felt strongly that national currencies were a source of identification with the nation. British government delegates hinted at this in explaining their reticence on the grounds that their existing monetary system was "approved by experience, and rooted in the habits of the people."[30] One British opponent, for example, spoke of the "spirit of nationality" that surrounds the pound sterling because of its long history as a "representative of value."[31] Similarly, a U.S. delegate to the 1867 Paris conference that discussed the plan made clear that it would be impossible to abolish national

---

27 Quotes from Karl Polanyi, *The Great Transformation* (Boston, 1944), 202, 196.
28 Quoted in M. Perlman, "In Search of Monetary Union," *Journal of European Economic History* 22 (1993): 318.
29 Henry Russell, *International Monetary Conferences* (New York, 1898), 117.
30 Quoted in Royal Commission on International Coinage, *Report* (London, 1868), 203.
31 John Bowring in Royal Commission, *Report*, 133.

names of currencies such as the "dollar" in the United States or "sovereign" in the United Kingdom because of the significance of these names to citizens of those countries. It was also clear that all governments had no interest in proposals that eliminated the different national emblems that existed on each nation's coins.[32] Indeed, U.S. proponents of the universal coin in the early 1870s were forced to recognize the attachment to these emblems when they met stiff opposition in Congress to their "practical, utilitarian" proposal to remove the eagle from silver coins and replace it with words indicating the intrinsic fineness and weight of the coin, a move designed to encourage the international acceptance of the coins.[33]

This whole episode thus made clear to liberals that their cosmopolitan ideals were not fully in keeping with the nationalist temper of the age. Although they did not embrace nationalism enthusiastically, liberals had to recognize its political power and influence, just as "free bankers" were also forced to. This is not to say proposals for supranational forms of money did not continue to resurface in liberal circles.[34] But they were acknowledged by most to be politically unrealistic given nationalist sentiments. It had become clear that any world monetary system had to be built on an "inter-national" basis — that is, on the foundation of nations and national currencies, as the gold standard was — rather than on more "cosmopolitan" principles.[35]

The cosmopolitan and individualistic ideals guiding Hayek's monetary proposals were thus not terribly different from the ideals of his liberal predecessors in the pre-1931 period. But while the latter increasingly resigned themselves to national currencies and the power of nationalism after the 1860s, Hayek was less inclined to do so. This partly reflected his fierce opposition to all forms of "collectivism," as already noted. But it also stemmed from a second source: his reaction against the experience of how national currencies came to be managed in the interwar period and after.

Popular Sovereignty and National Currencies

Of the reasons why nationalists supported the gold standard in the pre-1931 period, the most difficult one for liberals of that age to sympathize with was the nationalist goal of enhancing the ability of the state to control the

---

32 Russell, *International*, 60, 62. 33 *Congressional Globe*, Jan. 17, 1873, 672, 679.

34 See, e.g., Edwin Kemmerer, "A Proposal for Pan-American Monetary Unity," *Political Science Quarterly* 31 (1916): 66–80; Jean Van De Putte, *A World Currency* (London, 1920).

35 The exceptions of the LMU and SMU have already been noted in a previous footnote and can be explained in this context partly on the grounds that they were linked to French imperial objectives in the case of the LMU and "pan-Scandinavian" sentiments in the case of the SMU.

domestic monetary system. Most economic liberals of course believed that the gold standard required control of the token coinage and the note supply. But the fact that the gold standard rested on state-managed national currencies was not something they preferred to call attention to. The chief advantage of the gold standard from their perspective, after all, was its automaticity and its compatibility with laissez-faire principles.

The goals of nationalists posed little challenge to liberals when the former sought simply to enhance the state's control of the monetary system in order to provide a more efficient monetary order and stable currency by joining the gold standard. This was the dominant approach of nationalists in the pre-1931 period. But throughout the nineteenth century there were also nationalist thinkers less enamored of the gold standard. These were figures with a strong commitment to "popular sovereignty," one of the principles of modern nationalism that had emerged from the French and American revolutions. In their view, there was no particular reason why this principle should not be extended to the monetary realm; that is, that "the people" should be allowed to manage the national currency. For this management to be free from external constraints, the currency could not be tied to gold but rather would need to be inconvertible.

Johann Fichte's *The Closed Commercial State*, written in 1800, provided the first developed example of this kind of thinking in nationalist circles. Inspired by the French experiment with assignats, he called for an inconvertible token money that would be actively managed by the state with the objective of promoting the welfare of its citizens.[36] In a more sophisticated fashion, the English nationalist Thomas Attwood developed proto-Keynesian ideas about how an inconvertible national currency could be printed in sufficient quantities to ensure full employment.[37] The well-known American economic nationalist, Henry Carey, also advocated an inconvertible national currency on the grounds that it would discourage international trade and remove any external constraint on the creation of domestic money to promote the economic growth of the nation.[38] One of Carey's prominent followers in Canada, Isaac Buchanan, developed a similar set of ideas, arguing that a currency based on a universal form of money such as gold was "disloyal" and "unpatriotic" because it would serve only an "alien" class "whose boast is that money capital owns no allegiance to country." A "patriotic" policy should thus be governed by the idea that

36 See, for example, Carleton Hayes, *The Historical Evolution of Modern Nationalism* (New York, 1931), 263–5.
37 See, for example, David Moss, *Thomas Attwood: The Biography of a Radical* (Montreal, 1990).
38 See, e.g., Walter Nugent, *Money and American Society, 1865–80* (New York, 1968).

money should be "a thing of or belonging to a country, not of or belonging to the world."[39]

These advocates of an inconvertible currency and an activist national monetary policy were seen in liberal economic circles as radical heretics. But liberals also recognized the potential influence of their populist message. To call attention to the dangers of the government and the people "managing money," liberals highlighted the costs – particularly to the poor masses – of the disastrous inflationary experiences of inconvertible currencies such as the assignats. Liberals used these experiences to argue that only a currency protected from "politics" could be a sound currency. This message did indeed strike a chord with many nationalists who had experienced inflationary inconvertible money.[40] It also was often received sympathetically by many nationalists in peripheral countries who sought to attract investment and who were also aware of the vulnerability of their currencies to capital flight.

But liberals were also forced to recognize that their arguments would not be accepted by all in an age when the state had assumed greater control over the monetary system and new nationalist ideas of popular sovereignty were current in the political realm. When the British government refused to consider his proposals, for example, Attwood highlighted the connection between his ideas and the claims of popular sovereignty, leading the campaign in the 1830s to widen the electoral franchise out of a belief that the people would surely embrace his ideas even if the elite did not. As Frank Fetter notes, fear among liberals of his potent combination of mass democratic politics and radical currency reform played a key role in garnering support for Peel's 1844 Bank Act and its effort to depoliticize the conduct of monetary policy.[41]

Liberal fears intensified as the electoral franchise did begin to be extended dramatically during the late nineteenth century and especially during and after World War I, giving the poorer classes more power to express their views on the management of the national currency. As Barry Eichengreen has noted, political parties supporting laborers in this period frequently were attracted to monetary policies that would more actively manage the

39 Isaac Buchanan, "Nothing Could Be More Practically Disloyal, Unpatriotic, and Un-Christian Than the Hard Money Legislation of England," mimeo, Jan. 1880, Manuscript Group 24, D14 v.108 070994, Canadian National Archives.

40 This was true, e.g., of the first major political economist in the United States, Daniel Raymond, who in most other aspects shared similar views as Fichte, Carey, and Buchanan. He argued that a convertible currency was necessary to avoid the experience of the reckless note issues by many U.S. banks in the early nineteenth century, an experience that he argued had often seriously hurt the masses. Charles Patrick Neill, *Daniel Raymond* (Baltimore, 1897), 35, 40–1.

41 Frank Fetter, *Development of British Monetary Orthodoxy, 1797–1875* (Cambridge, 1965), 177–80, 212–14.

national currency to address problems of unemployment and economic growth, and their growing power posed an important challenge to supporters of the gold standard.[42] In the 1920s, liberals attempted to counter their influence through the establishment of a network of independent national central banks and the promotion of orthodox financial policies. This project was, of course, ultimately unsuccessful. In the wake of the financial crisis in the early 1930s and world depression, the gold standard collapsed and liberal conceptions of orthodox monetary management were abandoned almost everywhere. The very structures that had been constructed under the gold standard – national central banks and homogenous national token currencies – came under the control of politicians and were used to serve more activist purposes. With the triumph of Keynesianism in the post-1945 period, this new approach became dominant across much of the world.

It is out of this experience that Hayek's call for the denationalization of money needs to be understood. As politicians sought greater control over the management of national currencies during and after the interwar period, the dangers of the alliance between liberalism and nationalism became apparent. In promoting the gold standard, liberals had created structures such as central banks with a monopoly of the note issue and token coinages that could be used for more interventionist purposes. In an era of nationalism, this had turned out to be risky strategy since many of those committed to the new "national" sense of political community came to see an inconvertible national currency as a tool contributing to the realization of popular sovereignty. Liberals had thus helped to construct monetary structures that could easily be used for goals that they opposed. Far from being a quaint but antiquated community en route to a more cosmopolitan world, the nation had become a dangerous end point.

As a consequence, it is no surprise that at this time Hayek and other liberals began to write for the first time about the dangers of "monetary nationalism."[43] They used this phrase to refer to the kind of activist monetary policies that became popular after World War I (usually without acknowledging that the gold standard, too, had been a "nationalist" monetary institution for many groups). It was also in this period that liberals – including Hayek's mentor Ludwig von Mises – began to ask whether the earlier liberal support for national currencies had been a mistake.[44]

---

42 Barry Eichengreen, *Golden Fetters* (Oxford, 1992).
43 See, e.g., Friedrich Hayek, *Monetary Nationalism and International Stability* (London, 1937).
44 See Ludwig Von Mises, *The Theory of Money and Credit*, trans. H. Batson (1924; reprint, New Haven, Conn., 1953), 396–9, and Vera Smith, *The Rationale for Central Banking and the Free Banking Alternative* (1936; reprint, Indianapolis, 1990).

During the Bretton Woods era, economic liberals who remained committed to orthodox monetary goals and the gold standard could take some comfort in the fact that the international monetary order still rested, at least via the dollar, on gold (even if countries used unorthodox adjustable pegs and capital controls to maintain this link). With the breakdown of the gold standard in the early 1970s, however, all currencies in the world became what Fichte, Attwood, and other "heretics" during the nineteenth century had dreamed of: pure fiat currencies. The breakdown of the gold standard highlighted to economic liberals how difficult it had become to "protect money from politics"[45] in the traditional way when the principal commitment of governments in an age of mass democracy had become activist monetary management aimed at domestic monetary objectives. The inflation of the following decade did little to calm their concerns about the dangers of the new world of universal fiat money.

These events of the 1970s – combined with discussions about European monetary integration at the time – appear to have prompted Hayek to re-evaluate his thinking about the merits of national currencies. Since the gold standard could not be reintroduced as a means of preventing politicians from controlling national currencies, he was led to wonder whether monetary discipline could be better achieved by eliminating national currencies altogether. If people were given "choice in currency" (either between government issued currencies or between privately issued currencies), Hayek argued, they would choose the most stable currency. Currency competition would thus discipline governments, forcing them to maintain the value of money they issued and restrain spending.

Hayek's re-evaluation of the national question thus partly reflected an underlying individualism and cosmopolitanism in economic liberal thought. At the same time, however, it reflected his reaction to the monetary experience since the interwar period. In an age of mass democratic politics, when politicians were beholden to what he called "special interests," Hayek believed the nation was no longer a community that could be trusted to manage money according to his ideals.[46] Whereas many nineteenth-century liberals had seen their acceptance of nationalism as politically necessary and often even desirable as the first step en route to a more cosmopolitan order, Hayek thus saw the need to make more of a choice; embracing national currencies might preclude the realization of his individualistic and cosmopolitan ideals.

---

45 Hayek, *Denationalization*, 16.
46 For Hayek, the denationalization of money also had particular appeal because of his skepticism about the value of any kind of government planning. Thus, he attacked not just Keynesians but also monetarists for believing that even conservative monetary planning was desirable.

TOWARD A DENATIONALIZATION OF MONEY?

To what extent is Hayek's vision for the future of the world monetary system likely to be realized in the coming years? There is little evidence of his proposals being introduced in the near future in "Northern" countries. Even those who support Hayek's limited proposal of co-circulation of national currencies, such as Toyoo Gyohten, concede that "[f]or the moment ... this is sheer fantasy."[47] To be sure, the British government's support for the "hard ecu" proposal – which it advanced in the context of the discussions of monetary union in the European Union – drew on Hayek's ideas. But it has received little support beyond Britain. The prospect of the growth of "e-money" has also generated some literature arguing that Hayek's vision of privately issued currencies is soon to become a reality in Northern countries because the new technologies will make it difficult for states to control the issuing of money. As I have argued elsewhere, however, this view underestimates the extent to which government authorities can, and most likely will, regulate the new "e-money."[48]

As many observers have noted, the strongest evidence that Hayek's vision may become a reality comes not from developments in Northern countries but rather from increasingly widespread "currency substitution" within many countries in the "South" and ex–Eastern bloc during the last two decades. In many of these countries, citizens have genuinely come to acquire "choice in currency" within the domestic monetary system as foreign currencies – usually the dollar – have increasingly replaced the local currency as the dominant currency in use. Hayek's limited proposal for the denationalization of money, thus, is not just of academic interest for people in these countries. It is in fact a reality that has been experienced to varying extents over the last two decades.

This currency substitution process has partly been what Hayek might approvingly call a "spontaneous" market-led one. Individuals – particularly wealthy individuals – have been prompted to reduce their holdings and use of the domestic currency by high rates of inflation, overvalued currencies, and/or political instability. In most cases, the national currency's role as a store of value has been replaced first, but the replacement process has often – particularly in situations of hyperinflation – also extended to money's role as a medium of exchange and unit of account. This market-driven process has frequently taken place without the state's consent, and in

---

47 Paul Volcker and Toyoo Gyohten, *Changing Fortunes* (New York, 1992), 310.
48 Eric Helleiner, "Electronic Money: A Challenge to the Sovereign State?" *Journal of International Affairs* 51 (1998): 387–409.

countries with weak state capacity, policymakers have seemed powerless to stop it.

But the currency substitution phenomenon has also often been encouraged by governments through their decisions to legalize foreign currency deposits in banks or even the use of foreign currencies as legal tender in everyday transactions. For the most part, these policy decisions have not been driven by any great enthusiasm for Hayek's thinking. Instead, defensive motives were more important. As financial markets have become more liberal and globalized, wealthy asset holders had found increasingly easy opportunities to take their assets abroad in response to unfavorable economic and political circumstances. This has been particularly true in Latin America, where the elite have long had what James Mahon calls "cosmopolitan" asset preferences.[49] Permitting the domestic use of foreign currency has been a way of trying to encourage this elite to bring their capital back home.[50]

The lack of enthusiasm for Hayek's vision in policymaking circles is hardly surprising. Hayek and many of his supporters often argue that the central barrier to their project's realization is the state's desire to maximize the revenue it derives from monopolizing money. But equally significant is the fact that the trend undermines the political role that national currencies are seen by many to play in nation-building. Not only is the internal coherence of the national economy undermined by the prevalence of dollarization as transaction costs increase. So too is the state's ability to manage the national currency – either through discretionary monetary policy or exchange rate policy – in a manner that responds to the preferences of citizens. Even the ability of the national currency to foster a sense of collective identity may be undermined in situations where currency substitution is widespread. Although Hayek's supporters usually focus primarily on the economic benefits to arise from their proposal, these broader political consequences are often of central concern to policymakers. After all, although this is an era when economic liberalism has triumphed, it is also an age when nationalism remains alive and well in most parts of the world.

For this reason, many governments, particularly those with strong nationalist orientations, have responded to the rapid growth of currency

---

49 James Mahon, *Mobile Capital and Latin American Development* (University Park, Pa., 1996), 47. Currency substitution has been experienced in many Latin American countries to a limited degree for decades before the 1970s.

50 Johannes Mueller, *Dollarization in Lebanon*, IMF Working Paper no. 129 (Washington, D.C., 1994), 10 n.1; Mohamed El-Erian, "Currency Substitution in Egypt and the Yemen Arab Republic," *IMF Staff Papers* 35 (1988): 93; Diana Brand, *Currency Substitution in Developing Countries* (Munich, 1993); Miguel Savastano, "Dollarization in Latin America," in Paul Mizen and Eric Pentecost, eds., *The Macroeconomics of International Currencies* (Cheltenham, 1996).

substitution with "de-dollarization" initiatives involving regulatory changes and dramatic stabilization plans designed to restore confidence in the national currency and reduce capital flight. Many of these initiatives have been quite successful; for example, Israel in 1985, and many ex–Eastern bloc countries in the early 1990s.[51] But others have been less successful or have been quickly reversed primarily because of the kinds of factors already mentioned. In weak states, policymakers have been forced to recognize their incapacity to influence citizens' behavior in this area, particularly when stabilization programs have not been perceived as credible. In other cases, the de-dollarization initiatives have promoted extensive capital flight which, in turn, has forced a re-evaluation of the strategy.[52] The denationalization of money has, thus, often persisted not because of any enthusiasm for the process but rather because of poor state capacity or the constraints imposed by capital flight in this age of financial globalization.

It is interesting to note that the introduction of stabilization plans to reduce currency substitution usually involve not just fiscal and monetary restraint, but also the creation of an independent central bank or even a currency board. In this way, these stabilization plans in fact achieve the objective Hayek sought: that of disciplining government policy and "removing money from the realm of politics." But, unlike Hayek's proposal, they do so in a way that allows economic liberal goals to work hand-in-hand with the more nationalist objective of re-establishing a degree of control over the monetary system. The introduction of currency boards is perhaps the most dramatic example of this phenomenon. By reintroducing the kind of discipline associated with the classical gold standard, currency boards are usually seen as dramatic examples of a repudiation of nationalist approaches to economic policy. But frequently they have been introduced for quite nationalist reasons: to re-establish a degree of control over the monetary system, to expel foreign currencies, to recultivate "pride" in the national currency, and to attract international investment.[53] Politically astute economic liberals have

---

51 For Israel, see Michael Bruno, *Crisis, Stabilisation and Economic Reform: Therapy by Consensus* (Oxford, 1993). For the ex–Eastern bloc, see Brand, *Currency Substitution*; Ratna Sahay and Carlos A. Vegh, *Dollarization in Transition Economies*, IMF Working Paper no. 95 (Washington, D.C., 1995).

52 See, e.g., the cases of Mexico (1982), Peru (1985), and Bolivia (1982), analyzed in Guillermo Calvo and Carlos Vegh, *Currency Substitution in Developing Countries: An Introduction*, IMF Working Paper no. 40 (Washington, D.C., 1992), and Sylvia Maxfield, "The International Political Economy of Bank Nationalization: Mexico in Comparative Perspective," *Latin American Research Review* (1992): 75–103. Also significant has been a kind of hysteresis where currency substitution becomes difficult to reverse even after a successful stabilization as private actors.

53 See, e.g., Tapio Saavalainen, *Stabilization in the Baltic Countries*, IMF Working Paper no. 44 (Washington, D.C., 1995), 3.

in fact recognized the potential nationalist appeal of currency boards, as an alternative to currency substitution, in this respect.[54]

The way that economic liberals have been able to work alongside nationalists in attempting to re-establish national currencies in situations such as this is reminiscent of the alliance between the two during the era of the gold standard. Supporters of Hayek might call attention to the dangers in this approach, arguing that these national currencies will ultimately be used for more interventionist purposes by democratic governments in an age when they are no longer disciplined by the gold standard. But the likelihood of governments pursuing monetary policies that liberals disapprove of in the contemporary era seems slim. During the last decade, there has been a dramatic convergence of views, particularly in the developing world, in favor of orthodox liberal monetary goals. One cause has been the fear of the discipline of international financial markets against governments who depart from these goals; the discipline of the new globalized financial markets, in other words, has to some extent replaced that of the gold standard. At the same time, this trend has also been caused by a disillusionment with the kinds of activist monetary policies pursued in the middle decades of this century in the context of both the rational expectations revolution in economics and the actual experiences of inflation that sometimes accompanied those policies.[55]

Democratic governments thus appear less of a threat to liberal goals in the contemporary age than Hayek suggested. In contrast to the experience earlier in this century, "the people" appear to be expressing a preference for the same goals as economic liberals in the monetary realm today in many regions of the world. Importantly, however, this loss of interest in activist monetary policy has not usually translated into a loss of interest in national currencies. In addition to their roles of providing seigniorage revenue and fostering national identities and internal economic coherence, national currencies are still linked closely to a sense of popular sovereignty; that is, even if money is not to be actively managed, the people would like to keep that choice in their own hands. Instead of abandoning national currencies, most governments have chosen to "protect money from politics"

54 Steve Hanke, *Monetary Reform for a Free Estonia: A Currency Board Solution* (Stockholm, 1992), 18, 21; Steve Hanke, Lars Jonung, and Kurt Schuler, *Russian Currency and Finance: A Currency Board Approach* (London, 1993), 141–2, 144; Kent Osband and Delano Villanueva, "Independent Currency Authorities: An Analytic Primer," *IMF Staff Papers* 40 (1993): 206.
55 Sylvia Maxfield, *Gatekeepers of Growth: The International Political Economy of Central Banking in Developing Countries* (Princeton, N.J., 1997); David Andrews and Thomas Willett, "Financial Interdependence and the State: International Monetary Relations at Century's End," *International Organization* 51 (1997): 479–511.

through the establishment of independent central banks, or in some cases currency boards (with the important exception of the EU, where there is a broader interest in building a supranational political community).

Ironically, this triumph of liberal approaches to monetary policy provides a further barrier in the way of Hayek's ideas gaining more political influence. Not only do nationalists oppose it, but so, too, do many economic liberals. This opposition stems in part from many detailed economic arguments about the pros and cons of free banking or currency substitution that I will not discuss here (except to say that they are often similar to arguments made by liberals in the nineteenth and early twentieth centuries in support of currency monopoly).[56] But equally important is the sentiment that, given the triumph of liberal goals in the monetary sector, those fighting for the denationalization of money seem to be fighting an old battle. Two decades after Hayek first published his proposal, national currencies have ceased to pose the kind of threat that he perceived in many contexts. Consequently, it seems politically much simpler to embrace national currencies – rather than incur nationalist opposition – and ensure that they are managed in an orthodox fashion.

This is, for example, the approach adopted by liberal policymakers within the International Monetary Fund (IMF) in their advice to new nations in Eastern Europe and the former Soviet Union. Analyses by IMF staff suggest that they do not see much of a case for discouraging currency substitution on strictly economic grounds.[57] But closer to political realities than Hayek's academic supporters, IMF officials have been forced to recognize the power of nationalism in this region and the importance that nationalists attach to the creation of a national currency.[58] Like their predecessors in the League of Nations, IMF officials have not only recognized the need to

---

56 See, e.g., Charles Goodhart, *The Evolution of Central Banking* (Cambridge, 1988); Paul Mizen and Eric Pentecost, eds., *The Macroeconomics of International Currencies* (Cheltenham, 1996).

57 See, for example, Calvo and Vegh, *Currency Substitution*.

58 For this importance, see, e.g., Marco Kranjec, "Introduction of a New Currency: The Case of Slovenia," *Development and International Cooperation* 11 (1995): 130, 141; Marko Skreb, "Monetary Independence as a Precondition for Macroeconomic Stability – the Case of Croatia," *Development and International Cooperation* 11 (1995): 163. As the IMF Managing Director Michel Camdessus acknowledged in the early 1990s while discussing currency arrangements among the Soviet successor states, the decision of newly independent countries to create national currencies may have many economic drawbacks but it is a decision that "lies at the heart of national sovereignty. For many countries, an independent currency is a potent symbol of nationhood, like the flag or the national anthem." Michel Camdessus, *Economic Transformation in the Fifteen Republics of the Former U.S.S.R.* (Washington, D.C., 1992). The IMF has also been supportive of efforts to create national currencies in many regions of the ex–Eastern bloc as a way to avoid the monetary instability associated with transitional common currency regimes. See, for example, John Odling-Smee, "Closing Remarks," in J. Zulu, Ian McCarthy, Susanna Almaina, and Gabriel Sensenbrenner, eds., *Central Banking Technical Assistance to Countries in Transition* (Washington, D.C., 1994), 136.

embrace national currencies but even helped to create them in new nations through technical assistance programs that include such detailed advice as how to best design banknotes to reflect nationalist identities and ideas.[59] As in the pre-1930s period, however, the price for their support of national currencies has been that these currencies must be run in an orthodox fashion.

Nationalists in these regions have often been willing to accept this price, not just because of the discipline of international financial markets and their commitment to orthodox goals. In contexts where the state is weak and the nation is being consolidated, the IMF's support for the project of maintaining a national currency has political value for them. This parallels the late nineteenth- and early twentieth-century experience when prominent liberal "money doctors" introducing the gold-exchange standard in peripheral regions were often welcomed by local nationalists who saw their missions as useful in helping to design and implement "modern" national currencies as well as to signal "credibility" to international investors.[60] It is not just liberals, thus, who often recognize the worth of an alliance with nationalists. As they did before the 1930s, nationalists, too, often see advantages from a close association with powerful liberals.

In sum, Hayek's ideas represent an important departure from liberal thought during the era of the gold standard, a departure triggered above all by his evaluation of the experience with national currencies managed by governments in an age of mass democracy. But while a considerable degree of interest has been generated by Hayek's proposals, supporters of them seem to underestimate the important political barriers that stand in the way of their widespread and enthusiastic adoption. Hayek himself often identified the prime obstacle as the state's desire to maximize revenue it derives from being the monopoly producer of currency. But this analysis neglects the way in which the creation of national currencies historically was linked not just to revenue goals, but also to the objectives of both Hayek's liberal predecessors and nationalists in the nineteenth and early twentieth centuries. Not only do many liberals today remain committed to the idea that states should retain this monopoly, but so, too, do nationalists. To nationalists, a national currency is much more than an economic instrument. It is also a political tool that is closely linked to the coherence, identity, and nature of citizenship within a nation. This is often acknowledged in passing in much of the economic literature on currency substitution and monetary reform,

59 Richard Abrams, *The Design and Printing of Bank Notes: Considerations When Introducing a New Currency*, IMF Working Paper no. 26 (Washington, D.C., 1995).
60 See, e.g., Drake, *Money Doctor.*

but rarely analyzed in depth.[61] Indeed, it appears that only in contexts where the state is already weak or particularly vulnerable to capital flight that Hayek's proposal is being realized in a substantial way.

CONCLUSION

The triumph of economic liberal ideas today encourages parallels to be drawn with the era before the 1930s when they also dominated world economic affairs. I have attempted to highlight, however, how one of the key intellectual leaders of the recent resurgence of economic liberalism – Friedrich Hayek – recently called for a monetary order very different than the gold standard that his liberal predecessors had endorsed during the nineteenth and early twentieth centuries. Despite its cosmopolitan laissez-faire image in liberal circles, the gold standard was a monetary institution that helped to consolidate the very state-controlled national currencies that Hayek's followers now seek to dismantle. Indeed, it was this feature of the gold standard that often garnered support for it in that age of nation-building and nationalism. Although economic liberals in the nineteenth and early twentieth centuries were not terribly interested in this link between national currencies and the broader political project of nation-building, they were forced to recognize its political significance.

In calling for the dismantling of the very monetary structures that his liberal predecessors helped to build, Hayek's proposal would certainly usher in a different world than that which existed in the pre-1930s period. Hayek emphasized the similarities: the creation of a world of denationalized money was an alternative route to achieve the same low inflation objectives and lack of discretionary government control over money as existed during the era of the gold standard. But that earlier liberal world monetary system was built solidly on the base of national currencies, currencies which also helped to consolidate the economic coherence of nations, the link between state and citizen, and even national identities. By contrast, a world of "denationalized money" would encourage a more deterritorialized sense of economic space, a different sense of citizenship, and even alternative identities. In regions already experiencing widespread currency substitution, these trends can in fact already be seen to some degree.[62]

---

61 See, e.g., Ruben Lamdany and Jorge Dorlhiac, "The Dollarization of a Small Economy," *Scandinavian Journal of Economics* 89 (1987), 93; Richard Abrams and Hernan Cortes-Douglas, *Introduction of a New National Currency*, IMF Working Paper no. 49 (Washington, D.C., 1993), 1; John Williamson, *What Role for Currency Boards?* (Washington, D.C., 1995), 42.
62 Benjamin Cohen, *The Geography of Money* (Ithaca, N.Y., 1998).

What are the sources of this new interest in the denationalization of money in the contemporary era? In Hayek's case, I have suggested the source was both an underlying individualism and cosmopolitanism in liberal thought, and a reaction against the way national currencies came to be used when mass democratic politics replaced the "oligarchic" politics characteristic of the era of the gold standard.[63] At the same time, I have also argued that the influence of Hayek's ideas in regions experiencing currency substitution should not be overstated. Currency substitution has become widespread in many countries during the last two decades *not* because of any great enthusiasm for Hayek's ideas in policymaking circles. Rather, the phenomenon has become extensive primarily in countries – particularly those characterized by persistently high inflation, overvalued exchange rates, and/or political instability – where policymakers have only reluctantly accepted it either because they recognize their inability to prevent it given weak state capacity or because it appeared to be a way of reducing extensive capital flight.

Lack of enthusiasm for Hayek's ideas in policymaking circles is understandable. Although this is an age when economic liberal ideas are prevalent, it is also one in which nationalism remains a potent force throughout most parts of the world. Like many of his liberal predecessors, Hayek seemed not to recognize the enduring broader political significance of national currencies for nationalists. Moreover, with activist monetary management increasingly being abandoned around the world, many economic liberals – assuming they even agree with Hayek's ideas – also see little reason to challenge the widespread political commitment to national currencies (except in contexts such as the EU where a broader supra-national political project exists). The easier route is to endorse national currencies, while ensuring that they are managed in an orthodox fashion. Thus, while Hayek's proposal suggests that a very different kind of relationship between monetary and political space might emerge than that which existed during the pre-1930s period, in instances such as these the similarities between the two eras seem more apparent than the differences. Both then and now, economic liberals have often been forced to acknowledge both the political significance of nationalism as well as the fact that the "national question" in currency affairs raises issues that go well beyond narrow economic concerns.

---

63 Quote from Brian Johnson, *The Politics of Money* (London, 1970), chap. 2.

10

International Financial Institutions and National Economic Governance

Aspects of the New Adjustment Agenda in Historical Perspective

LOUIS W. PAULY

OVERVIEW

In its early years, the International Monetary Fund (IMF) promoted exchange rate stability through its central role in the "par value" system created at Bretton Woods. The mandate enshrined in its Articles of Agreement left plenty of room for interpretation, but its central mission was narrowly focused. The par value system came crashing down in the early 1970s, and the Fund adapted its main tools – consultation procedures that evolved into an apparatus for multilateral economic surveillance and conditional financing arrangements – to a new environment. In practice, the mission advanced with these tools, as well as with various forms of technical assistance provided to members centered on promoting the cause of open, contestable, well-governed, and transparent markets. Although that mission continues to emphasize those markets within member-states that most directly link the current account of national payments balances with one another, during the past two decades the Fund has increasingly concerned itself with structural factors shaping the capital account.

Early in 1998, its Managing Director stated that the Fund's central objectives now encompassed the following:

- restructuring financial sectors, where owners and managers can be genuinely accountable for the prudent operation of banks, "where loans are made on the basis of objective commercial criteria,"

For comments on this chapter, I am grateful to the participants in the conference, "The International Financial System: Past and Present," sponsored by the German Historical Institute and held at Princeton University in April 1998. Particular thanks are owed to Jacques Polak. Although he and I agree on many things, he has never hesitated to pinpoint aspects of my work on the Fund and the League with which he disagrees. In light of his comments on this chapter, I have tried to clarify parts of my analysis. We nevertheless continue to see some things differently. Responsibility for the

- promoting transparent, independently audited corporate balance sheets, and consolidated financial statements in the case of business conglomerates "so that markets can monitor corporate performance,"
- creating "a more level playing field for private sector activity" by dismantling monopolies, eliminating government-directed lending, increasing the transparency of foreign trade procedures, and revising government procurement and contracting regulations.

"For the IMF, which for fifty years essentially confined itself – in accordance with its mandate – to helping its member countries accept essential monetary and macroeconomic discipline," Michel Camdessus concluded, "these are entirely new frontiers – both vast and promising."[1] He was not alone in exploring these frontiers, however, as a range of other international financial institutions (IFIs) – from the World Bank and the regional development banks to the Bank for International Settlements – appeared simultaneously to be moving in the same direction.

If one looks back slightly more than fifty years, however, those frontiers cease to seem entirely new ones for international organizations. The adaptation of today's IFIs hearkens back to debates on the external implications of national industrial systems that took place under the auspices of the League of Nations during the interwar period. It also resonates with seminal debates on the direction of U.S. foreign economic policy in the 1944–7 period. In short, the incipient agenda for the IMF and other IFIs represents the recovery and revitalization of an earlier policy agenda, an ambitious but ultimately abandoned attempt to link the restoration of international capital markets with the promotion of what we might call a universal code of conduct for national economic governance.

It is worth probing the historical parallel. The main point of comparison involves a perennial issue in the history of modern capitalism: official sanctioning and regulation of industrial and financial cartels versus governmental policies inclined toward the break-up of cartels and the stimulation of competition. In this regard, the role of intergovernmental institutions became a matter of controversy during the interwar, post–World War II, and

chapter as it now stands rests entirely with me. An earlier version of the chapter, without the commentary, appeared as "Good Governance and Bad Policy: The Perils of International Organizational Overextension," *Review of International Political Economy* 6, no. 4 (winter 1999): 401–24; for permission to publish this revised version, I am grateful to the editors of that journal. My research has been assisted by a generous grant from the Social Sciences and Humanities Research Council of Canada.

1 *IMF Survey*, Feb. 9, 1998, 38; also see IMF, *Good Governance: The IMF's Role* (Washington, D.C., 1997); Manuel Guitián, "The Role of the IMF in an Integrating World," remarks presented at the University of Toronto, Center for International Studies, Feb. 27, 1998.

present periods. In each case, prominent voices during each period explicitly advocated a return to what seemed the golden era of a globalizing economy, an era that ended abruptly and catastrophically in 1914. At the core of that advocacy during the two earlier periods lay the illusion that a broad international consensus was near at hand on the proper role of government on the issue of restrictive business practices. History may help us discern whether the situation has changed today.

This chapter begins with a brief orientation to the instrument of multilateral economic surveillance, especially as wielded by the IMF and especially as it evolved in tandem with the vast expansion of international capital movements after the breakdown of the post–World War II exchange rate system. The chapter then reviews earlier work on the external consequences of cartels and other industrial practices advanced by the Economic and Financial Organization of the League of Nations. The League's contribution was modest, to be sure, and the issue was never central to its long-forgotten economic work. The chapter then shows, however, that key themes from the League's analysis carried directly over into the intense debate that followed World War II on the extent to which the United States should extend to the world its own internal microeconomic preferences. That debate was muffled by the onset of the Cold War. The new "economic governance" agenda of the IFIs masked the fact that the debate was revived, not transcended, after the Cold War ended.

ANALYTICAL CONTEXT

Multilateral surveillance – a process of intergovernmental collaboration mediated by international organizations and aimed essentially at rendering compatible certain national economic policies having consequences beyond national borders – exists today in a number of arenas. In none is it more fully developed than in the international monetary field, where an established mediator – the International Monetary Fund – was available for just such a purpose when the need arose.

Pragmatically built on the base of its post–World War II experience in consulting with certain member-states on exchange rates and exchange restrictions, IMF surveillance came to rest on an explicit legal obligation binding all members in 1976. Over time, the scope of that obligation expanded. In the wake of burgeoning capital market growth and periodic national and systemic financial crises, the surveillance mandate of the Fund was gradually broadened to cover the full range of economic policies capable of generating unsustainable imbalances in national current accounts and, in practical if not formal terms, increasingly in national capital accounts. Especially when linked to conditional financing arrangements, Fund surveillance therefore came logically to be associated in both public and specialist discourses with the notion of deep structural adjustment inside national economies as they became ever more integrated with one another.

From a systemic point of view, the ultimate rationale for the complex realities of that association rests on the deliberate policy objective of states to build a stable and increasingly prosperous global economy. The underlying project thus remains a political one. It is not "market-led" and never has been. It was set in train by practical statesmen and their advisers, energized mainly by impulses emanating from the United States after World War II. With no clear master plan but a reasonably coherent (by its own historical standards) American foreign policy line, a shifting and decentralized cast of political actors and their supporters in a widening array of powerful states drove that train. That they often appeared unprepared for the unintended consequences of their sometimes explicit and sometimes implicit policy decisions should not confuse us as to the intended trajectory of those decisions. Economic depression and war were the poisons. International economic interdependence promised a more effective antidote than any other on offer. In today's terms, economic globalization was the means to an end, not the end itself.

The key to the success of the project was – and remains – the maintenance of *domestic* coalitions adequate to the task of coping with the *domestic* political consequences of deepening economic interdependence. On any given issue, questions arise as to how external actors, acting in their own interests, can best assist in bolstering such coalitions. Unilateral, bilateral, regional, and multilateral options suggest themselves. The conference diplomacy and economic staff work of the League of Nations were primitive multilateral instruments. From the beginning, the economic surveillance function of the IMF has combined a multilateralist spirit with a unilateralist impetus. As the scope of the IMF expands, the question is whether that combination can hold. Can it succeed in bolstering supportive domestic coalitions for the systemic experiment in globalization in both follower states *and* leading states? Organizations like the IMF are complex, and their agendas reflect the interaction of many forces. Only a true cynic, however, would entirely discount the possibility that the expansion of multilateral surveillance beyond its traditional macroeconomic terrain and onto the field of industrial governance was mainly driven by the familiar political logic of interdependence. The question of whether the precise form, tone, and venue of that expansion reflected wisdom nevertheless remains open for analysis and legitimate debate.[2]

I do not propose here to examine the roots of IMF surveillance in any depth, a task I set for myself elsewhere.[3] To provide a framework for the historical material that follows, however, it is important at least to cast a glance at a number of complicated and subtle issues related to Fund surveillance in general and to its linkage with Fund conditionality in particular cases. It is also important to acknowledge the distance thus far traveled in the gradual evolution of Fund competence (both legal and practical) beyond the current account of its member-states and into their capital accounts.[4]

A simple idea from open-economy macroeconomics provides an initial sense of the internal choices states make when they seek to harness the benefits of economic openness without incurring unacceptable costs. It is evident in theory, if not always in practice, that there is a trade-off faced in the assignment of policy priority to exchange rate stability, capital mobility, or monetary autonomy. The sum of the choices in this regard made especially

---

2 The policy debate is already prominently joined. See Martin Feldstein, "Refocusing the IMF," *Foreign Affairs* 77, no. 3 (1998): 20–33; and Stanley Fischer, "In Defense of the IMF," *Foreign Affairs* 77, no. 44 (1998): 103–5.

3 For amplification of the themes of this section, see Louis W. Pauly, *Who Elected the Bankers? Surveillance and Control in the World Economy* (Ithaca, N.Y., 1997), and "The League of Nations and the Foreshadowing of the International Monetary Fund," *Essays in International Finance* 201, Princeton University, International Finance Section (Dec. 1996): 1–47.

4 Jacques Polak disagrees below about the extent to which Fund surveillance should be seen as historically unique. I concede that roughly analogous economic and financial operations of the Secretariat of the League of Nations were primitive, lacked a legal mandate, and proved completely ineffective in halting the slide into depression and war. These facts reflected the circumstances that informed and surrounded them. The informal and pragmatic character of the missions of League economists, mainly to countries depending on the League for direct or indirect financial assistance, mirrored the culture of the British civil service that more than any other shaped the League's Secretariat. Their ineffectiveness, especially in the 1930s, testified to the absence of a policy consensus among the great powers of the day as well as to flaws of institutional design. The League's hortatory annual World Economic Surveys during the 1930s differed in many ways from the IMF's definitive World Economic Outlooks, but they shared certain policy and normative aspirations. The League's free trade/sound money advice proffered to members in international conference settings during the 1920s, and more directly to Central European countries aided by the League in the 1920s and 1930s, surely bears distinct similarities to the more discreetly delivered advice of the Fund during contemporary surveillance procedures. Conversely, the legal character of the IMF's core mandate as well as its insistent pursuit after the debt crises of the 1980s and 1990s surely testifies in substantial part to the dominant culture of American governance and to the policy priorities of the United States and other leading members of the Fund. Moreover, just as was the case in the interwar period, the essential weakness of instruments wielded by an intergovernmental organization vis-à-vis powerful member-states is today well understood, legal mandates notwithstanding. I do not doubt that the contemporary period can plausibly be depicted to reflect "progress" in certain economic aspects of human affairs, especially when it is contrasted with the 1914–45 period, and I consider surveillance-type instruments to be necessary in a world that aspires to deeper economic and financial integration. But historical analogies, with their imperfections suitably specified, permit analysts to probe such ideas and to test the limits of dominant interpretive frameworks. See Richard E. Neustadt and Ernest R. May, *Thinking in Time* (New York, 1986).

by leading states during the past two decades helps to explain the growth of contemporary international capital markets and the refocusing of the IMF's mandate on sustaining those markets.

Recognizable precursors to such markets existed in the early years of the twentieth century. World War I destroyed them. During the interwar period, leading states tried with an increasing sense of urgency to turn the clock back. In the 1920s, a general consensus had been achieved at the level of principle, which today would be labeled classically liberal except that it assumed the successful restoration by governments of a workable gold standard. The effort to put principle into practice failed catastrophically.

Following World War II, the victors attempted once again to restore international economic openness, but this time on the foundation of preponderant American military power and a gradual movement toward integrated national markets. The project was intimately linked with the domestic politics of the welfare state, and the specter of the Great Depression was ever present in the background. After the Cold War began, the military calculation became more complex but economic *and* financial openness soon moved to the center of the foreign policies of most advanced industrial states. Although they rarely made stark or irrevocable decisions to favor financial openness above all other economic objectives, they did over time adjust a widening range of internal policies to promote and accommodate the expansion of international capital flows.[5] They also reshaped the mandates of international institutions in this light.

In short, from the late 1940s through the early 1970s leading states moved away from one set of policy trade-offs toward another. After World War II, they sought both exchange rate stability and monetary autonomy, and they were willing to tolerate limits on capital mobility in order to achieve those objectives. As that system was breaking down, they gave priority to capital mobility and monetary autonomy and proved themselves willing to abandon exchange rate stability as a central goal. Only one priority remained constant. Still held responsible for national security broadly defined – and in practice defined mainly by interest group politics in combination with general electoral demands for satisfactory macroeconomic performance – states retained their right to craft internal monetary policies as they themselves saw fit. The abandonment of exchange rate stability and the implicit privileging of international capital mobility has sometimes been viewed as a straightforward caving-in of government policy to the interests of financiers and multinational corporations. There is no doubt that such interests were in

5 Eric Helleiner, *States and the Reemergence of Global Finance* (Ithaca, N.Y., 1994).

the ascendancy throughout the postwar period, but the denouement of the Bretton Woods system may more plausibly be depicted as the path of least resistance for national policymakers of the day. Through a re-setting of priorities, they clearly hoped to export some of the costs of uncoordinated national policies while continuing to tilt in the direction of market-opening.

From the mid–1970s onward, a widening group of states collectively encouraged the further deepening of the channels through which capital could flow among their economies. The growth of international capital markets occurred even as some states, mainly in Europe, sought to restore a degree of exchange rate stability for themselves by limiting their own monetary autonomy within regional or bilateral arrangements. In the 1980s, however, all found that further capital market deepening necessitated a greater degree of coordination in their financial regulatory and supervisory policies, or at least a greater degree of policy consistency upon which nationals and their foreign economic partners could count. In the Latin American debt crisis, the IMF proved a handy and adaptable tool for ameliorating financial losses in creditor states while encouraging domestic financial reform in debtor states. With its legitimacy deriving from a charter approved by almost all countries of the world, the promise of symmetry inherent in its surveillance operations, the ability to place conditions on the use of its resources, and a high degree of credibility in the markets themselves, the instrument of the IMF was available to be deployed again in the financial wake of the end of the Cold War. By then, and in contrast to the situation prevailing at the time of the IMF's establishment, capital decontrol had come to define a basic normative objective of the system. Derogations from the norm, which continue to be plentiful, came ever more clearly to be viewed as temporary in nature. Here is, indeed, the frontier in a long and continuing multilateral effort to expand and adapt the surveillance instrument of the IMF to new circumstances.

Foreshadowed in the Fund's early experience with shepherding members availing themselves of "Article XIV" escape hatches to the obligation of liberalizing payments systems so that national current accounts could interact freely, the Fund's capacity to provide surveillance for the system as well as for all members was formalized in the Second Amendment to its Articles, which took effect in 1976.[6] Unwilling collectively to accept the domestic strictures of a pegged exchange rate system, and willing to risk a high degree of exchange rate instability, those members hoped that Fund surveillance

---

6 Harold James, "The Historical Development of the Principle of Surveillance," *IMF Staff Papers* 42, no. 4 (Dec. 1995). For a fuller treatment, see Harold James, *International Monetary Cooperation* (Washington, D.C., 1996).

would enhance the openness and fluidity in national payments systems deemed essential to the expansion of international trade and, increasingly, investment.

In legal terms, the Fund's existence thereafter rested on the principle that member-states were accountable to one another for the external effects of a widening range of domestic economic policies. (In theory, and consistent with the main lines of the Fund's history, those policies could be seen to include all those capable of influencing exchange rates.) The fact that most of these effects were now in practice transmitted rapidly through deepening international capital markets is a necessary condition to the extension of the Fund's surveillance apparatus ever more assertively into the arena of financial policy. The sufficient condition is rooted in the apparent policy preferences of the true architects of those markets, the United States and other leading states acting collectively and collaboratively.

Consistent with a long line of thought concerning the political exigencies of economic interdependence, I have elsewhere depicted an imaginary spectrum of possible policy environments. On one side would lie intentionally dis-integrated national financial markets; on the other, stable global markets resting on strong and effective instruments of global governance. I also made the obvious point that the policies required actually to live near either end of the spectrum were well-nigh impossible to imagine emanating from national political systems bearing even a remote resemblance to those in existence today. I argued that states, especially leading states, have demonstrated by their actual policy choices throughout the post–World War II era clear interests in capturing the benefits of deepening financial market integration *without* fundamentally compromising their ultimate political authority over that process. Multilateral institutions like the IMF, I concluded, are born in precisely such an environment. In precisely such an environment, moreover, unilateral political choices sometimes too delicate to articulate clearly are tempered by the ever-present threat of cross-border financial crisis. That tempering sharpens the mandate of institutions like the IMF to guide the development of collaborative principles and practices and to provide systemic oversight that retains maximum scope for policy independence for leading states. And if they fail to meet their difficult charge, as some have before and others might again, such institutions are in place to serve their masters in their final role, the role of scapegoats.

The new agenda for which IMF surveillance, conditional financing arrangements, and their analogs in other IFIs were apparently being adapted in the late 1990s reflected the crisis-prone nature of the political project commonly labeled "global financial integration." The project itself brought ever-deeper national and regional norms of economic behavior into tension with one another. Some observers depicted the resulting process of adjustment as a kind of institutional, regulatory, and behavioral arbitrage. Others saw a long and ever more subtle search for a stable balance of power across still-distinct national or regional political economies. The continuing debate along such lines was not new. Also not new was the attempt to use international organizations to help *define* and *promote* norms of good governance – financial, corporate, and official. But assigning them the task of *enforcing* norms upon which tacit disagreement remained among leading states was something else entirely. In principle, the former conduces to constructive international collaboration. In practice, the latter threatens to discredit the collaborative project as a whole. We witnessed this dilemma earlier in the twentieth century.

THE LEAGUE OF NATIONS AND INDUSTRIAL ORGANIZATION AND BUSINESS PRACTICE

In the early 1920s, the League of Nations helped various central European states recover financial stability in the aftermath of World War I. In the most prominent cases of Austria and Hungary, the actual nature of the intervention by League staff was more intrusive than that contemplated today in typical IMF financing programs. Both programs involved an infusion of hard-currency funding sourced in private external markets. In the Austrian case, other governments guaranteed those loans, but in both cases a League-appointed commissioner supervised inward and outward flows of foreign exchange until the loans were repaid. As these "programs" were running their course, League officials began to devote time and considerable energy to thinking more generally about the linkages between financial reform, economic reconstruction, market openness, and the recovery of a stable peace. By current standards, their efforts to articulate sound and universally applicable principles of economic organization and policy look unsystematic, even primitive. Moreover, a crucial split developed both inside the staff of the League and among League member-states on the issue of precisely how modern industrial economies should be organized at the producer level. Although never a key issue for the League's Secretariat, they did wrestle with the most important issues involved and their leaders did later reflect on that effort. Both the effort and the reflection are illuminating.

In the age of conference diplomacy, it seemed obvious that the best way to build interstate consensus on appropriate norms of economic behavior was to work toward and then convene a great meeting of the right sort of people. Alexander Loveday, on the staff of what became the League's Economic, Financial, and Transit Department in the 1920s and later director of that Department, concluded after the League's demise that on economic questions its procedures were defective for three reasons. The policymaking Economic Committee of the League "conceived itself to be under an obligation to treat the world as a unity"; it "confined itself to the elaboration of doctrinal principles of a general order"; and it sought to "achieve the formal acceptance and enforcement of the principles it elaborated by means of international conventions, or alternatively it sought the solution of present ills in international negotiations under which each state was asked to make some apparent sacrifice for the common good."[7] Such defects were not obvious, however, during the League's heyday.

In 1925, the League's Assembly began laying the groundwork for an International Economic Conference, which would eventually take place in Geneva two years later. The agenda for the Conference was vast, but throughout the period leading up to it, issues of industrial organization continually arose. At a time when high levels of protectionism and monetary instability still impeded international trade and the restoration of free capital movements, these issues were never paramount, but they were also never ignored. Private agreements among firms designed to stabilize production and consumption in key industries were, after all, a fact. The questions surrounding them covered a broad terrain, ranging from their economic effects to their impact on democracy to their utility in building a peaceful world order. In the background, of course, were intense debates that had roiled national governments ever since the term "cartel" was first used in this context. (In his classic study, Ervin Hexner set the date as 1879.[8]) In the background too, were organized business interests from various countries which could be counted on to line up on either side of each such question.

With the United States, the Soviet Union, and some forty-six member-states of the League in attendance, the Geneva Conference opened in May 1927. Various resolutions concerning industrial organization were debated, but no consensus existed on the issue of cartels. Following a great deal of preparatory work by the League's Secretariat, all that could be agreed, but agreed unanimously, was that industrial "rationalization" could promote "a better distribution of wealth" if it was "coordinated and far-reaching."[9]

---

7 Alexander Loveday, "Some Lessons from the Economic Activities of the League," unpublished, undated paper (likely 1946–7), 8. Personal papers, box 176, Nuffield College, Oxford.
8 Ervin Hexner, *International Cartels* (Chapel Hill, N.C., 1945), 3.
9 Wallace McClure, *World Prosperity as Sought Through the Economic Work of the League of Nations* (New York, 1933), 225–9.

National legislation on industrial agreements should not necessarily be prejudiced against them, since they might indeed be "actuated by a sense of the general interest." Moreover, since national approaches in this regard differed significantly, "effort toward international supervision seemed premature." Behind the delicate words lay a Continental European response to the position long since promoted by the unofficial American delegation to the League. Geneva would not be the venue for internationalizing the Sherman Act. It might, however, be the place for a less ambitious attempt to bend private interest to public purpose.

"The central industrial problem, that of the international cartel, proved to be the subject of widely differing opinion, which prevented the adoption of resolutions that were of a far-reaching character." Therefore, the cause of greater "clarity" in this arena would have to be pushed through an informal agreement to improve the "machinery of the League." Conference delegates enjoined the Economic Committee and the Secretariat "to undertake in a very comprehensive way the collection of industrial information, upon which alone effective and coordinated production could be achieved."[10] This path offered the best chance that over time the League would be able to find consensus among its members, and, where such consensus existed, to articulate "a comprehensive code of policy behavior."[11] In terms of enforcement, it is worth noting, it was widely assumed that market forces would suffice. Clear ideas would help, but a natural competition would in any event push the world toward what today's descendants of the Geneva process would label "best practice."

Per Jacobsson, then a member of the League's Secretariat and later the managing director of the IMF, thought he saw the beginning of an historic conceptual rapprochement in 1927:

[The Geneva Conference] reached a synthesis of the two main economic ideas of the last century expressed on the one hand, by the Manchester School concentrating upon the advantages of free competition and, on the other hand, by manifold movements aiming at improvement in social conditions and insisting upon the rights of society as a whole.[12]

This proved to be wishful thinking, and issues of industrial organization get to the heart of the matter.

It is conventional for textbooks on the international economy to assign pride of place to the issue of trade. The flow of commodities, goods, and

---

10 Ibid.
11 James Arthur Salter, *Memoirs of a Public Servant* (London, 1961), 198–9.
12 Per Jacobsson, *The Economic Consequences of the League* (London, 1927), 53.

services across borders is the central analytical concern, a reflection no doubt of its prominence in the real world of international business, politics, and diplomacy. Cross-border investment complicates the scheme, but is still usually assessed in a trade context. In light of the trade-investment interaction, international finance then takes its usual place in our textbooks as the hand-maiden, whose job it is to assist and facilitate but who must always be viewed with suspicion, since her capacity to break down at awkward moments can threaten the "real" economy.

The 1927 Geneva consensus was in many ways much more ambitiously multilateral on trade and financial matters than the so-called "Washington consensus" was widely taken to be in the mid-1990s. At the heart of the Geneva consensus was a general agreement at the level of principle that trade restrictions were bad and a restoration of accommodating international capital flows on the basis of a reliable exchange rate mechanism was good. Indeed, twenty-nine of the national delegations at Geneva solemnly agreed to abolish all import and export restrictions among them within six months! Jacobsson's suggestion, however, was that the consensus ran deeper. He was wrong, but his error points to a central fault line that runs through the putative consensus of his day as well as ours. Some at Geneva believed passionately that modern capitalism should and could be regulated at the level of the producer; furthermore, to the extent that "great natural lines of production did not stop short at frontiers," they believed it would eventually be necessary to move requisite regulatory authority beyond the national level.[13] Others, however, believed even more fervently that such views were mortal threats to freedom, democracy, and national self-determination.

The depth of the chasm between the two views was plumbed during the two decades following the Geneva Conference. It is not coincidental, moreover, that the less ambitious multilateral architecture erected almost exactly twenty years later ignored the issues of industrial organization and regulation raised at Geneva. Before the onset of the Great Depression, however, and well before the rise of American ideological hegemony, the idea received a serious airing.

On October 4, 1928, the International Federation of League of Nations Societies convened in Prague around an agenda designed to follow up the deliberations in Geneva. Eighteen national delegations were present, as were representatives from twenty-two nongovernmental organizations. Officials from the League's Secretariat helped organize the three-day event and served

13 McClure, *World Prosperity*, 219.

as rapporteurs.[14] In one summary account, a League staffer captured the tenor of the meeting.

Extremists who predicted economic cataclysm for Europe if all protective duties were not abolished...sat side by side with advocates of European Customs Union.... A draft resolution to the effect that international cartels should send periodically to the Economic Committee of the League of Nations reports on their activities [was defeated] but traces of it can be found in [a] resolution asking the National Committee of the Federation to study the question of the control of cartels. The Conference also calls on the Economic Committee [of the League] to study the question of the control of international industrial agreements.[15]

Under the watchful eye of the International Chamber of Commerce, with which it had long and close relations, the League's Secretariat subsequently did compile such a study. By focusing on agreements that transcended national boundaries, however, the study avoided the central normative issue upon which leading member-states disagreed. In Hexner's terms, they were able to evade the central question of whether all private collective marketing schemes are undesirable, for "neither friends nor enemies of cartels like such clarification."[16]

In 1930, the League published two volumes surveying the legal and economic aspects of international industrial agreements. Focusing on prominent cartels of the day in such sectors as steel and associated finished products, copper, mercury, and other minerals, aniline dyes, and electric lamps. The studies suggested that the stabilization or raising of prices, and thus profits, was not always the effect of the cartel movement, or even their ultimate objective. "Rationalization," the prevention of "over-production," and the avoidance of excessive reliance on price-clearing mechanisms of distribution came closer to the mark, although generalizations proved impossible to sustain. Wallace McClure, whose 1933 book on the economic work of the League reflected his experience there as an adviser to the U.S. State Department in the 1920s, saw these studies leading to the following conclusion: "The benefits of such rationalization as is signified by the international cartel await adequate international machinery for public control."[17]

Further work along this line was shared by the League Secretariat and the International Labor Office. The issue of commodity cartels was on the agenda of the ill-fated World Economic Conference of 1933, and the

14 League of Nations, Registry File #10A-3672; Carton R.2663, League Archives, Geneva.
15 Ibid.   16 Hexner, *International Cartels*, 10.
17 McClure, *World Prosperity*, 277.

associated discussion was followed up with a report from a League Committee in 1937. By then, however, the issue had become deeply embedded in the high politics of war preparations. While the overarching ideological contest was being addressed on the battlefield, however, League staff continued to push the matter forward.

During the wartime sojourn in Princeton of the League's economic and financial staff, Gertrud Lovasy, a junior League staffer who would later work at the IMF, was assigned the task of compiling a study of international cartels. Her draft memorandum was circulated in 1945 and returned with many comments. Alexander Loveday, then director of the Princeton staff, subsequently opposed publication since he felt it needed deeper grounding in the actual operation of cartels.[18] At the dissolution of the League, a revised document was taken over by the Department of Economic Affairs of the United Nations. Mimeographed copies were circulated to delegations preparing for the UN Conference on Trade and Employment. Still marked "preliminary" and bearing the caveat that "on no point has it been revised by the United Nations Secretariat," it was published in 1947.[19]

To contemporary eyes, Lovasy's study does not seem particularly controversial. Mainly descriptive and historical, it summarizes issues that the League had been following ever since 1927. It also, however, clearly set out the diversity of national approaches to cartels and related restrictive business practices, and underlined controversies still unresolved in a number of national cases. In the U.S. case, for example, the study noted that the Webb-Pomerene Act of 1918 continued to be widely interpreted as carving out an exception to the Sherman-Clayton antitrust tradition to allow U.S. firms to participate in foreign cartels as long as this did not affect the domestic U.S. market. Publicly taking exception to this interpretation, however, the Anti-Trust Division of the Justice Department expressed the view that so-called Webb-Pomerene associations were intended "to strengthen American competition against foreign cartels."[20] More broadly, the study contrasted the dominant American policy approach with the preference of other states to accept cartels and regulate them as well as with the more ambitious efforts to establish intergovernmental cartels, especially in certain commodity markets. This seemingly balanced study and its reception, however, needs to be viewed in the political context of the times.

---

18 Letter from Loveday to Lester, dated Dec. 17, 1945. League of Nations, File 10601, 43539; Carton R.4221, League Archives, Geneva.

19 Gertrud Lovasy, *International Cartels: A League of Nations Memorandum* (Lake Success, N.Y., 1947).

20 Ibid., 33.

In September 1944, President Franklin Roosevelt instructed Secretary of State Cordell Hull in the following terms:

The Sherman and Clayton Acts have become as much a part of the American way of life as the due-process clause of the Constitution. By protecting the consumer against monopoly these statutes guarantee him the benefits of competition. . . . The antitrust statutes aim at the elimination of monopolistic restraints in inter-state and foreign commerce. Unfortunately, a number of foreign countries, particularly in continental Europe, do not possess such a tradition against cartels. On the contrary, cartels have received encouragement from some of these countries. Especially is this true with respect to Germany. . . . Cartel practices which restrict the free flow of goods in foreign commerce will have to be curbed.[21]

The cartel issue had become bound up in public consciousness with the great task of defeating the Nazis, whose ability to wage war was inextricably linked in public consciousness to now-infamous German cartels. Even so, only two months after Roosevelt's letter the International Chamber of Commerce (ICC) attempted to bring a measure of nuance back into the building debate on the shape of the postwar world.

The Chamber convened a major conference on the subject in Rye, New York, in November 1944. One report setting the agenda for the meeting surveyed agreements between independent private parties to regulate production, promote orderly marketing, coordinate prices, and exchange technical information. To the extent such agreements could have an impact on international trade, the report argued, they could be viewed in either a positive or a negative light. While Roosevelt's views adequately expressed one perspective, another was available. Such agreements could "improve quality, lower costs, and, by keeping supplies at a level which will satisfy and stimulate demand, maintain and increase employment, further peaceful relations in trade, enable living standards to be raised, open and expand markets in an orderly and progressive manner." The ICC therefore recommended further study and business-government consultation in order "to establish rules and standards to govern such agreements in international trade."[22]

The same conflict between the policy goal of articulating clear and generally applicable principles in this regard, and the practical exigencies of life "in the markets," underlay all associated study and reflection inside the League since 1927. The final League memorandum on the subject took special pains to highlight the direction of likely U.S. policy after the war was concluded. Citing Congressional testimony from Assistant Secretary of

---

21 Letter dated Sept. 6, 1944, quoted in full in Hexner, appendix VI.
22 Hexner, *International Cartels*, appendix VII.

State William Clayton, the memorandum underlined the American plan for the establishment of an "International Office for Business Practices." The Office would:

> assist in the prevention of undesirable cartel practices by serving as a central depository of information and reports from participating governments and other sources, by initiating the study of problems relating to the activities of private international business organizations and the application of the agreement on restrictive trade practices, with a view to making recommendations to participating governments, and by furnishing information or undertaking such investigations as may be feasible to aid participating governments.[23]

League staff, in turn, concluded:

> Although the United States Government does not expect acceptance of the program by all other nations, it rejects the alternative line of international policy.... Past experience, it contends, does not support the view held in some countries that, under appropriate government supervision, cartels may serve useful purposes.[24]

As things turned out, de-cartelization became a central element in the policies guiding the initial period of Allied occupation of Germany and Japan. Nevertheless, the onset of the Cold War soon provided a rationale for the U.S. government itself to foster the participation of American firms in certain cartel arrangements, notably in the petroleum industry.[25] At the international level, however, Clayton's basic idea survived and became embedded within the Havana Charter. The new International Trade Organization was to include a Commission on Business Practices. But the ITO could not be ratified, and the interim General Agreement on Tariffs and Trade (GATT) left to carry the mantle failed to sustain the idea.

In a discursive passage on the myriad theoretical and institutional impediments to a clear interstate consensus on a notion of "workable competition," the final League study presaged the difficulties that would bedevil all attempts to revive the idea during the next fifty years. Indeed, a direct line can readily be drawn from the intellectual core of the League study to the incipient effort of the GATT's successor, the World Trade Organization, to negotiate a binding agreement on trade-related antitrust measures, or what some have called "a global competition policy."[26] In the midst of continuing disagreement even among leading states, sometimes explicit but most often implicit, on the actual meaning of such concepts as

---

23 Lovasy, *International Cartels*, 34–5.   24 Ibid.
25 See Diane Kunz, *Butter and Guns: America's Cold War Economic Diplomacy* (New York, 1996), 225–7.
26 The analytical literature is now immense. For a recent general study, see Edward M. Graham and J. David Richardson, eds., *Global Competition Policy* (Washington, D.C., 1997).

contestable markets, efficiency, and fairness, the central parallel goes back even further.

[We hereby create a working group] to study issues raised by Members relating to the interaction between trade and competition policy, including anti-competitive practices, in order to identify any areas that may merit further consideration.

Virtually echoing their predecessors at the Geneva Conference of 1927, so the world's leading trade ministers ended their first meeting as governors of the World Trade Organization in 1997.[27]

THE POSTWAR ECONOMIC ORDER

A keen scholarly effort has been under way for many years now to encapsulate, in theoretically and politically meaningful terms, the nature of the compromise at the heart of U.S. foreign economic policy after World War II ended. That compromise has had a new edge since 1989, when certain questions preempted in 1947 were reopened. Ikenberry, for example, has argued that in the early postwar years the United States sought to construct a liberal multilateral system that, on the one hand, would rely on instruments of collective security to manage the threat of military conflict and, on the other hand, would use markets to force constructive adjustments to international economic exchange. Within a short period of time, however, the system leader found itself constrained by the institutionalized reality of European welfare states and the necessity of maintaining a military "empire by invitation."[28] Ruggie labeled this same end-position "the compromise of embedded liberalism," wherein a preference for liberal, market-led solutions to the collective action problems of international life is continually adapted to the necessity of governmental interventions in pursuit of national goals.[29] Along similar lines, Kunz probes deeply into the character of the internal American contest over a postwar foreign policy orientation. She contrasts a traditional preference for governmental noninterference in the workings of markets, especially financial markets, with the revival of the idea that national government should actively promote U.S. business

27 Ibid., 5. Compare to: "National economies have become more and more interdependent. . . . Among them, a world economy has been formed. The common problem uniting all of the resulting problems may be stated in these terms: to give to the world economy its fundamental law." Geneva, 1997? No, the concluding sentences of a 6,500-page "Inquiry on Production, 1920–25," published by the International Labor Organization and cited in McClure, *World Prosperity*, 279.
28 G. John Ikenberry, "Rethinking the Origins of American Hegemony," *Political Science Quarterly* 104, no. 3 (1989): 375–400.
29 John Gerard Ruggie, "International Regimes, Transactions, and Change: Embedded Liberalism in the Postwar Economic Order," *International Organization* 36, no. 2 (1982): 195–231.

interests overseas, and finally with the new multilateralist option of intimately linking U.S. security objectives together with universal tariff reductions and the international regulation of unfair trade practices.[30]

The contemporary resurrection of Assistant Secretary Clayton's idea of an international Commission on Business Practices, or at least a binding agreement on restrictive business practices and their remedies, takes us right back not only to 1927 but also to the initial post–World War II debate on the international economy, both inside the United States and more broadly. There is no easy answer as to why it was defeated when Clayton himself revived, as I suggested above, an idea with a much longer pedigree.[31] For present purposes, however, let me simply assert that its defeat reflected a distinct lack of consensus among leading states on such basic issues as the purpose of markets, the limits of international liberalism, and the very meaning of such concepts as efficiency and fairness. For support, I would simply point once again to the seventy years of controversy surrounding the term "cartel" following the International Economic Conference of 1927.

The central question now is whether Clayton's idea stands a chance today *because* such a consensus finally exists. Is such a consensus not distinctly implied if the IMF seeks to ensure "loans are made on the basis of objective commercial criteria," transparent auditing standards, "level playing fields," the "dismantling" of monopolies, and the elimination of government-directed lending? There is no doubt that the growth and expansion of international capital markets provides a necessary condition to reconsidering such complex and deeply political issues. But does the so-called Washington consensus, or what Harold James has labeled the "commandments of the modern decalogue," now really extend this far?[32] Moreover, if such a consensus truly is evolving, is it already sufficiently robust to justify enforcement by the IMF?

At a time when the word "globalization" is omnipresent and the logic of policy and structural convergence seems self-evident, it is ironic that the rapidly growing body of scholarship in the fields of comparative and international political economy points in another direction.[33] Recent studies, for

---

30 Kunz, *Butter and Guns*, 6.

31 Analogous ideas, of course, percolated in the background throughout the Cold War. In the context of its work on the developmental impact of multinational enterprises, for example, the United Nations Conference on Trade and Development proposed a Code on Restrictive Business Practices in 1981. In addition, the OECD has long advanced a series of work programs on related issues.

32 James, *International Monetary Cooperation*, 607.

33 Paul N. Doremus et al., *The Myth of the Global Corporation* (Princeton, N.J., 1998); Suzanne Berger and Ronald Dore, eds., *National Diversity and Global Capitalism* (Ithaca, N.Y., 1996); Helen Milner and Robert Keohane, eds. *Internationalization and Domestic Politics* (Cambridge, 1996); Paul Hirst and Grahame Thompson, *Globalization in Question* (Cambridge, 1996); Sylvia Ostry and Richard

example, conclude that corporate governance and financing structures combine to form unique patterns of industrial organization around the world, that these patterns continue to differ markedly along national lines (especially among the leading economies), and that continual processes of adaptation are more often driven by internal pressures than external ones. Leading Japanese, American, and German corporations, in particular, continue to differ systematically in the relative priority they assign to the immediate interests of their shareholders, in the centrality of their banking relationships, in their exposure to impersonal capital markets, in the nature of the accountability of their managers, in their approach to vertical integration, and in their general orientation to the issue of horizontal concentration. Students of corporate organization, in short, continue to turn up evidence of national diversity on basic questions of efficiency and fairness, findings which correlate with those of many counterparts who study competition policy.[34]

Let me put a finer point on this conclusion. In his influential *The Competitive Advantage of Nations*, Michael Porter concluded as follows:

Leniency toward cartels is a trap. . . . Cartels dampen and suspend the self-reinforcing process of upgrading that grows out of domestic rivalry. . . . A strong antitrust policy, especially in the area of horizontal mergers, alliances, and collusive behavior, is essential to the rate of upgrading in the economy. Mergers, acquisitions, and alliances involving industry leaders should be disallowed. . . . A strong policy bias should favor internal entry, both domestically and abroad, instead of acquisition. Direct interfirm collusion should be illegal. . . . Leniency toward mergers and alliances (and monopolies) . . . are part of a disturbing trend toward viewing competition as "wasteful" or "excessive" that has gained currency during the last decade, as it did in the 1930s.[35]

R. Nelson, *Techno-Nationalism and Techno-Globalism* (Washington, D.C., 1995); Winfried Ruigrok and Rob van Tulder, *The Logic of International Restructuring* (London, 1995); Richard Samuels, *"Rich Nation, Strong Army"* (Ithaca, N.Y., 1994); U.S. Congress, Office of Technology Assessment, *Multinationals and the US Technology Base*, OTA-ITE-612 (Washington, D.C., 1994); David C. Mowery, *Science and Technology Policy in Interdependent Economies* (Boston, 1994); Mark Mason and Dennis Encarnation, eds., *Does Ownership Matter?* (Oxford, 1994); Richard R. Nelson, ed., *National Innovation Systems* (New York, 1993); Bengt-Ake Lundvall, ed., *National Systems of Innovation* (London, 1992); Andrew Sobel, *Domestic Choices, International Markets* (Ann Arbor, Mich., 1994).

34 Graham and Richardson, *Global Competition Policy*. The editors conclude, inter alia, that "lack of consensus on substantive standards constitutes a major dilemma of competition policy. The murkiness of much of the underlying economics exacerbates a second, related dilemma. Not only are substantive standards differences across nations, they have also been significantly revised over time within some nations" (550). Even the evident rhetorical consensus on the evils of cartels noted throughout the book continues to be compromised, as also noted, by a less evident but more real lack of consensus on the wisdom of export cartels and on the appropriateness of important sectoral exemptions (552). See also Edward M. Graham, *Global Corporations and National Governments* (Washington, D.C., 1996).

35 Michael Porter, *The Competitive Advantage of Nations* (New York, 1990), 663.

A more eloquent statement of the traditional and dominant American ideological position would be hard to find. These days, and especially in the
midst of the Asian financial mess, corporate executive and national policymakers around the world now publicly sing from the same hymnbook. Many
careful and highly qualified observers think that history is now converging
decisively toward American norms. Detailed comparative scholarship simply
raises a caution flag. It suggests that social scientists should interpret with a
grain of salt the "evidence" of a new global consensus delivered at Davos or
at annual meetings of the IMF, especially as it pertains to the microeconomic
structures of modern capitalism.

The bitter experience of the League of Nations in this realm provides a
cautionary tale. Shortly after closing up the League's economic and financial
organization, Alexander Loveday pinpointed what he considered to be the
central flaw in its original design:

The world was not in any very meaningful way a unity. The primary function of
any international organization should be not to postulate but to promote its unity.
It is composed of nations at all stages of cultural and economic development and
to endeavour to force the same principles of action down the throats of all, babes
and full grown men alike, will choke the one and undernourish the other.[36]

Chastened by the onset of international economic depression, Loveday
watched the League "willingly and resolutely" abandon "the conception
of universalism" and move away "from the restrictive idea of its pre-1914
forefathers that an international organization should confine its activities
to international problems." In its last years, the organization he led would
spend most of its time "with strictly national affairs."[37] Through "research,
ad hoc commissions on carefully designed subjects, meetings of experts on
different subjects the purpose of which was simply to exchange views and
experience, and the preparation of models," he saw the League modestly
but constructively "making peoples world-conscious by tracing the working of the fundamental economic forces that underlay national phenomena,
by showing the similarity of the economic problems with which different countries were beset, and more generally by supplying to each state
information about others."[38]

---

36 Loveday, "Some Lessons," 8.   37 Ibid., 13.

38 Ibid., 16. Again, I agree that such activities did not constitute a formal legal obligation on the
    part of League member-states to consult with one another, but they were not entirely distinct from
    consultations procedures, supported by research, that evolved within the early IMF on policy matters
    under its purview. Those procedures, in turn, were well established when leading states concluded
    in the mid-1970s that a formal commitment to multilateral economic surveillance was required.

TOWARD A NEW ORDER?

The continuities evident in debates since the 1920s over, on the one hand, the restoration of global capital markets and, on the other, restrictive business practices and their international remedies usefully frame attempts to understand the new structural adjustment mission of the IFIs. As noted above, throughout the postwar period, advice resulting from surveillance activities of international institutions like the Fund has often been controversial. It has also often been ignored, not only by great powers but by smaller states as well. Most of the time, peer pressure has been the only sanction. In some cases, however, the possibility of enforcing policy prescriptions has been enhanced by financial desperation. Policy advice can then sometimes be transformed into lending "conditions."

Fund "conditionality," in particular, has always been controversial. Indeed, controversy is inherent in an objective political dilemma: A debtor state confronts circumstances where it is unable internally to generate the funds it needs and unable to attract the kind of no-conditions-except-repayment funding available from foreign private lenders, while creditor states are politically unwilling or unable to provide open credit-lines on their own treasuries. Long before the term came into common usage, Keynes confronted the central dilemma associated with conditionality, when in 1944 the United States rejected his plan for an international clearing union. He confronted it again in 1946, when he went to Savannah, Georgia, for the first board meeting of an IMF that he still hoped might evolve into an institution approximating his original politically neutral vision. "I went to Savannah to meet the world," Keynes later recounted, "and all I met was a tyrant."[39] In fact, he worried publicly that the Fund and the World Bank would "grow up politicians; your every thought and act shall have an *arrière-pensée*; everything you determine shall not be for its own sake or on its merits but because of something else."[40] The remark was prescient.

In an intrinsically political process, albeit one mediated by a technocratic staff that places a high value on the objective of neutrality, the Fund has over time been pushed by both sides of the financing transaction to adapt its conditionality to changing circumstances. Conditions couched in the language of macroeconomic policy and its imperfectly measurable outcomes

---

39 R. F. Harrod, *The Life of John Maynard Keynes* (London, 1951), 639.
40 D. E. Moggridge, *Maynard Keynes: An Economist's Biography* (London, 1992), 831. He added privately, "The Americans at the top seem to have no conception of international co-operation; since they are the biggest partners they think they have the right to call the tune on every point. If they knew the music that would not matter so much; but unfortunately, they don't."

were once seen as adequate to discipline states confronting international payments shortfalls and to reassure creditors. Beginning in the 1970s, however, in the wake of commodity price shocks and galloping inflation, Fund economists found themselves up against deeper structural impediments to successful macroeconomic adjustment. Systemic structures, like the market power of the oil cartel and the inflationary bias in U.S. policies, it could do nothing about. But it did have leverage with regard to internal structures within debtor countries, structures like marketing boards that fixed internal prices and exacerbated the need for external financing. A subtle but steady movement in the Fund's own policies began.

In 1979, new guidelines for its financing arrangements enjoined the Fund to "pay due regard to the domestic social and political objectives, the economic priorities, and the circumstances of members." To that diplomatic and politically soothing balm, however, was appended the phrase, "including the causes of their balance of payments problems."[41] The door was opened to "structural" conditionality, and during the early 1980s, both the Fund and the World Bank would walk through that door with member-states from the developing world. The Bank soon began providing non-project related "structural adjustment loans." In 1986, the IMF created its own "structural adjustment facility" (SAF) under which drawing could be made at subsidized rates and lengthened terms by the sixty-one low-income countries. IMF and World Bank programs were to be coordinated and hinged on "policy framework papers" negotiated by the IFIs and national governments that promised to develop more efficient internal markets over a medium term. In 1988, the IMF's SAF was supplemented with an "enhanced structural adjustment facility," which increased the aggregate amount of permissible drawings by a single member, albeit only on the basis of more far-reaching and more precisely specified adjustment efforts.

In the 1990s, the IFIs found themselves in the center of efforts to provide official financing for states in transition from socialism to capitalism, and in those cases too, the adjustment of internal structures at the root of payments imbalances came into play. As in the case of low-income countries, in a world

---

41 James, *International Monetary Cooperation*, 521. James's general treatment of the evolution of IMF conditionality is comprehensive and accessible. For more detailed treatments, see Joseph Gold, *Conditionality*, Pamphlet Series, 31 (Washington, D.C., 1979); John Williamson, ed., *IMF Conditionality* (Washington, D.C., 1983); Manuel Guitián, *Fund Conditionality: Evolution of Principles and Practices*, Pamphlet Series, 38 (Washington, D.C., 1981); Joseph Gold, *Exchange Rates in International Law and Organization* (Washington, D.C., 1988); Jacques J. Polak, "The Changing Nature of IMF Conditionality," *Essays in International Finance*, 184, Princeton University, Department of Economics, International Finance Section (1991).

where formal sovereignty still has meaning, creditor states could not confront those structures directly. They were also unable or unwilling to open their own treasuries. By accident, then, the IFIs became the chief promoters of norms of "good governance." In the case of the IMF, the thrust of that evolution has been enhanced by the exigencies of an equally accidental financial crisis-management function as international capital markets grew explosively after the late 1970s.

That evolution, now characterized by crisis-induced moments of institutional and policy innovation, continues to confound efforts to place rigid demarcation lines around particular IFIs. It also continues to arouse passionate debate both inside and outside the institutions between those who see it eroding traditional principles, rendering them into unaccountable foreign aid agencies, and overstretching the competence of their staffs. That debate becomes more contentious as what Jacques Polak calls "secondary objectives" multiply in the actual practice of Fund conditionality.[42] As Harold James has noted, "Complaining that the institutions are damaged by the crisis is rather like claiming that car crashes have a bad effect on seat belts."[43] It may nevertheless be true that the IFIs, and the Fund in particular, are in dangerous territory when it comes to certain aspects of their new governance agendas.

Recall my starting point that the member-states of the Fund have collectively made a broad choice since the 1970s to advance the cause of international financial integration. At a minimum, that choice raises the risk that national financial disasters can become systemic financial crises. At a maximum, it promises to accelerate economic growth. But private finance is more fickle than public finance, and the experience of an increasing number of states suggests that Keynes's fears remain apt if not precisely targeted. For creditor states, global finance is an opportunity moderated by a risk. For debtor states, it can be the new tyrant when creditors come to expect conformity to economic standards reflecting their own internal values. But what happens when core values diverge among creditor states themselves?

The economic policy trade-offs implied in the assignment of priority to international capital mobility were recognized in 1944. Even clearer to the architects of the Bretton Woods system was the associated political conundrum. Capital mobility represented a threat to the authority of the modern

---

42 Ibid., 24–33. Polak notes that these have included poverty alleviation, environmental objectives, the containment of military expenditures, and human rights. The new governance agenda apparently seeks to add many more items to this list.

43 James, *International Monetary Cooperation*, 527.

state itself when stable exchange rates were deemed to be necessary conditions for international as well as domestic economic recovery. For different reasons, however, the political calculus can be similarly complicated when a general preference for international capital mobility is combined with an inability or an unwillingness to stabilize a systemic exchange rate regime. The last time something like this defined the status quo, during the interwar period, the strong competed to define the deepest structural rules of the game. We comfort ourselves now with the belief, perhaps it should be called the hope, that today's great powers actually agree on those rules. That hope seems to provide a solid enough basis for the IMF and other IFIs dominated by leading states to be empowered to intervene ever more intrusively in the domestic political and social arrangements of relatively weak states. It is possible, however, that a Pandora's box has been opened.

The consensus on precisely what structures are compatible with markets deemed to be both efficient and fair may not be as deep as it seems. Few historians would make the claim that the industrial development of today's great powers was unambiguously marked by "loans made on the basis of objective commercial criteria," by transparent balance sheets, by the dismantling of monopolies, by "level playing fields," or by fair "government procurement and contracting regulations." Even today, the proposition that they themselves are fully prepared to accept common standards on each point is open to doubt. In such an environment, it is appropriate that the basic norms required for a continued deepening of the great postwar experiment in international economic interdependence be negotiated in the forum of the WTO. In the absence of marked progress in that forum, however, the weak will have cause to resent the imposition by the IFIs of standards that the strong are reluctant to impose upon themselves. They may also begin plausibly to depict that imposition as an effort by the strong to protect their own financial interests as well as to lock in the competitive advantages that accrue to first-movers in the industrialization process.[44]

We do not need to rediscover as the League of Nations did that the important question concerning the universal evolution of deep structural standards is not "efficient and fair for what" but "efficient and fair for whom." Symmetry in the distribution of the adjustment burdens associated with global economic interdependence was a key principle of the Bretton Woods

---

44 On related issues that became especially salient in the wake of the Asian financial crisis of the late 1990s, see Louis W. Pauly, "What New Architecture? International Financial Institutions and Global Economic Order," *Global Governance* 7, no. 4 (2001), 469–84.

system, albeit one honored mainly in the breach. In the post–Bretton Woods environment, it remained a normative ideal.[45] It would seem wise to bring that principle back to center stage before accelerating the movement to articulate and enforce international standards of industrial organization and business practice.

45 See Joseph Gold, "Symmetry as a Legal Objective of the International Monetary System," in *Legal and Institutional Aspects of the International Monetary System: Selected Essays*, 2 (Washington, D.C.: International Monetary Fund, 1984). Gold notes, "Is freedom for all members to choose their exchange rate arrangements compatible with the idea of interdependence that is the *idée reçue* of many multilateral international organizations? The freedom granted to members by the Second Amendment implies the necessity of a strong central authority to avoid abuse. The success of the Fund in achieving the symmetrical treatment of members will depend on the skill with which it performs the functions that are described in the Second Amendment, not simply as surveillance, but as 'firm surveillance' (304). A step toward symmetry in practice occurred during the LDC debt crisis of the 1980s, when banks and official agencies in industrial countries were required to incur losses linked directly to programs of sustainable adjustment in certain indebted states.

Index